A Norfolk Rhapsody

A Norfolk Rhapsody

Ralph Vaughan Williams in King's Lynn

Jill Bennett | Elizabeth James

POPPYLAND PUBLISHING

Copyright © Jill Bennett and Elizabeth James

First published 2022 by Poppyland Publishing, Lowestoft, NR32 3BB

www.poppyland.co.uk

ISBN 978 1 909796 94 2

Picture credits, where known, are either in the public domain or under a Creative Commons Licence (source in caption) with the exception of the following:

Emery collection
James, C.
James E.
Lowestoft Maritime Museum
Middleton, B.
Peter Brooks collection
Picture Norfolk
Poppyland Photos
Ralph Vaughan Williams Society
Roberts, A.
Surrey History Centre
True's Yard Fisherfolk Museum

Typeset in Avenir Book 9.5/12.5pt

Printed by Severn Printing.

Front cover: North End, King's Lynn.
Anne Roberts.
Back cover: The Baden Powell sailing past Kings Lynn May 2020 (top), The old Guildhall today (bottom).
Anne Roberts.
Frontispiece: The fisher fleet, King's Lynn c1900.
Anne Roberts.

Contents

Acknowledgements

Thanks to Hugh Cobbe, director of the Vaughan Williams Charitable Trust, for permission to use the material from Ralph Vaughan Williams's notebooks and for giving us his invaluable comments on the text; to Mark Leslie, editor of the Lynn News, for permission to quote from reports of Vaughan Williams' visits to King's Lynn; to Lindsey Bavin and all the staff at True's Yard Fisherfolk Museum in King's Lynn, the Lynn Museum (Norfolk Museums Service) including their permission to use the taped reminiscences of Duggie Carter's family from 1976 and other help; the staff at King's Lynn, Hunstanton and Gaywood Libraries. In the Archives search room at King's Lynn Town Hall, we must thank Susan Maddock, and the staff at the search room in the Norfolk Record Office in Norwich. We are also indebted to the Vaughan Williams Memorial Library and the English Folk Dance and Song Society for permission to use invaluable material from The Full English, the online collection of material from Vaughan Williams' and others' collections. Also to Surrey History Centre for their permission to quote Lucy Broadwood's diaries.

We are grateful to Mike Herring for allowing us to use his taped research of 1967 into traditional music in the North End.

For the background to the history of the North End we must thank especially Dr Paul Richards, the late Jeanne Wheeler, and the late Jean Tuck. For information on Bob Jackson of Sheringham and his railway career thanks are due to Dave King curator of the North Norfolk Railway Museum at Sheringham, and to the Midland and Great Northern Railway Society. To Alan Helsdon, who shared our research for many months particularly into the singers and their families and the Revd Alfred Huddle's background. Thanks to Peter Salt for scouring Kelly's Directories for us and other research, and to Sally Turff for patiently reading through the text for us and helping us to make it clearer and more consistent.

Thanks to Mike Emery of Sheringham for information and pictures of his great grandfather, who sang to Vaughan Williams. Also to Lesley Lougher and Cynthia of South Street, Sheringham, who tracked down three of Vaughan Williams' post war addresses in Sheringham for us, and Jeff Link who identified a fourth, and John Osborne who designed the front cover.

Finally, our heartfelt thanks to Colin James and the late Noel Linge for their support and encouragement over our years of research, writing and discovery.

Foreword

The English folksong became a fundamental ingredient in the music of Ralph Vaughan Williams as he developed his own characteristic voice and sought to establish a national music distinct from the pervasive influence of the 19th century Austro-Germanic tradition. By making song-collecting expeditions to likely haunts, he and others, such as George Butterworth and Cecil Sharp, were just in time to rescue songs handed down by oral tradition but already threatened by industrialisation and urbanisation, and soon to be further imperilled by the modern radio age. Starting in 1903, Vaughan Williams sought out singers in Essex, around his childhood home Leith Hill Place in Surrey, in Sussex, Berkshire, Yorkshire, Kent and, in 1905, in Norfolk where, between 7 and 14 January, he visited Tilney, Sheringham and King's Lynn.

Records survive of these expeditions in notebooks now in the British Library, in which he noted the tunes and some of the words which were sung to him, though with little else recorded except possibly the odd circumstantial note. In this book Jill Bennett and Elizabeth James give us a detailed account of Vaughan Williams' week in Norfolk, describing his peregrinations around King's Lynn, mostly to parts which have since been rebuilt, and the singers whom he met. The songs which were sung to the composer appear with complete texts and tunes in chapters devoted to particular singers, or groups of singers such as those living in the King's Lynn Union Workhouse. The authors have been able to take advantage of True's Yard Fisherfolk Museum to discover much about the singers whom Vaughan Williams encountered during his visit and, of course, have had access to Vaughan Williams' own notebooks. As a result, they have created an in-depth picture of the visit, and to an extent that does not I believe exist for any other of the composer's song-collecting expeditions.

The outcome of the expedition for the composer was telling. He wrote three Norfolk Rhapsodies using some of the tunes he had collected at King's Lynn (notably *The Captain's Apprentice* in the first and *Young Henry the Poacher* in the second), though sadly the third Norfolk Rhapsody is lost. Perhaps the most widely felt result of the visit was his adaptation of *Young Henry the Poacher* as the hymn-tune he named *King's Lynn* which he set to words by G K Chesterton (*O God of earth and altar*) in *The English Hymnal*. He was working on this historic collection as the Music Editor at the time, and it was published in 1906, the year following his King's Lynn visit. This tune has remained in common use ever since and is still to be found in all the major hymn books. The 1905 visit remained very sharp in the composer's own memory, for he returned to King's Lynn for the festival in 1952 and gave a talk illustrated by two singers about the songs he had collected there. All in all, Vaughan Williams' foray into Norfolk in 1905 had a wide significance both for him and for all those who love his music.

Hugh Cobbe
Director
The Vaughan Williams Charitable Trust
March 9th 2022

Introduction

"The first Norfolk Rhapsody … is a deeply considered work.… The sum total is a moving piece of music which inspires and retains affection as well as admiration."

Hubert Foss' study of RVW in 1950

Just over a week before Ralph Vaughan Williams came to King's Lynn, the town was alive with new year celebrations for 1905. There were suppers and concert parties and services.   At Central Hall the people at the watchnight lantern service were treated to Mrs Perry singing *A Mother's Prayer*; *Knocking, Knocking*; and *Throw Out the Lifeline*. Mr W Easter sang *The Old Arm Chair*.[1] No mention of the old songs which were sung in the pubs and the workhouse—the newspaper reporter had either not heard them or dismissed them as of no interest. Why sing the old songs when the shops were advertising 'the latest music promptly stocked'?

Luckily for us Ralph Vaughan Williams, 13 months into his enthusiastic collecting of folk songs, came to West Norfolk a week later expressly to hear those old songs and note them down from the singers. He was uniquely well qualified to do it both by training, temperament and character. What he heard excited and inspired him.

Through him, we can still hear the songs of a lost fishing community and their contemporaries. Through their songs he created great music which speaks to audiences across the world.

Musicologists tend to skim over the week that Vaughan Williams spent in King's Lynn. But it was a week he never forgot and recalled clearly when he returned to the town nearly half a century later. He said he "reaped a rich harvest" when he came to Lynn.[2] This is why we have tried to retrace his steps, find out more about the people he met, and see how his music was infused with the melodies and ideas he heard in the yards, the workhouse and the pubs of old King's Lynn.

Those songs might well have vanished for ever had he not come to West Norfolk in 1905. We would have been left with hearty anthologies of the music of Merrie England or Victorian parlour ballads as a picture of English folk music here. But Vaughan Williams was one of those uncovering a rich and rapidly vanishing heritage.

So where was RVW in his musical career by the time he came to King's Lynn on 5 January 1905?

Notes

1   *Lynn News*, 7 January 1905.
2   *Lynn News and Advertiser*, 25 July 1952.

A Composer in The Making

"That foolish young man, Vaughan Williams, who would go on working at music when he was so hopelessly bad at it."

Aunt Etty, one of RVW's Darwin relations

Ralph Vaughan Williams was born in 1872 in Down Ampney, in Gloucestershire. His father Arthur Vaughan Williams was the vicar there, son of Judge Edward Vaughan Williams, the first Judge of Common Pleas. His mother was Margaret Wedgwood, great granddaughter of the famous Josiah Wedgwood, the pottery designer and entrepreneur. Her great uncle was Charles Darwin, the author of *The Origin of Species*.

It was a happy household but short-lived. Arthur died when Ralph was two years old. His widow took their three children, Hervey, Ralph and Meggie, to live at Leith Hill Place, the Wedgwood family home near Dorking, with her sister Sophie. It was a big country house overlooking the Surrey Downs[1] and the children were brought up, according to James Day, "with strict but kindly discipline. Margaret Vaughan Williams taught her children respect for the persons and needs of others, whatever their position in life, by precept, example and occasionally by punishment if necessary; in doing so she influenced her younger son so profoundly that kindness and consideration remained indelible features of his character throughout his life. Two of the cardinal offences were disrespect for the servants and tale-bearing; the virtues encouraged were directness, independence of outlook and industry."[2] Those qualities would not be lost on the men and women he met many years later in Norfolk, where the slightest hint of arrogance would doubtless have closed the door to their music and songs.

Ralph showed a talent for music as a child and was taught the piano and then the violin ("my musical salvation", he called it in his musical autobiography of 1950).[3] He was very impressed that his great aunt Emma had studied the piano with Chopin.[4] He was playing conventional classical pieces by composers such as Mozart, Haydn, Handel and early Beethoven. A visiting teacher at his preparatory school in Rottingdean, West Sussex, gave him a Novello book of Bach, which he considered a great treasure. He also recalled that it was at Rottingdean that he heard his first piece of folk music, *The Cherry Tree Carol*. His reaction, he wrote later, was more than simple admiration for a fine tune.[5]

Vaughan Williams as a young man.

All Saints Church, Down Ampney, Gloucestershire. Churchcrawler.

Not all members of the family thought he could make a career out of music. One of his Darwin cousins, Gwen, recalled his Aunt Etty, his father's older sister, talked about "that foolish young man, Ralph Vaughan Williams, who would go on working at music when he was so hopelessly bad at it." In a letter she took up the theme again: "He has been playing all his life, and for six months hard, and yet he can't play the simplest thing decently. They say it will simply break his heart if he is told that he is too bad to make anything of it."[6]

From Rottingdean he went to Charterhouse School, and from there directly to the Royal College

opposite: Leith Hill.
Anne Roberts.

1

of Music in 1890. In the holidays before he started, he heard Wagner's music for the first time and was clearly impressed. Wagner was a dominant composer of the musical world, his ideas enormously influential. What was left to explore in classical music in the wake of such a genius?—so ran the received wisdom at the time. It wasn't very encouraging for the new generations of composers, who were looking for a new direction.

At the Royal College of Music Vaughan Williams said he wanted to learn composition under Sir Hubert Parry because Parry's music had something peculiarly English about it. "So I was quite prepared to join with the other young students of the RCM in worshipping at that shrine, and I think I can truly say that I have never been disloyal to it."[7] Parry had written that a composer must write music as his musical conscience demands.[8] That lesson stayed with the young music student. Writing sixty years later, RVW said he still thought *Blest Pair of Sirens* was his favourite piece of music written by an Englishman.[9]

In 1892 he went to Cambridge to read history but kept up his lessons with Parry while he did so. He was awarded a second-class degree in history in 1895 but also took a Bachelor of Music the year before. His musical education was broadening all the time through playing, conducting, talking with leading musicians of the day. He used to visit the Darwins, as did the writer E M Forster. Gwen Raverat (nee Darwin) recalled, "We must have seen a good many Great Men in our youth, but most of them seemed to me very uninteresting…. But, of course, these two were not great men then; this is what you have to go through to become great."[10]

Then he returned to the Royal College, of which Parry was now director. Ralph had lessons from Charles Villiers Stanford, an Irishman who was also in the vanguard of seeking inspiration from 'national' music. "Stanford was a great teacher, but I believe I was unteachable," Vaughan Williams wrote. "I made the great mistake of trying to fight my teacher."[11] But his tutors were also his fellow students, particularly Gustav von

Royal College of Music.
David Iliff.

Holst, who became a close and much valued friend and musical critic. The students would all meet at a little teashop in Kensington and discuss "every subject under the sun from the lowest note of the double bassoon to the philosophy of Jude the Obscure."[12]

In 1895 he got his first job as an organist at St Barnabas' Church in South Lambeth. But he was still studying. Stanford suggested he should go to Italy and hear opera at La Scala. Vaughan Williams wanted to go to Berlin. So after he married Adeline Fisher in Hove in October 1897, the couple went there on a working honeymoon. He took instruction from Max Bruch, who, he said later, gave him more encouragement than he'd ever had.[13] When he came back, he left his organ post at St Barnabas' Church in London, and started to grow as a composer not by studying, but by doing.

A Land Without Music

In those early years of Vaughan Williams' musical life, English music was regarded as non-existent. England was labelled "a land without music" by the German musicologist Schmitz. Many years before that Dr Charles Burney, who had spent nine years in the 18th century as organist at St Margaret's in King's Lynn, had said that there was no distinctively English music. "Though the natives of Ireland and Wales can boast of National tunes, both plaintive and spirited, that are characteristic, pleasing and distinct from each other, the English have not a melody which they can call their own except the hornpipe and the Cheshire round," he wrote.[14] Developments in music had all been happening in Germany, Italy and Austria. Fashionable music had to be that which was imported, especially from the countries which the well-heeled visited on their Grand Tour.

This was a theme which Ralph Vaughan Williams picked up in his lecture at the King's Lynn Festival in 1952, as reported in the *Lynn News and Advertiser*:

Three hundred years ago it (folksong) belonged to everyone. Then came the eighteenth century with the rise to power of the landed gentry followed by the industrial revolution. It was at that time that the landed gentry became "complete artistic snobs. Their young men made the grand tour and came back with Italian singers, French fiddlers and German composers. But meanwhile the humbler folk remembered their own beautiful songs and ballads.

Many of the humble folk could not read and the songs were handed down by word of mouth, being preserved by oral tradition. They were passed down from father to son, to become a national heritage belonging to us all. Then came the Education Act of 1870," said Dr Vaughan Williams, "and we learned to read. The result was a flood of cheap and nasty verse allied to cheaper and nastier music." The old ballads were deemed out of date and as they only existed in the hearts and minds of the singers they began to disappear as the younger generation grew up. "We began to lose our songs and became instead a land without music," commented Dr Vaughan Williams. But a band of devoted musicians who realised their value set to work to collect those which had not been irretrievably lost. This movement started in the mid nineteenth century and reached its climax at the beginning of the twentieth.[15]

So although at home, Victorians were great lovers of and enthusiasts for music, original composition was in the doldrums, apart, perhaps from the works of Sir Arthur Sullivan and the young Edward Elgar. Hector Berlioz, the French composer, came to London and observed: "There is no town in the world where so much music is consumed as London."[16] But there were few major English composers at the time.

Parry and Stanford started to redress the

Adeline Fisher by Henry Lamb, 1906.

Sir Hubert Parry, depicted on a cigarette card, 1914.

W.D. & H.O. Wills cigarette card.

balance. But was it enough just to be English and a good composer? Where was your inspiration to come from? How did you produce a school of music which was not just another set of works developing the ideas of Wagner or Brahms but written in London? On the continent, composers like Mahler, Bartok, Grieg, Sibelius and Dvorak had been looking to the folk music of their own countries.

But there were doubts that any 'genuine' folk music remained in England, and Parry feared what remnants that did exist were rapidly disappearing. At the first general meeting of the Folk Song Society, he said:

> There is an enemy at the door of folk music which is driving it out—namely the popular music of the day—and if we compare the genuine old folk music with the songs that are driving it out, what an awful abyss appears! The modern popular song reminds me of the outer circumference of our terribly overgrown towns, where the jerry-builder holds sway, and one sees all around the tawdriness of sham jewellery and shoddy clothes, the dregs of stale fish and pawn shops, set off by flaming gin palaces at the corner of the streets…

> The old folk music is among the purest products of the human mind. It grew in the hearts of the people before they devoted themselves assiduously to the making of quick returns. In the old days they produced music because it pleased them to make it, and because what they made pleased them mightily, and that is the only way good music is ever made.[17]

Parry's pupils, notably Vaughan Williams and Gustav Holst, picked up the baton and ran with it.

Lucy Broadwood and the Early Folk Song Society Collectors

While Vaughan Williams was at college and starting out on a career in music, a group of enthusiasts had set about collecting English folk songs. The movement had started in the mid 19th century and gained a new momentum in the 1890s. One of the first connections for Vaughan Williams was Lucy Broadwood, who was to become the secretary of the Folk Song Society.

The Broadwood family lived at Lyne, near Horsham, not far from Leith Hill Place. Lucy Broadwood, (born August 1858), who was a friend of the Wedgwoods and Vaughan Williams' mother Mrs Margaret Vaughan Williams, had herself been out in the field collecting. She was also at the heart of the music establishment as a member of the great Broadwood piano family, who sponsored the Broadwood series of concerts in London. She was a leading member of the Folk Song Society, founded in 1898. Her uncle, The Revd John Broadwood, collected and published *Old English Songs as now sung by the Peasantry of the Weald of Surrey and Sussex* in 1843. It was one of the first collections of its kind made in England. Mr Broadwood included the flattened 7th which contemporary musicians might have regarded as 'wrong' but he said, "Musically it may be wrong but I will have it exactly as my singers sang it."[18] The collection was reprinted in 1889 as *Sussex Songs* and included more songs added by Lucy.

Lucy Broadwood ventured out collecting with J A Fuller Maitland, who was married to one of her cousins, and was the music critic of the *Times*. They published *English County Songs* in 1893. The collection included 95 songs, some of them appearing in print for the first time. In the introduction, Lucy and Fuller Maitland wrote: "In all parts of the country, the difficulty of getting the old-fashioned songs out of the people is steadily on the increase, and those who would undertake the task of collecting them—and a most engaging pursuit it is—should lose no time in setting to work. In almost every district, the editors have heard tantalising rumours of songs that "Old So-and-So used to sing, who died a year or two back". It is true that when once started, the greater number of the singers find a good deal of difficulty in leaving off, for they are not unnaturally pleased to see their old songs appreciated by anybody in these degenerate days."[19]

These were sentiments which were to be echoed by RVW so closely that he was clearly taking a lead from Lucy Broadwood. Many years later, in 1923, he wrote to her, "I remember years ago at St George Square when I was v. raw how you showed me Purcell and Bach and many things I did not know and also folk song—*it was you who first introduced me to it.*" (*our italics*).[20] In another letter he wrote, "You did give me a copy of the Folk Song Journal—it is a delight to me every day—I am using *Poor Mary*, and *The Young Serving Man* at the lecture I give in Bournemouth next week. I have also largely quoted from your preface. I hope you do not mind."[21]

Lucy Broadwood was a founder member of the Folk Song Society and both of RVW's tutors, Parry and Stanford, were vice presidents along with Sir John Stainer and Sir Alexander Mackenzie. J.A. Fuller Maitland and Leeds-based collector Frank Kidson, who published *Traditional Tunes* in 1891, were committee members, as were A.P. Graves and Mrs Laurence Gomme, who had specialised in collecting children's songs and games. The adoption of its first report in 1899 was moved by Sir Edward Elgar. The society started off with one foot firmly in the art music (what we would call classical music) establishment of the day, the other in the little-known territory of collecting from the ordinary people of the British Isles.

Few collectors managed to straddle those two worlds successfully. But both Lucy Broadwood and Ralph Vaughan Williams did. No wonder in his search for new musical expression as a composer, Ralph would consider English folk songs an avenue he wanted to explore. Lucy Broadwood, an accomplished singer and pianist in her own right, was also a well-to-do hostess who did a great deal to help talented musicians on their way, enabling them to meet people who might be helpful to them. She took a keen interest in Ralph Vaughan Williams' career, pasting reviews of his concerts in her diaries. In December 1904 she kept a review which said, "Among the band of young English composers who are now making their voices heard in the land, there is no-one more talented than Mr R. Vaughan Williams, who gave a concert at Bechstein Hall last night … This music is strong, melodious and original."[22]

Ralph Vaughan Williams and his wife Adeline were frequent visitors to Lucy's flat in Carlisle Mansions and he valued her opinion on his compositions. In her diary she notes offering him advice on his *Sea Symphony*, in which she felt the orchestra was overwhelming the singers. They sat going through it for a day, he making changes to the orchestration.[23]

Ralph was part of Lucy's circle; and she was keen to get more collectors out looking for singers and noting the songs they sang. One of the people who took that on board was the principal of the Hampstead Conservatoire, Cecil Sharp. He joined the Folk Song Society in 1901 and became a keen and active member and went on to become a leading figure in the revival of folk dance and song. He had already begun to note traditional dances, notably Morris dances he had seen first at Headington Quarry near Oxford.

In September 1903 Cecil Sharp had his first great success in folk song collecting. He heard *The Seeds of Love* sung by John England in Hambridge in Somerset that September when he went to visit his friend The Revd Charles Marson, who had suggested he might find some songs to note in the area. Sharp published his songs from Somerset in 1904.[24] Vaughan Williams was fired up by that. Fifty years later he wrote in the preface to the third edition of Sharp's *English Folk Song: Some*

Lucy Broadwood.
Surrey History Centre.

Cecil Sharp, 1916.
One Hundred English Folksongs.

Conclusions:

We knew, vaguely, that we had some traditional tunes in this country and that some of them, such as *Dives and Lazarus* and *My Bonny Boy* were very beautiful. But such a wealth of beauty as this volume, containing, to mention a few, *High Germany*, *The False Bride*, *Searching for Lambs* and *The Crystal Spring*, was something we never dreamed of. And where did it all come from? It was not a bit like Purcell, or Arne or Bishop or Sterndale Bennett. Nor apparently could we trace it to watered-down reminiscences of Schubert or Mendelssohn. It must therefore be indigenous.

But Sharp believed and we believe, that there, in the fastnesses of rural England, was the well-spring of English music; tunes of classical beauty which vied with all the most beautiful melody in the world, and traceable to no source other than the minds of unlettered country men, who unknown to the squire and the parson were singing their own songs, and, as Hubert Parry says, "liked what they made and made what they liked.[25]

There was a sense of urgency in the drive to collect folksongs. The Revd Sabine Baring-Gould, who was noting songs in the West Country, wrote in 1905 that there were not enough collectors in the field. "Few counties in England have been worked," he wrote. "Sussex has been well explored by the late Revd John Broadwood and then by Miss Lucy Broadwood; Yorkshire by Mr Frank Kidson; Northumberland by Dr Collingwood Bruce and Mr John Stokoe. Mr Cecil Sharp is now engaged in Somersetshire and Dr Vaughan Williams in Essex. Who will undertake Lincolnshire, Dorset, Hampshire and other counties?"

That call was partly taken up by two brothers, H.E.D. (Henry) and R. Hammond in Dorset and George B. Gardiner in Hampshire. Later the Australian-born pianist and composer Percy Grainger collected in Lincolnshire. But it was Vaughan Williams who wanted to spread his net more widely in East Anglia.

Most of the people who sang to the Edwardian collectors were old and Sharp believed their songs and tunes, learned in the 1840s, would be extinct in a decade. Sharp was keen to get publicity for the cause and gave a series of lectures in 1903. His friend Thomas Lennox Gilmour, who worked for the *Morning Post*, reported his lecture on folk songs in 1903. From then on the newspaper continued to publicise Sharp and his activities.

1904 brought further key developments which spurred Lucy Broadwood, Ralph Vaughan Williams and Cecil Sharp into action. J.A. Fuller Maitland gave a series of three lectures at the Royal Institution of Great Britain in Albemarle Street in Piccadilly on British Folk Song. Lucy Broadwood records in her diary that she went to all three on January 16th, 23rd and 30th. The programme for the third lecture is attached to the diary page, with a synopsis of that day's lecture.

The modern scales—Tonic relationships —the major scale not identical with the Ionian mode—one tune to many songs—one song to many tunes—*hints on the collection and arrangement of folk songs (our italics)*. The talk was illustrated by Miss Florence Bulleid and Mr James Campbell McInnes.[26]

Lucy records that Sharp went to the middle lecture.

On 30 January she wrote,

In the morning wrote a long letter to the *Morning Post* re folk songs. Heard from Mrs R. Vaughan Williams and answered. In afternoon went to J.A.F.M. last folk song lecture. Miss Bulleid sang her ballads admirably.

On 2 February she wrote in her diary:
My long letter on Folk Song together with one from Cecil Sharp and another letter came out in the *Morning Post…*

Heard from J.C. McInnes. Wrote to Cecil Sharp. In afternoon I went to Bach choir practice and I fetched Ralph Vaughan Williams in a cab and went via St Pancras to Hertford … (his) lecture in the Town Hall, very full, on

British Folk Song which I illustrated with 7 long ballads. Enthusiasm and interest shown. Returned by train…

Two days later both RVW and Sharp are in touch with her again. The next day she:

heard from Mr Sharp, R.V. Williams, F. Kidson and other folk song people.

In evening went to sup with Ralph Vaughan Williams to meet Mr Cecil Sharp. We discussed the Folk Song Society and made a scheme for reviving its dying embers.[27]

Vaughan Williams starts collecting folk songs

All this was just nine weeks after Ralph had had his first real taste of successful collecting. In late 1903 he had been lecturing on folksong at Brentwood in Essex. Afterwards he was invited to a vicarage tea party at Ingrave near Brentwood by the Misses Heatley, who said they knew of a local man who knew some old songs. His name was Charles Pottipher and at this polite gathering, dressed in his best suit, he was clearly reluctant to sing. But Vaughan Williams went to see him at his cottage the following morning, 4 December 1903, and Mr Pottipher sang him *Bushes and Briars*. "I had never heard it before but I had known it all my life," he said later. He noted it down and also five other songs: *The Storm*, *Princess Royal*, *Here Comes Little David*, *The Cruel Father and the Affectionate Lover* and *The Sheffield Apprentice*.

So began two years of folk song collecting expeditions. In 1903 he went to Ingrave; Henry Burstow, a Horsham man, sang to him at Leith Hill Place, the family home. Isaac Longhurst sang to him at Broadmoor, Mr Garman at Forest Green in Surrey.

In 1904 he was out collecting in earnest and found 250 songs in Essex, (mainly in the Ingrave area), Sussex, Surrey, London, Wiltshire, Yorkshire and Kent. By the end of the year, according to Ursula Vaughan Williams, he had a year of achievement to look back on. "In fact he probably did not look back at all but spent his evenings studying maps, for as usual he was out all day collecting songs, mostly in Sussex, though on New Year's Eve he went as far as Gravesend."[28]

The subject of finding folk songs was still under discussion in the letters pages of the *Morning Post*. A Mr Stephen Gowe wrote complaining of a poverty of songs in Essex. Ralph took up this challenge and wrote to the paper:

Sir,

My attention has been drawn to the paragraph in your issue of October 1st referring to my letter in the Morning Post in which I described how I noted down a large number of folk songs in Essex. It may interest your readers to know that the village where I made my collection was Ingrave, near Brentwood. My thanks are due to the Misses Heatley of Ingrave Rectory for discovering singers in the parish who still sing "the old ballads", and introducing me to them, so that I could note down the songs as they sang them. It is interesting to note that though these ladies have lived in Ingrave for several years and are intimate with the village people, they had no idea that the folk song survived there until I suggested the possibility to them some time ago.

Now I believe that Ingrave is not an exceptional village from that point of view. I imagine if every village, not only in Essex, but all over England, were investigated, an equally rich store of traditional song will be found; but it will not be found without some trouble. The younger singers, it must be confessed, very seldom sing the old country ballads, it is the elder people to whom we must go and they are often shy, or have forgotten the old songs, or they will require a little persuasion and to be assured they are not being laughed at.

But if anyone cares to undertake the search he will find the results amply repay him. I am sure that your readers would be astonished at the beauty and evident antiquity of many of the tunes which I have noted down, many of them being founded on "the old Church modes". The collections of *Songs of England* and the like give no idea of the real nature of English folk music; indeed I believe we are only now beginning to realise what a store of beautiful melody has existed in our country; and this is not a mere individual opinion, but is supported by a perusal of the collections of folk music made in Sussex and Somerset by such well known authorities as Miss Lucy Broadwood and Mr Cecil Sharp.

But whatever is done in the way of preserving traditional music must be done quickly; it must be remembered that the tunes, at all events, of true folk songs exist only by oral tradition, so that if they are not soon noted down and preserved they will be lost for ever.

This is the work that the "Folk Song Society" is attempting to do. The Society has already published six numbers of its "Journal" each containing about forty traditional ballads collected from all parts of England, besides which the Society has an immense quantity of material still in manuscript which it is only prevented from publishing for lack of funds. May I add that the secretary of the society is Miss Lucy Broadwood, 84 Carlisle Mansions, Victoria Street, SW. and that if any of your readers know any traditional ballads or any information concerning them, they would be doing a good work by sending them to the hon.sec., when they will be considered by the editing committee: or if anyone knows of traditional songs but does not feel able to note them down correctly, I

RVW noting down songs.
Anne Roberts.

myself should be happy, wherever possible, to come and note down the songs from the mouths of the singers.

Yours etc. R.Vaughan Williams.[29]

Notes

1 Now owned by the National Trust.

2 Day, J. (1963 reprinted 1998) *Vaughan Williams,* Oxford: OUP, p.4.

3 Foss, H. (1950) *Ralph Vaughan Williams, A Study,* London: Harrap, p.19.

4 Wedgwood, B. and Wedgwood, H. (1980) *The Wedgwood Circle 1730-1897: Four Generations of a Family and Their Friends,* Southampton: Eastview Editions, pp.344-50.

5 Holmes, P. (1997) *Vaughan Williams.* London: Omnibus Press, p.9.

6 Raverat, G. (1952) *Period Piece: A Cambridge Childhood.* London: Faber and Faber, p.273.

7 Ibid. 3.

8 Ibid.

9 Ibid.

10 Ibid. 6 p.273.

11 Ibid. 3 p.27.

12 Ibid. p.28.

13 Ibid. p.30.

14 Burney, C. in Rees, A. *Rees' Cyclopaedia s.v. Simplicity in Music* (1802-1820).

15 *Lynn News and Advertiser,* July 1952.

16 Berlioz, H. (1963) *Evenings in the Orchestra* Fortescue. C.R. (trans.), London: Peregrine Books, p.222.

17 *RVW Society Journal*, 14 February, 1999.

18 Flattening the seventh note of the scale indicated that the singers were using modes rather than conventional major or minor scales. Learned musicians of the time doubted that the English 'peasantry' could possibly use or understand them.

19 Broadwood, L.E. and Fuller Maitland, J.A. (1893) *English County Songs.* London: J.A. Cramer and Co Ltd, preface p.iv.

20 Letter 3 April 1923, in Lucy Broadwood collection, Surrey History Centre.

21 Letter 2 October 1902, in Lucy Broadwood collection, Surrey History Centre.

22 Lucy Broadwood's diary 1904, ibid.

23 Lucy Broadwood's diary 18 October 1910, Surrey History Centre.

24 Schofield, D. (2004) Sowing the Seeds: Cecil Sharp and Charles Marson in Somerset, *Folk Song Journal* 8 (4).

25 Sharp,C. (1907, 4th edition 1965) *English Folk Song: Some Conclusions.* Mercury Books Appreciation of Cecil Sharp by RVW.

26 Lucy Broadwood's diary 1904, Surrey History Centre.

27 Lucy Broadwood's diary 1904, Surrey History Centre.

28 As quoted by Williams V. U. (1964) *R.V.W. A biography of Ralph Vaughan Williams.* London: Clarendon Paperbacks.

29 Ibid. p.69.

The Compleat Collector

"It will greatly facilitate the work of the Hon Secretary if contributors of Folk Songs to the Society will observe the following rules when preparing their MSS."

Lucy Broadwood, secretary of the Folk Song Society

The Notebooks

Before we embark on the story of Vaughan Williams' remarkable visit to West Norfolk, it is worth looking at how he noted songs, and the background to folk song collecting at the time.

Ralph Vaughan Williams noted all the tunes he found in Norfolk in a small field manuscript notebook, taking down the tunes as the singers sang them to him. It's clear that he had time to note some songs more carefully than others, especially when he was noting from a group of singers together. Sometimes he notes, "I am doubtful about this" or observes that the singer was very hoarse. He notes down words when he hasn't heard the song before; sometimes there are fragments, where perhaps the older singers can't remember all the words themselves. It was then for Vaughan Williams and often Lucy Broadwood and Frank Kidson to search out the remainder. Often the words went back to broadside sheets, of which all three had substantial collections. At the time, part of the collector's essential background information was a knowledge of broadsides, the printed sheets of ballads and songs hawked round the country by pedlars and street singers.[1]

His note of what he heard was, as far as one can tell, a faithful record. He didn't judge the musicianship of his singers and players, adjusting where they might have been 'wrong' to a trained musician's ear. Maybe it was the influence of the Revd John Broadwood, who had insisted he would

have the tunes as his singers sang them. It's one of the qualities which makes his collecting so valuable. He also notes variations in the tunes as they were sung to him, often as the singer adjusted the tune to the words. As you read these tunes, you can imagine the people singing them and hear the shape and cadence of Norfolk dialect in them. His respect for those men and women of West Norfolk permeates the way he noted their songs, and his later recollections of them.

There are other notebooks in Vaughan Williams' papers, but they appear to be the 'neat' transcriptions from the field notebook he took with him whenever he was out and about. He remarks on his own bad handwriting, so it appears that either Lucy Broadwood or possibly his wife Adeline would copy out tunes when they were being prepared for publication or comparison with versions collected elsewhere. He also had a scrapbook which had some words and notes in it.

The original field notebook was kept by his second wife Ursula Vaughan Williams until she died. It is now in the British Library.

In this book, we have used the song titles noted by Vaughan Williams, which were those given him by the singers he met. Some were known or published by other titles elsewhere, but we are staying with the Norfolk versions. He tended to note in the keys of G or D and their related keys for convenience (a natural choice for a string player). He clearly did not expect singers to sing them in those keys, choosing instead a

opposite: Ballard seller in Pilot Street.
Anne Roberts.

Example of Vaughan Williams notebook—On Board a '98, Mr Leatherday, King's Lynn Union, 9 January 1905.
British Library.

pitch which suited them. The tradition was to sing unaccompanied, and there is no note of anyone using an accompanying instrument on his West Norfolk visits. When he collected elsewhere, he noted the instruments if people played them.

An interesting feature of the King's Lynn notes is that he does not record having heard any of these songs in a pub. They are either written down as heard "in King's Lynn", "in the North End" or "in the union". Again, his custom in other places, both before and after the King's Lynn visit, is to note if he has heard a song in a pub, so it is fair to conclude that he went to his singers' homes or to the union. No doubt there was plenty of singing in the pubs, but that was not where Vaughan Williams headed to note down songs. In Lucy Broadwood's advice to collectors, she asks for the name of the singer, the date and place to be recorded, and as he has followed it elsewhere, there is no reason to suppose he did not do so in King's Lynn.[2]

It is evident that he had to write quickly and sometimes was not sure of a tune when a singer was hoarse or possibly was elderly and unable to sing well. Occasionally his

hasty note is difficult to transcribe with certainty, and we have had to make a judgement on what he was writing.

He was not using a phonograph at the time to record songs, even though he did so on later expeditions he made in South Norfolk and the Broads with George Butterworth.

Broadside Ballads

One of the essential tools of a folk song collector's trade was a knowledge of broadside ballads, published by printers in the cities and commonly sold in the streets and fairs by ballad sellers.

Broadsides were the street literature of the country for four centuries. When few people could afford books, they were a source of information, comment and entertainment. They were ephemera: most were thrown away after reading or pasted on walls or cupboard doors. A few were in collections. Some reproduced songs which were popular at the time; others were like newspapers, reporting court cases and current events. Like today's tabloid newspapers, they had brash headlines and did a roaring trade when sensational court cases were going on. Some of the publishers had their own writers to turn such events into doggerel; others put old ballads or popular songs into print. Many of the crime-based ballads have a moral at the end: don't go poaching, or thieving, or you will end up in the same way as the unfortunate souls in the ballad. Dreadful murders seemed to be good earners for the publishers. The story of William Corder's trial for the murder of Maria Marten in the Red Barn sold more than one and a half million copies. There was also a brisk trade in sentimental ballads, as singers enjoyed a good love story then as now.

The publishers and printers of these broadsides included James Catnach, who originated in Alnwick and then went to London at the Seven Dials, and John Pitts, who had his Toy and Marble Warehouse there. One of the capital's largest slums, the Seven Dials became the centre for the ballad wholesalers; Dickens described it in his early Sketches by Boz as "Seven Dials! The region of song and poetry—first effusions and last dying speeches: hallowed by the names of Catnach and of Pitts." Pitts and Catnach were great rivals, but there were others in the same trade: Henry Parker Such and William Fortey among them. The ballads were supplied by the ream (480 sheets) or sometimes by the yard to men and women who then sold them to the public.

The ballad sellers sang their wares on the street. There are records of ballad sellers in King's Lynn in the 19th century, so some might have provided the words of the ballads sung in the town. Others might have come from ships in port, or from visiting pedlars and showmen. The ballads cost a ha'penny or a penny and they were widely distributed. They rarely had tunes printed with them, although would sometimes specify a well-known air of the time, which is often of little help to us now. The diarist Samuel Pepys had a collection of broadsides.[3]

By the time Vaughan Williams was collecting, both Frank Kidson and Lucy Broadwood had collections and RVW had some of his own, which are now in the Vaughan Williams Memorial Library. Kidson, in particular, felt a good knowledge of broadsides was essential to a folk song collector.

Vaughan Williams had limited time for collecting and will sometimes refer to a broadside source for the words of a song. Unfortunately, this can deny us the local turn of phrase in some, but possibly gained him precious time for noting more songs. It also had the benefit of filling in the gaps in the singers' memories. Many had not sung these songs for some years and did not necessarily remember all the words.

Of the King's Lynn songs, Vaughan Williams noted only 19 full, or reasonably full, sets of words. In some others he notes just a first verse, which has enabled us to seek out the likely broadside or other version he had heard. But some are noted only as tunes, and broadsides have to be the first port of call for the most likely lyrics. The broadside writers' language tends to be more flowery and less direct than that honed by oral tradition.

The Folk Song Society

Lucy Broadwood was the secretary of the Folk Song Society and already had some years of experience of collecting by the time Ralph Vaughan Williams ventured into the field. Over the previous 15 years, there had been a growing number of people interested in collecting 'genuine old ballads' and the formation of the Folk Song Society came out of their work. Some collectors were out in the field themselves, armed with manuscript books and a determination to seek out the singers and their songs. They had also built up a network of correspondents who sent them further

The Long Song Seller from a daguerrotype by Beard.
London Labour and London Poor by Henry Mayhew Vol. I, pub.1861.

Example of a popular ballard song book published for home consumption.
public domain, pub 1880.

material. Lucy Broadwood developed a wide correspondence with people who had songs to offer, lamenting the fact that as a woman she could not venture into pubs alone in search of songs. She set out guidelines for collectors which Vaughan Williams followed. This was her advice in the 1906 Folk Song Journal:

TO COLLECTORS AND CONTRIBUTORS OF FOLK SONGS

Collectors are reminded that the Society's leaflet, *Hints to Collectors*, has proved useful to beginners, and may be had at three half-pence the copy from the Hon. Secretary.

1. Write on only one side of the sheet of paper, whether words or music. It is of the greatest importance that Tunes should be written with *unmistakeable clearness in the first instance*. NAMES and ADDRESSES should be unmistakeable to the reader not familiar with them.

2. In the case of TUNES, write the title of the song to which it belongs *above the tune, in the middle of the sheet*. On the *right side* of the tune, and above it, write:

"Sung by (Mr., Mrs. Or Miss -------) at (King's Lynn, Norfolk.)

Noted by (John or Edith --------) *Date* (Sept.,1905)"

On the *left side* of the tune write the *tempo* or *mode* of the air, if wished.

3. In the case of WORDS, the song should have its title written above it, and the verses should be properly divided. Notes on the words should be marked with an asterisk, etc., and written at the foot of the sheet.

4. All DETAILS concerning age, occupation of the singer, the source of the song, and so forth, are of interest and importance. But they should be written *on a separate sheet of paper* headed with the name of the song to which they refer, together with any general remarks that the contributor wishes to make on the song itself.

5. Each TUNE should be firmly attached to its own WORDS, and sheet with DETAILS.

6. Contributors should keep copies of their MSS.

7. All communications should be initialled on the envelope "F.S.S."[4]

This is largely what Vaughan Williams did, although sometimes the "unmistakeable clearness" is not always evident as he became more pressed for time and had to make his notes quickly!

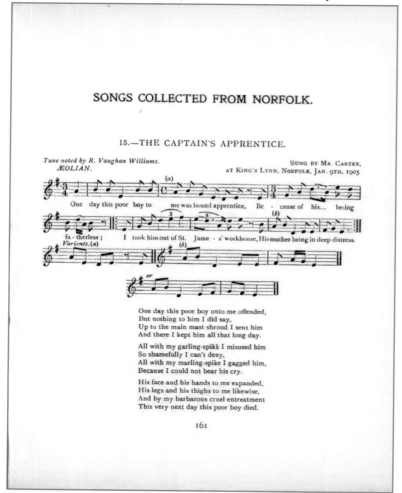

Page from The Folk Song Society Journal 1906, No. 8, Vol. II, Part 3, where RVW first published some of his King's Lynn collection.

British Library.

Notes

1   Broadwood, L.E. and Fuller Maitland, J.A. (1893) *English County Songs.* London: J.A.Cramer and Co Ltd, preface p.iv.

2   There is a strong tradition in King's Lynn that RVW collected songs at the pub called the *Tilden Smith.* It is not mentioned in any of his notebooks or letters. However, in the 1950s the BBC chose the pub for a programme about folksong, using local singers at the time. This could have led to the assumption that Vaughan Williams had collected there, which is not borne out by the manuscripts. As he was staying in a temperance hotel, he might well have repaired to the *Tilden Smith* for a drink in the evening! There is also evidence from a contemporary newspaper report of a licencing hearing that the pub had no music licence at the time.

3   Shepard, L. (1962) *The Broadside Ballad.* London: Herbert Jenkins Ltd.

4   *Folk Song Society Journal* (1906) 8, (II, 3) p.i.

First Stop The Fens: Two Days in the Tilneys

"In times past every English village was a nest of singing birds."
Cecil Sharp, folksong collector, writing in English Folksong: Some Conclusions

Maybe it was as a result of Vaughan Williams' letter in the *Morning Post*, or maybe through Lucy Broadwood's indefatigable work for the F.S.S. that in 1905 Ralph made his way to Tilney All Saints just a few miles outside King's Lynn. There is no evidence of why he went to Northwest Norfolk. Maybe it was through someone getting in touch with Lucy Broadwood or Cecil Sharp; maybe the vicar of Tilney All Saints, the Revd John Henry Newnum, responded to the circular letter Cecil Sharp had sent to clergy encouraging them to search out old songs sung by their parishioners. Maybe Kate Lee, the first secretary of the Folk Song Society, had encouraged a Norfolk expedition because of her experience of collecting in the Broads, where her husband had a yacht, and in Wells next the Sea.[1]

Maybe the invitation came directly from the first singer he met, the sexton at All Saints church in Tilney All Saints, John Whitby.[2] He may have come from a singing family. On 5 January 1905, a W. Whitby was noted as singing at the Dividing Club Dinner at Tilney Fen End.[3] Perhaps this is why, in the first week of January 1905, we find Ralph Vaughan Williams noting down John Whitby's songs. The composer had high hopes of this foray into the Fen villages, for it was in country areas he expected to find songs surviving. It was an expectation shared by the other collectors at the time. Cecil Sharp wrote in 1907 that "as recently as thirty or forty years ago every country village in England was a nest of singing birds."[4]

According to Kelly's 1904 Norfolk Directory, Tilney All Saints was a mile from Clenchwarton Station on the former Midland and Great Northern Joint Railway[5] and this may have been how Vaughan Williams arrived. Tilney St Lawrence lies a few miles to the south, beyond the present A47 from King's Lynn to Wisbech, and was the larger of the two villages. It had two blacksmiths and wheelwrights to All Saints' one and, where All Saints had a village shop, St Lawrence boasted a "grocer and draper". Most of Kelly's commercial entries for the Tilneys were farmers growing grain and vegetables.

Mr John Whitby the sexton

Vaughan Williams noted that his first singer, John Whitby, was sexton at Tilney All Saints. By 1911 he was also Parish clerk, a post which had been held in the 1904 Directory by Robert Whitby. Robert Whitby, born in 1847 at Walpole St Andrew, was John Whitby's brother; by 1891 he was living in Tilney All Saints but is only ever described by the censuses as an agricultural labourer. John Whitby himself was aged 63 in 1901, born, like Robert, at Walpole St Andrew, six miles from Tilney. He was still living there with his wife and daughter, both named Rachel, and simply described as "groom and gardener". By 1911 he was a widower, still living at Walpole with his 21-year-old granddaughter Elizabeth Peeling who was described as (his) housekeeper. Whitby may have been a widely spread name locally, as the 1904 Directory also shows a William Whitby, beer retailer, in Tilney St Lawrence and a Walter Whitby, blacksmith, in Walpole St Peter.

opposite: The village fiddle player.
Anne Roberts.

17

John Whitby sang 10 songs:

As I was a-Walking
Bold Carter
Green Bushes
It was one Morning
Lord Bateman
Lord Lovel
The Crafty Ploughboy
The Red Barn (Maria Marten)
The Streams of Lovely Nancy
The Yorkshire Bite/Lincolnshire Farmer
Young Jockie

Mr Whitby's repertoire has quite a "rural" flavour and he may well have aired it at harvest celebrations and other community festivities.[6] It includes two ancient but frequently encountered narrative ballads: *Lord Bateman* and *Lord Lovel*. The latter might perhaps have been well-liked locally because of the proximity of Lovells Hall, a couple of miles from Tilney and just inside the parish boundary of the next village, Terrington St Clement.

Lord Bateman

Mr Whitby January 7th 1905

Lord Bateman was a noble lord   a noble lord of high degree   But he was ta-ken and put in prison   Till of his life he was quite wear-y

Lord Bateman

Lord Bateman was a noble lord
A noble lord of high degree
He shipped himself on board a ship
Some foreign country he would go see.

He sailed east, he sailed west
Until he came to proud Turkey
When he was taken into prison
Until of his life he was quite weary.

In this prison there grew a tree
It grew so stout, it grew so strong,
And he was chained all by the middle
Until his life it was almost gone.

The turnkey had one only daughter
The fairest that all eyes did see
She stole the keys of her father's prison
And said Lord Bateman she would set free.

'Have you got houses, have you got land?
Does half Northumberland belong to you?
What would you give to that fair young lady
That out of prison would set you free?'

'I have got houses, I have got land,
And half Northumberland belongs to me
All this I would give to the fair young lady
That out of prison would set me free.'

She took him to her father's hall
And gave to him the best of wine
And all the healths she drank with him
'I wish Lord Bateman that you were mine.'

'Seven years I will make a vow
Seven years I will keep it strong
If you will wed with no other woman
I will wed with no other man.'

Seven years been gone and past
And fourteen days to keep it strong
She packed up all her gay clothing
And said Lord Bateman she would go see.

And when she came to Lord Bateman's castle
There she boldly rang the bell
'Who's there, who's there?' cried the proud young porter
'Who's there I pray unto me tell.'

'Is this, is this Lord Bateman's castle?
And is his Lordship here within?'
'Oh yes, it is Lord Bateman's castle,
And he's just returned with a new bride in.'

'Tell him to send me a slice of bread
And a bottle of the best wine
And not to forget the fair young lady
That did release him when he was confined.'

Away, away, went this proud young porter
Away, away, away went he
Until he came to Lord Bateman's chamber
Then on his bended knees fell he.

'What news, what news, have you my porter?
What news have you brought to me?'
'There is one of the fairest creatures
That ever my two eyes did see.

She has got rings on every finger
And on one she has got three
She's as much gay gold about her middle
As would buy half Northumberlee.

She bids you send her a slice of bread
And a bottle of the best wine
And not to forget that fair young lady
Who did release you when close confined.'

Then up and spoke the young bride's mother
Never heard to speak so free
'You'll not forget my only daughter
If so Sophia has crossed the sea.'

Lord Bateman then flew into a passion
And broke his sword in splinters three
'She came to me with horse and saddle
And she may go back with coach and three.'

Then he prepared another wedding
With both their hearts so full of glee
'I'll give up all my father's riches
If so Sophia has crossed the sea.'

This ballad was widely collected across the country. Both Frank Kidson and Lucy Broadwood published versions of it in the 1890s and it was published as a broadside in 1624. The story seems to have appealed to many singers despite the 19 or in some cases 21 verses! Lucy heard it in Northamptonshire and Cecil Sharp collected it in December 1905 in Somerset.

RVW knew Lucy Broadwood and J Fuller Maitland's *English County Songs* so it seems likely that he was content to note the first verse and rely either on their versions or on the broadside. He had collected a version himself at Billericay Union in April 1904 from John Denny, two months later from Mr Wetherill in Bourne End. In 1908, Peter Knight of Hickling sang him the *Turkish Lady*, which sounds like the same story. This is the version in *English County Songs*.[7]

Tilney Church where John Whitby was sexton.
Colin James

It was one morning

Mr Whitby, Tilney All Saints, January 7th 1905

It was one morn - ing in the spring   I went on board   to serve   my_ king   I left my

dear - est   dear   be - hind   Who oft times told   me her heart was mine.

It was one morning

Oh very early all in the spring,
I went on board for to serve the king,
Leaving my dearest dear behind
She oft-times told me her heart was mine.

Oh then I hugged her all in my arms
I thought I got ten thousand charms
For promise vows and kisses sweet
Promised to marry next time we meet.

Oh when I was sailing all on the raging seas
Taking of all opportunities
Sending of letters to my dearest dear
But one from her I could not hear

Oh then I returned back to old England
I went unto her father's house,
Her father axed me oh what I mean
'My daughter a long time has a-married been.'

So cursed be all gold and silver too
And all false women that don't prove true
I'd sooner be where the bullets fly
Than be in a false woman's company.

One verse noted by Vaughan Williams from Mr Whitby. It is similar to the verse which was noted as the start of *Early, Early in the Spring* by Cecil Sharp in Somerset in 1906 from James Thomas at Cannington. The story is also told on broadsides. It appears as *The Disappointed Sailor* in W.H.Logan's *A Pedlar's Pack of Ballads and Songs* published in Edinburgh in 1869. Admiral Vernon's attacks on Cartagena in the West Indies took place in 1740 and 1741 (and are described, incidentally, in Smollett's novel, *Roderick Random*) but the song was current for the next 150 years, though sometimes in abbreviated form, according to Roy Palmer. This the version he refers to from *A Yacre of Land*:

It was early, early in the spring
I went on board to serve the King
I left my dearest dear behind
Who oft times told me her heart was mine.

When I came back to her father's hall
Enquiring for my jewel all
Her cruel old father this replied,
'Her mama says O if you deny.

'Oh she has married another man
A richer man for all his life
A richer man for all his life
O he had made her his lawful wife.'

'O God curse gold and silver too
And all false women that won't prove true,
For some will take and then will break
All for the sake of richeree.

'Oh stop young man, don't talk too fast
The fault is great but none of mine
The fault is great but none of mine
Don't speak so hard of the female kind.

'If you had gold you might have part
As you have none you have gained my heart
You gained it with a free goodwill
So keep my vows and hold them still.'

'Oh since hard fortune around me frowns,
I'll sail the ocean around and around,
I'll sail the ocean until I die
I'll quit my ways on a mountain high.'

A.L. Lloyd uses broadsides to fill out the narrative with yet another version, but using the same first verse. Both seem reminiscent of a Dorset song called *The Single Sailor* collected by the Hammond brothers between 1905 and 1908 from J. Baker in Bere Regis.[8]

When I was sailing on the sea
I sometimes found opportunity
To write a letter to my dear
But not one word from her did I hear.

When we arrived off Cartagena Town
The cannon-balls flew up and down
But all the dangers that I could find
Her sweet young face still run in my mind.

When I got back to old England's shore
I went straightway to my love's door
Her cruel old father made this reply
'My daughter does your love deny.

'She's married to a merchant all her life
So you may seek some other wife.'

I cursed all gold and silver too
I cursed young women who cannot be true
As first make vows and then them break
And marry a merchant for riches' sake.

I wish I was back off Panama shore
Where thundering cannon loud do roar
I'l sail the ocean until I die
Although the waves run mountains high.

Bold Carter

Mr Whitby, Tilney All Saints, January 7th 1905

Bold Carter

Come all you wild young men
And a warning take by me
Never lead your life astray
Into bad company.

Bold Carter is my name
And hard is my intent
Till I got pressed by a press merchant
And on board a man o'war got sent.

We hadn't sailed long
Before the first thing that we spied
It was five French ships came a sailing to the war
And at length they were going to draw nigh.

We hoisted our main colours
Our bloody, bloody flag we let fly
Singing every man stand to his gun
For the Lord knows the day he must die.

Our captain got wounded most wonderfully sore
And so did the most of his men
Our whole ship's rigging got all shot away
So at last we were forced to give in.

Our decks were all sprinkled with blood
And the great guns so loud they did roar
I wished myself back at home again
With my Polly that I left upon the shore.

She's a tall and handsome girl
She's a black and roving eye
And here upon the deck where I lay shot
For her sweet sake I must die.

Here's adieu to my father and my mother
Crying friends and relations too
I should never have crossed the salt seas so wide
If I had not been ruled by you.

RVW noted the words of *Bold Carter* from Mr Whitby's singing. This appeared in the *Journal of the Folk Song Society* Vol. III p.116. Roy Palmer says it first appeared as *The Valiant Sailor* in 1744 as one of 'three excellent new songs' in *The Irish Boy's Garland*, which was printed in Edinburgh and sold in Swan Close a little below Cross-Well, north side of the street.'

Lord Lovel

Mr Whitby January 8th 1905

Lord Lo-vel he stood at his cast-le gate, A comb-ing his milk white steed, When up__ came La-dy__ Nan-cy Bell To wish her lover good speed speed__ speed

Lord Lovel

Lord Lovel he stood at the castle gate
Combing his milk white steed,
When up came Lady Nancy Bell
To wish her lover good speed, speed, speed.

So where are you going Lord Lovel she cried
Oh where are you going, she said;
I'm going my lady Nancy Bell
Strange countries for to see.

When will you be back, Lord Lovel, she said
Oh when will you come back said she
In a year or two – or three at most,
I'll return to my fair Nancy.

But he had not been gone a year and a day
Strange countries for to see
When languishing thoughts came into his head
Lady Nancy Bell he would go see

So he rode and he rode on his milk white horse
Till he came to London town
And there he heard St Pancras bells toll
And the people all mourning round.

Oh what is the matter? Lord Lovel he said
Oh what is the matter said he.
A Lord's lady is dead the woman replied
And some call her Lady Nancy.

So he ordered the grave to be opened wide
And the shroud he turned down
And there he kissed her clay cold lips
Till the tears come trickling down.

Lady Nancy she died as it might be today
Lord Lovel he died as tomorrow
Lady Nancy she died out of pure, pure grief
Lord Lovel he died out of sorrow.

Lady Nancy was laid in St Pancras Church
Lord Lovel was laid in the choir
And out of her bosom there grew a red rose
And out of her lover's, a briar.

It grew and it grew to the church steeple too
And then it could grow no higher
So their (sic) it entwined in a true lovers' knot
For all true lovers to admire.

These words are from a broadside published by Such sometime between 1863 and 1885. Other publishers reproduced it in London and Edinburgh. Mr Whitby may have been attracted to the tale because of Lovel Hall and Lovel Cottage, taking their names from one of the manors in Terrington St Clement, which is one of Tilney All Saints' neighbouring villages. Lovel is also one of the titles of the Cokes of Holkham Hall.

Maria Marten

Mr Whitby

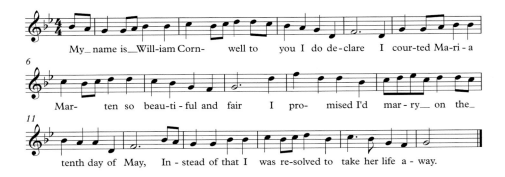

My_ name is_Will-iam Corn- well to you I do de-clare I cour-ted Ma-ri-a

Mar- ten so beau-ti - ful and fair I pro- mised I'd mar-ry_ on the_

tenth day of May, In - stead of that I was re-solved to take her life a - way.

Maria Marten

Come all you bold young thoughtless men
A warning take by me
And think of my unhappy fate
To be hanged upon a tree.

My name is William Corder
The truth I do declare
I courted Maria Marten
So beautiful and fair.

I promised her I'd marry her
All on one certain day
Instead of that I was resolved
To take her life away.

I went unto her father's house
Upon the eighteenth day of May
Come, my dearest Ria
And we'll fix the wedding day.

'If you will meet me at the red barn
As sure as I have life
I will take you down to Ipswich Town
And there make you my wife.'

He went straight home and fetched his gun
His pick-axe and his spade
He went unto the red barn
And there he dug her grave.

With heart so light she thought no harm
To meet him she did go
He murdered her all in the barn
And he laid her body low.

And all things being silent
They could not take no rest
Which appeared in her mother's house
When suckled at her breast.

Her mother had a dreadful dream
She dreamed it three nights o'er
She dreamed that her dear daughter
Lay beneath the red barn floor.

They sent her father to the barn
And in the ground he thrust
And there he found his daughter dear
Lay mingling with the dust.

Come all you young thoughtless men
Some pity look on me
On Monday next will be my last
To be hanged upon a tree.

This was a sensational murder and trial which was swiftly put into verse by the ballad sellers. William Corder was convicted of the murder of Maria Marten in 1828 and he was hanged at Bury St Edmunds. Catnach sold one and a half million copies of the ballad and the doleful accounts of Corder's crime, imprisonment and death. It was made into a Victorian melodrama and occupied many column inches in newspapers across East Anglia. As late as 1941 Arthur Mee wrote that

Maria Marten

while he was writing the Suffolk volume of *The King's England* series, 'the old melodrama of Maria Marten, founded on the crime, was drawing half of London to see it.'[9]

Vaughan Williams noted the first verse which Mr Whitby sang to him:

My name is William Cornwell to you I do declare
I courted Maria Marten most beautiful and fair
I promised her I'd marry on the 10th day of May
Instead of that I was resolved to take her life away.

He had heard the song from Mr Booker at Kingsfold in December 1904. George Hall, who learned his songs in Huntingdonshire, sang this version to collector R.A. Gatty at Hooton Roberts in 1907. Vaughan Williams linked this tune to the tune for *Come all ye Faithful Christians* when it was published in the *Journal of the Folk Song Society* Vol. II p.174. (From *Everyman's book of English Country Songs* by Roy Palmer pub. J.M.Dent, 1979) Other singers who sang this to him were Hoppy Flack at Fowlmere in Cambridgeshire in 1907 and Christopher Jay at Acle in 1908.

This is the full broadside and account of the *Confession and Execution of William Corder, the Murderer of Maria Marten, 1828* from the Seven Dials Press in the CSL collection:[10]

'Since the tragical affair between Thurtell and Weare, no event has occurred connected with the criminal annals of our country which has excited so much interest as the trial of Corder, who was justly convicted of the murder of Maria Marten on Friday last.

The Confession (Bury Gaol, August 10th, 1828 – condemned cell.

(Sunday evening, half past eleven.)

"I acknowledge being guilty of the death of poor Maria Marten, by shooting her with a pistol. The particulars are as follows—when we left her father's house, we began quarrelling about the burial of the child: she apprehended the place wherein it was deposited would be found out. The quarrel continued about three quarters of an hour upon this sad (sic) and about other subjects. A scuffle ensued, and during the scuffle, and at the time I think that she had hold of me, I took the pistol from the side pocket of my velveteen jacket and fired. She fell, and died in an instant. I never even saw her struggle. I was overwhelmed with agitation and dismay – the body fell near the front doors on the floor of the barn. A vast quantity of blood issued from the wound, and ran on to the floor and through the crevices. Having determined to bury the body in the barn (about two hours after she was dead sic) I went and borrowed a spade of Mrs Stow, but before I went there I dragged the body from the barn into the chaff house and locked the barn. I returned again to the barn, and began to dig a hole, but the spade being a bad one and the earth firm and hard, I was obliged to go home for a pick-axe and a better spade, with which I dug the hole, then buried the body. I think I dragged the body by the handkerchief that was tied round her neck. It was dark when I finished covering up the body. I went next day and washed the blood from off the barn floor. I declare to Almighty God I had no sharp instrument about me and no other wound but the one made by the pistol was inflicted by me. I have been guilty of great idleness, and at times led a dissolute life, but I hope through the mercy of God to be forgiven,

William Corder"

Witness to the signing by the said William Corder,

John Oridge.

Condemned cell, 11 o'clock Monday morning, August 11th 1828

The above confession was read over carefully to the prisoner in our presence who stated most solemnly it was true, and that he had nothing to add or retract from it – W.Stocking, chaplain; Timothy R. Holmes, Under Sheriff.

The Execution

At ten minutes before 12 o'clock the prisoner was brought from his cell and pinioned by the hangman, who was brought from London for the purpose. He appeared resigned, but was so weak as to be unable to stand without support; when his cravat was removed he groaned heavily, and appeared to be labouring under great mental agony. When his wrists and arms were made fast, he was led round twards (sic) the scaffold, and as he passed the different yards in which the prisoners were confined he shook hands with them, and speaking to two of them by name, he said, 'Goodbye, God Bless You.' They appeared considerably affected by the wretched appearance that he made and "God Bless You!" "May God receive your soul!" were frequently uttered as he passed along. The chaplain walked before the prisoner, reading the usual Burial Service, and the Governor and Officers walking immediately after him. The prisoner was supported to the steps which led to the scaffold; he looked somewhat wildly around and a constable was obliged to support him while the hangman was adjusting the fatal cord. There was a barrier to keep off the crowd amounting to upwards of seven thousand persons, who had at this time stationed themselves in the adjoining fields, on the hedges, the tops of houses, and at every point from which a view of the execution could be best obtained. The prisoner, a few moments before the drop fell, groaned heavily, and would have fallen, had not the second constable caught hold of him. Everything having been made ready, the signal was given, the fatal drop fell, and the unfortunate man was launched into eternity. Just before he was turned off he said in a feeble tone, "I am justly sentenced and may God forgive me.'

William Corder.

The Murder of Maria Marten by W.Corder

Come all you thoughtless young men a warning take by me
And think upon my unhappy fate to be hanged upon a tree
My name is William Corder, to you I do declare
I courted Maria Marten, most beautiful and fair.

I promised I would marry her upon a certain day
Instead of that I was resolved to take her life away
I went into her father's house the 18th day of May
Saying my dear Maria we will fix the wedding day.

If you will meet me at the Red Barn, as sure as I have life,
I will take you to Ipswich Town, and there make you my wife.
I then went home and fetched my gun, my pickaxe and my spade,
I went into the Red Barn and there I dug her grave.

With heart so light, she thought no harm, to meet him she did go,
He murdered her all in the barn, and laid her body low;
After the horrible deed was done, she lay weltering in her gore,
Her bleeding, mangled body he buried beneath the Red-barn floor.

The Red Barn, Polstead.

Now all things being silent, her spirit could not rest,
She appeared unto her mother, who suckled her at breast,
For many a long month or more, her mind being sore oppressed,
Neither day or night she could not take any rest.

Her mother's mind being so disturbed, she dreamt three nights o'er
Her daughter she lay murdered beneath the Red-barn floor,
She sent her father to the barn, when he the ground did thrust,
And there he found his daughter mingling with the dust.

My trial is hard, I could not stand, most woeful was the sight,
When her jawbone was brought to prove, which pierced my heart quite;
Her aged father standing by, likewise his loving wife,
And in her grief her hair she tore, she scarcely could keep life.[11]

Adieu, adieu, my loving friends, my glass is almost run,
On Monday next will be my last, when I am to be hanged;
So you, young men, who do pass by, with pity look on me,
For murdering Maria Marten, I was hanged upon a tree.

The Streams of Lovely Nancy

Mr Whitby January 1905

The Streams of Lovely Nancy

The streams of lovely Nancy are divided in three parts
Where young men and maidens take their sweethearts
And the drinking good liquor causes their hearts to sing
And the sound of yonder valleys cause the rocks for to ring.

At the top of this mountain, there my love's castle stands
It's all overbuilt with ivory on yonder black sand
Fine arches, fine porches, and diamonds so bright,
It's a pilot for a sailor on a dark winter's night.

On yonder high mountain, where the wild fowl do fly,
There is one amongst them that flies very high,
If I had her in my arms, love, in the diamond's black land
How soon I'd secure her by the sleight of my hand.

At the bottom of this mountain there runs a river clear,
A ship from the Indies did once anchor there
With her red flags a flying and the beating of her drum
Sweet instruments of music and the firing of her gun.

So come all you little streamers that walk the meadows gay
I'll write unto my own true love, wherever she may be
For her rosy lips entice me with her tongue she tells me so
And an angel might direct us right, and where shall we go?

Complete words from the singing of George Dowden of Lackington in Dorset, who sang it to Cecil Sharp in 1905. Found also in Sussex. Lucy Broadwood suggested it could be a Cornish song. The Revd Sabine Baring-Gould collected a West Country version called *The Streams of Nantsian*.[12] Later Hammond collected it in 1905 and Cecil Sharp in 1906. Vaughan Williams only noted the words of the first verse from Mr Whitby.

As I Was a-Walking

Mr Whitby Jan 1905

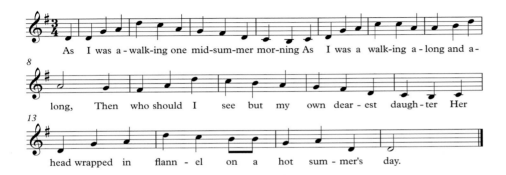

As I was a-walk-ing one mid-sum-mer mor-ning As I was a walk-ing a-long and a-long, Then who should I see but my own dear-est daugh-ter Her head wrapped in flann-el on a hot sum-mer's day.

As I Was a-Walking

As I was a walking one midsummer morning
As I was a walking along and along
Who should I see but my own dearest daughter
With her head wrapped in flannel on a hot summer's day.

"Oh Mother, dear Mother, come set you down by me
Come set you down by me and pity my case
For my wounds are now aching, my poor heart is breaking,
And I in a low spirit must die."

*"So rattle your drums, and play your fife over me,
So rattle your drums as we march along
Then return to your home and think of that young girl
O there goes a young girl cut down in her pride."*

"O mother, dear mother, come send for the clergyman
O send for the doctor to bind up my wound,
And likewise my young man that his heart may not wander,
That he may see me before I'm screwed down."

So rattle etc..

As I Was a-Walking (cont)

"And when I am dead to the church they will carry me
Six jolly fellows to carry me along,
And in each of their hands a bunch of green laurel
So they might not smell me as they're walking along.

So rattle etc….

And when I am dead to the church they will carry me
Six pretty maidens to bear up my pall,
And in each of their hands a bunch of primroses
Saying there goes a true-hearted girl to her home.

So rattle etc…

This comes from the same family of songs as the *Unfortunate Lad* and Mr Anderson's song, *As I was a walking down by the black hospital*. I have used the words collected by Vaughan Williams' friend and fellow composer George Butterworth. A version from Hampshire collected by Francis Jekyll in 1909 is included in *The Penguin Book of English Folk Songs* edited by A.L. Lloyd and Vaughan Williams and published in 1959. This is their note on the song:

> At the end of the eighteenth century a homilectic street ballad spread in England concerning the death and ceremonial funeral of a soldier 'disordered' by a woman. It was called *The Unfortunate Rake* (in Ireland) or *The Unfortunate Lad* (on the broadside printed by Such). It is still a common song in the British Army, though printed versions are few. English sets have been reported from Yorkshire (*Folk Song Society Journal* Vol. I p.254) and Hampshire (Vol. III p.292). Our song represents a later development in which the sexes are reversed, but the ceremonial funeral is retained. Versions of this form have been recorded from Oxfordshire and Somerset (JFSS iv p.326) as well as the present Hampshire version. In America, the song has been adapted to the cattle range (*The Cowboy's Lament* or *The Streets of Laredo*) and the gambling hall (*St James Infirmary*.) The motive of the ceremonial funeral remains constant, despite all the transformations of the chief character.

Mr Whitby would have been astonished at how far the ballad had travelled.

Green Bushes

Mr Whitby Jan 1905

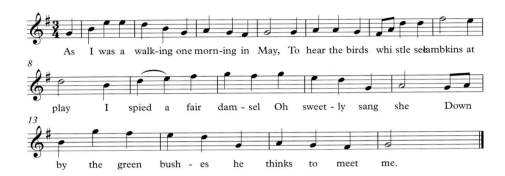

Green Bushes[13]

As I was a-walking one morning in May
To hear the birds whistle, see lambkins at play,
I spied a fair damsel Oh sweetly sang she
'Down by the green bushes he thinks to meet me.'

'Oh where are you going, my sweet pretty maid?'
'My lover I'm seeking, kind Sir,' she said,
'Shall I be your lover, and will you agree
To forsake the old love and foregather with me?'

'I'll buy you fine beavers, a gay silken gown,
With furbelowed petticoats flounced to the ground
If you'll leave your old love and following me
Forsake the green bushes, where he waits for thee.'

'Quick, let us be moving from under the trees
Quick let us be moving, kind sir, if you please
For yonder my true love is coming, I see,
Down by the green bushes he thinks to meet me.'

The old love arrived, the maiden was gone,
He sighed very deeply, he sighed all alone,
'She is on with another, before off with me,
So adieu ye green bushes for ever,' said he.

'I'll be as a schoolboy, I'll frolic and play,
No false hearted maiden shall trouble my day
Untroubled at night I will slumber and snore
So adieu ye green bushes, I'll fool it no more.'

This version of the song is from Lucy Broadwood's *English County Songs* p.170 published in 1893. She heard it in Devon. RVW had heard the song from Mr and Mrs Ratford at Ingrave in April 1904, and in 1922 Cecil Sharp also collected it. A.L. Lloyd says in *Folksong in England*, p.32, that the dominant version in England, Scotland and Ireland was spread by theatre companies travelling with Buckstone's play *The Green Bushes* written in 1845. King's Lynn resident Jean Tuck recognised the song when we sang it in King's Lynn in 2013.

The Lincolnshire Farmer

Sung by Mr John Whitby, Tilney All Saints, January 8th 1905

Good peo-ple att-end and soon you shall hear It is of an old far-mer lived in Lin-coln-shire; A York-shire boy he kept for his man for to do all his bus-iness as you shall un-der-stand.

The Lincolnshire Farmer

Good people attend and you shall hear
It's of an old farmer lived in Lincolnshire
A Yorkshire boy he kept for his man
For to do all his business and you will understand.

Now early one morning he called for his man
For to go to the fair, as you will understand,
Saying, "Boy, the old cow you shall take to the fair,
For she is in good order and her I can spare."

Away the boy went with the cow in a band,
To go to the fair, as you shall understand,
As he was going he set with three men
And he sold his old cow for six pounds ten.

Away then they went to an alehouse to drink
And there the three men paid the boy down his clink
There sat an old highwayman drinking his wine
Said he to himself, 'All that money is mine.'

The boy then unto the landlady did say,
'What am I to do with my money, I pray?'
'I'll sew it into your coat lining,' said she,
'For fear on the highway you robbed shall be.'

The boy took his leave and home he did go
The highwayman he followed after also,
And soon o'ertook him all on the highway
'Oh well overtaken, young man,' he did say.

'Will you get up behind me?' the highwayman said,
'How far are we going?' the poor boy replied.
Four miles and further, for ought that I know.'
So it's jump up behind and away they did go.

They rode till they came to a green shaded lane,
'Oh now my young man I must tell it you plain,
Deliver your money without any strife
Or else I will soon make an end of your life.'

When he found that he had no time for dispute
He quickly alighted without fear or doubt
He tore his coat lining the money spilled out,
And all in the long grass he strewed it about.

The highwayman he jumped down from his horse
But little he thought it was to his loss
For while he was gath'ring the money from the grass
To make him amends he rode off with his horse.

He hallooed and shouted and bid him to stand
The boy would not hear him but still galloped on
Unto his own master, and to him did bring
A saddle and bridle and many a fine thing.

Now as the boy John he was riding home,
The servant was standing all in the front room,
She runs to her master and says 'Here's a loss,'
Says she 'The old cow has turned into a hoss.'

The saddlebag opened, within was a hole
They took sixty pounds out in silver and gold.
Says the boy to his master, 'I hope you'll allow,
That master, dear master, I've well sold your cow.'

The boy with his valour and courage so rare
Three parts of the money he got for his share
So now the highwayman he's lost a great store
And he may go robbing until he gets more.

This is another version of the tale sung as *The Yorkshire Farmer* or the Yorkshire Bite by Mr Anderson. The song was also collected in Herefordshire and Suffolk. When it was published in the *Folk Song Society Journal* Vol. II p.174 Vaughan Williams explained that he had used the words in full from Mr Anderson's version, collected later in the week in King's Lynn, to complete Mr Whitby's. Frank Kidson says the more usual title of the song is *The Crafty Ploughboy* or *The Highwayman Outwitted*; but from 20th century recordings it seems to have remained as *The Yorkshire Bite* in Norfolk and Suffolk. The words were on a Pitt broadside and on later ballad sheets, including the *Pedlar's Pack of Ballads* of 1868.

Young Jocky

Mr Whitby Jan 1905

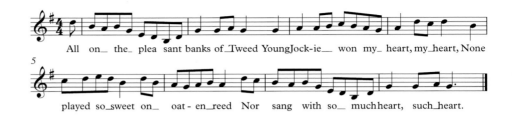

All on_ the_ plea sant banks of_Tweed YoungJock-ie_ won my_ heart, my_heart, None played so_sweet on_ oat - en_reed Nor sang with so_ much heart, such_heart.

Young Jocky

Young Jocky walked out one light summer's morning
He carelessly laid himself against a green
He had not laid there long before his true love come by
And on her lovely Jocky cast an eye.

And the little lambs play round them all in the morning dew.

This song does not seem to have wide currency. RVW gives us this one verse. The following version was collected in 1912 by Dorothy Marshall from Mrs Humphrey "learned before she was 16" in Storrington, Sussex.[14]

Young Jocky walked out on a fine summer's morn
And sat himself down beneath a green thorn
He had not long been there when a fair maid came by
And on this gentle shepherd cast a languishing eye.

She says my gentle shepherd have you seen my two lambs
Have you seen my two lambs that so carelessly strayed
Oh yes my lovely fair maid I saw them go by
They are down in yonder green woods indeed it's no lie.

She thanks him with a curtsey and turned herself round
Young Jocky followed after and lodged in the downs
She came to the groves but no lambs could she find
But still this young shepherd kept wondering her mind.

'Tis a sad disappointment on a poor silly maid
She little thought he played his games so artful and gay.

Soon this young couple married as I've heard many say
Down in yonder cottage the dwell both night and day
They live and love together all joys to renew

Stephen Poll

Vaughan Williams' next contact was the fiddler Stephen Poll of Tilney St Lawrence, whom he described as a labourer aged about 80. He was however nearer 70 than 80 as he was born c1836 [15] at Tilney All Saints where his two eldest children, Florence and William were also born. By 1870 Stephen and his wife Frances had moved to Tilney St Lawrence, where they had four more children but by 1901 Frances had died and Stephen was at home with his youngest son, another Stephen. As an instrumentalist and caller of dances, Stephen senior was no doubt well known to John Whitby.

Mr Stephen Poll sang one song (The Foxhunt) and played four tunes:

Gypsies in the Wood
Ladies' Triumph
Low backed Car
Trip to the Cottage

The Village Fiddler.
Library of Congress.

Trip to the Cottage

Stephen Poll, Tilney St Lawrence January 7th 1905

Trip to the Cottage

The tune was found in Ireland and in Dorset and Shropshire. The last professional piper in Farney, Louth, Philip Goodman, had it in his repertoire in 1898. One of the earliest recordings was by Cecil Sharp on a wax cylinder in 1908 from the playing of John Locke, a gipsy fiddler.

Ladies' Triumph

Stephen Poll, Tilney St Lawrence, January 7th 1905

Ladies' Triumph

One of the tunes was the widespread *Ladies' Triumph*, more commonly just *The Triumph*, of which versions have been collected around the country, including a Dorset one from Thomas Hardy, who describes the dance in *Under the Greenwood Tree*. This and a version from Northumberland are included in the English Folk Dance and Song Society's *Community Dance Manual* but although obviously based on the same tune, neither resembles Poll's very closely.

No other version of the tune seems to have been collected in Norfolk under that name, but Poll's tune does closely resemble *Shave the Donkey* as played by Walter Bulwer of Shipdham on the fiddle in 1959. (Bulwer's two-part tune is simpler than Poll's three-part tune, more or less the first two parts, reversed, with the third omitted.) Certainly Stephen Poll's version of *Ladies' Triumph* fits the dance of the same name beautifully.

The Country Dance by Walter Shirlaw.
Metropolitan Museum of Art.

Gypsies in the Wood

Stephen Poll, Tilney St Lawrence January 7th 1905

Gypsies in the Wood

Gypsies in the Wood accompanies the simple longways dance of the same name. As a song (Roud 13187) it is associated with a children's singing and clapping game, starting with the lines, "My mother said I never should; Play with the gypsies in the wood". An early collected example was noted from Alice Gillington from Hampshire and published in *Old Hampshire Singing Games* in 1909. It is impossible to say how closely connected Poll's tune is to the song, but the words could certainly be sung to it. As a dance, *Gypsies in the Wood* was adopted as a Molly dance and noted as such by Cyril Papworth and Russell Wortley during their collecting in Girton and Comberton in Cambridgeshire.[16]

Gypsies Cooking on an Open Fire by Thomas Rowlandson.
Yale Center for British Art.

The Low Backed Car

Stephen Poll, Tilney St Lawrence January 7th 1905

The Low Backed Car

The Low Backed Car was a popular Irish song. The tune appeared in *O'Neill's Music of Ireland* published in 1903 number 387. It was later recorded by various artists and the sheet music was published.

Frustratingly RVW doesn't often tell us much about his singers but he did make a special note about how Stephen Poll learned the dances and tunes he played for village gatherings. This was the note he made:

Country dances played by Mr Poll

He used to learn them at Lynn Fair, when a new dance was danced he would learn it by dancing in it—then later ask for the same again and then knew the tune and the dance and could start top. He used to fiddle for dances—the old country dances used to have more money in them because each couple as they got to the top would give him a penny. He described one song as a "good old solid song".

The Foxhunt

Stephen Poll, labourer, at Tilney St Lawrence, January 7th 1905

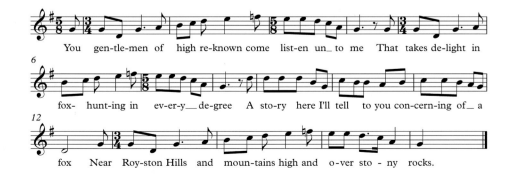

You gen-tle-men of high re-known come list-en un__ to me That takes de-light in

fox- hunt-ing in ev-er-y__de-gree A sto-ry here I'll tell to you con-cern-ing of__ a

fox Near Roy-ston Hills and moun-tains high and o-ver sto - ny rocks.

The Foxhunt

You gentlemen of high renown come listen unto me
That takes delight in foxhunting in every degree
A story here I'll tell to you concerning of a fox
Near Royston Hills and mountains high and over stony rocks.

Bold Reynard being in his hole and hearing of those hounds
Which made him for to prick his ears and tread upon the ground
Methinks me hears some jubal hounds pressing upon my life
But before that it's time they shall come I'll tread upon the ground (?)

They hunted full four hours or more through parishes sixteen;
They hunted full four hours or more till they came by Parkworth
Green
O now if you'll only spare my life I'll promise and fulfil
To touch no more your feathered fowls nor lambs in yonder field.

Bold Reynard's beat and out of breath and treading of those grounds
Thinking he must give up his life before those jubal hounds
So here's adieu to ducks and geese likewise young lambs also
They've caught old Reynard by his brush and they would not let him
go.

RVW noted these words from Mr Poll in full. In his note about Mr Poll learning dance tunes at Lynn Fair, he says he describes one song as a 'good old solid song'. He doesn't specify this one, but it is the only song that RVW wrote down from Mr Poll. The song is in the *Journal of the Folk Song Society* Vol. II p.104, where it is next to a version collected in Launceston from Mr. Burns, an employee of the local urban district council. The note with them says the words are almost the same except that the 'green' in Norfolk becomes 'Parkworth'.

Notes

1   "I hadn't the first idea how or where to begin. First of all I asked the clergyman and the doctor, but they couldn't assist me at all. I did not know any of the people about, so the only thing to do was to be audacious. Accordingly, I wandered down one morning to the Quay, where I had noticed that four old fishermen always stood… At last, with a rather trembling heart, I boldly went up to one of them and said, "Do any of you sing?". Bearman C.J.'Kate Lee and the founding of the Folk Song Society' *Folk Music Journal* (1999) 7 (5) pp.630-631.

2   As RVW stayed in the Cozens Temperance Hotel in King's Lynn' on his visit, it would argue that the person who invited him was not in a position to put him up. It seems unlikely, therefore, that the parson was behind the invitation. More likely perhaps, that it was someone of modest means.

3   *Lynn News,* 5 January, 1905.

4   Sharp, C. J. (1907 reprint 1965) *English Folk Song: Some Conclusions* 1st ed.. London: Methuen, rep. Wakefield: E.P. Publishing, p.133.

5   The present A17 follows the old line

6

7   Broadwood, L. and Fuller Maitland, J. (eds.) (1893) *English County Songs.* Unknown.

8   Brocklebank, J. and Biddie Kindersley, B. (eds.) (1948) *A Dorset Book of Folk Songs from a collection by H.E.D. Hammond.* London: The English Folk Dance & Song Society, p.6.

9   Mee, A. (ed.) (1941) *Suffolk Our Farthest East,* London: Hodder and Stoughton, *p.322.*

10   As quoted in Sola Pinto,V. and Rodway, A.E., (1957) *The Common Muse.* London: Chatto and Windus.

11   Ibid.

12   Woods, F. (1983) *English Traditional Verse.* London: OUP.

13   Words from George Butterworth's notebook. Butterworth and RVW were great friends and both were collecting before the First World War. Butterworth was killed during the war and left all his music and manuscripts to Vaughan Williams.

14   From the Full English.

15   Calculated from 1881 census.

16   Notes on these two tunes kindly contributed by Chris Holderness.

King's Lynn: The Unexpected Treasure House of Song

"There I reaped a rich harvest."

Vaughan Williams recalling his visit to King's Lynn

Vaughan Williams says he was disappointed with his venture into the Tilneys, and apparently intended to leave the area. But by chance he met the Revd Alfred Huddle, and that turned a disappointing visit into one where he found a treasure trove of songs. For Mr Huddle asked if he would like to hear the fishermen of the North End of King's Lynn.

Vaughan Williams talked about his visit to King's Lynn in a lecture to the Musical Convention of Choirmasters, School Teachers and Music Teachers in Norwich. The *Lynn Advertiser* reported Vaughan Williams' recollections: "After visiting the country places around, and getting nothing, he was about to leave the district in despair..."

Why 'in despair'? Vaughan Williams had heard ten songs from Mr Whitby and used some of them in several compositions later. Mr Poll also yielded four tunes and a song. So why was this a poor result in his eyes?

Maybe we must go back to the small circle of collectors and musicians in London for the answer. Both J.M. Fuller Maitland and Lucy Broadwood were talking about how to tell whether a song was a 'genuine' folksong.[1] We know Vaughan Williams was particularly keen on tunes in the old modes rather than those in modern scales. So maybe he didn't feel he was getting the 'real thing', those vanishing melodies of the common people.

But then came that chance meeting with Alfred Huddle, as reported by the *Lynn Advertiser*:

A curate at King's Lynn asked him if he would like to see the fishing people… He said he should, and he was taken into some of the worst slums he had ever been into in his life. He was there very forcibly reminded of the fact that the appeal of the folk song was to the ear and not to the nose. (Laughter) Instead of going away he stayed a week. He met some very hard working and very poor fishermen and they sang to him when they could get away from their work. He noted down 78 genuine ballads in one week (Applause) [2]

The densely populated yards of the North End must have been unlike anything Vaughan Williams had spent time in before. Much effort was made by people living there to keep the yards clean and tidy. But fish

North Street 1958: This is the north side of the street. The curved front of the tobacconist's on the right was on the corner of Pilot Street; Bennell's shop next to it was a shoe repairer's. The next shop front visible, next to the arch into Whitening's Yard, had been a butcher's, but in 1933 was a fish and chip shop. The white building is on the corner of North Place; in 1933 it was Polly Goodson's grocery shop. Between it and the "chippie" were the narrow arched entries of three more yards.
True's Yard.

opposite: St. Ann Street.
Anne Roberts.

39

St Nicholas' Chapel, from the south-east.
Colin James

Cozens Hotel where RVW stayed during his week in King's Lynn and from here he wrote to his cousin enthusing about his finds.
Colin James

processing and other trades must have given the area an all-pervading smell. Even today, when shellfish are being processed, the aroma reaches across North Lynn. No wonder Vaughan Williams remarked on it.

When he spoke at the King's Lynn Festival in July 1952, he again referred to the fortunate meeting with the Revd Alfred Huddle, the curate at St Nicholas' Chapel. The *Lynn News and Advertiser* reported: "He met a clergyman who was intimate with the North End fishermen. They both went to hear them sing... And, said Dr Vaughan Williams, I reaped a rich reward there."[3]

His excitement about those riches was evident in a brief letter he sent to his cousin, Ralph Wedgwood, on 15 January 1905, from the Cozens Hotel where he stayed.

I am collecting the most wonderful songs among the fishermen here.[4]

Vaughan Williams clearly enjoyed telling one story about his stay, as related by Ursula Vaughan Williams:

Early in January he stayed at King's Lynn in a small commercial hotel, where to his surprise the landlady greeted him as an old friend and asked tenderly after his dogs. He found out, after a bewildering conversation, that she was certain he had stayed there before with a troupe of performing dogs when a circus had been visiting the town, and nothing he could say would convince her otherwise. He came to the conclusion that she suspected him of having failed with his performers and disposed of them,

probably in some horrible and brutal way which he was unwilling to confess."[5]

Vaughan Williams may have had an additional clue to the possibilities of singing among the fishing community: a memo, from a list perhaps written by Lucy Broadwood, of a possible source of songs in Lynn. The cryptic reference appears on a substantial list of names in a scrapbook, which may or may not have been his own. It reads: "Bayley Hilda's Yard—Norfolk Street King's Lynn?"[6] He met a John Bayley later in the week.

To understand the extraordinary week of collecting which Vaughan Williams spent in Lynn, it is vital to understand the distinctive community of the North End of King's Lynn to which he was introduced. Modern King's Lynn holds few clues to the old North End. Just as the songs themselves are not complete without the people who sang them and the part the music played in their lives, so in turn those lives are incomplete without the background against which they were lived.

The North End of King's Lynn

Before large-scale redevelopment in the 1960s, the North End of King's Lynn was curiously set apart from the rest of the town. Nevertheless, even in 1905 it had been subject to many changes over the previous half century, which impacted on the lives of those older North Enders, including some of the 1905 singers, who had grown up in a community even more closely defined in area. Most notable of these changes were the knock-on effects of re-routing the Great Ouse outfall in 1852 and the ensuing creation of the docks. The changes can be seen by comparing the detailed 25-inch Ordnance Survey maps of the mid 1880s with the simple street and river layout on the 1830 map[7], familiar to Mr Carter, Mr Anderson, Mr Harper and Mrs Howard from their childhood.

The old North End was shaped by three streets. Pilot Street and St Ann Street ran south to link it with the town centre; North Street ran east-west joining these two to each other. In these streets and the yards behind them lived the families who made their living by fishing. The 1851 census shows the fishermen's homes interspersed with other trades and shopkeepers, but their role was to supply the needs of the fisher families and all were part of a distinct community.

Before the shifting westward of the Great Ouse outfall, anciently laid out land plots behind the houses on the west side of St Ann Street backed almost onto the Ouse foreshore. At the northern end of the street a right angle with North Street was dictated by the tributary Gaywood River, which before the creation of the first dock in 1869 flowed almost directly behind North Street. Its mouth, known as the Fisher Fleet, housed the fishing boats. Until 1803 both streets were jointly known as Northirne, an old English term for "north corner". On the St Ann Street and North Street corner itself, a defensive fort, once equipped with cannon, was set up in the 16th century. This corner is still called St Ann's Fort and a fragment of ancient wall can still be seen, but by the 19th century it performed no defensive function. The area is chiefly characterised now by an entrance to the docks.

Pilot Street ran parallel with St Ann Street on the inland side of the splendid medieval St Nicholas' Chapel. This chapel, built to service the whole northern half of the town, was daughter church or chapel of ease of the parish and priory church of St Margaret.[8] Pilot Street was the North End's main artery, until its near obliteration in the 1960s. It passed the eastern end of North Street and continued north to cross the Gaywood River or Fisher Fleet by a bridge, which appears occasionally in the earlier records as Fishers Bridge. In medieval times the street was dignified at this point by a gate called Doucehill Gate, but the road went nowhere beyond it except to the marshes and former saltings. It follows therefore that, unless one had business with the fishing community itself, outsiders had no reason to traverse either Pilot Street or North Street, and rarely did.

Some of the fishermen of Pilot Street, North Street and St Ann Street lived in houses fronting those streets but many more in the narrow yards behind, where the former long land plots behind the houses had been filled with small cottages. The same thing was happening in the town centre to cope with a growing working population, as it did, often to dire effect, in the great industrialised cities. Some, though by no means all, were one-up, one-down cottages of the kind preserved today at True's Yard, often blind-backed against the yard boundary. Some were named after neighbouring pubs and some, such as Watson's and Begley's Yards, probably bore the names of their builders and creators. All the cottages in a yard would share two or three privies and a water supply. The pressure on the limited urban sanitation played a role in the fearful epidemics which beset Lynn in the 19th century. There is some evidence to suggest that, at least by the 20th century, the North End was a healthier place to live than the town centre in terms of untimely deaths. Nevertheless, a startling rate of Victorian infant mortality in the North End is demonstrated by the answers to a 1911 census question which asked householders how many children they had had and how many of them were still alive in that year.[9]

The first changes in the North End began in 1852 with the diversion of the River Great Ouse into a new outfall further westward, to reduce the problem of silting.[10] When the river rushed through into its present course it initiated more than a straighter route into the Wash. The Alexandra Dock, opened in 1869, was constructed behind St Ann Street and St Ann's Fort, where the old river bed joined the new. Beyond it a necessary westward extension to the Gaywood River or Fisher Fleet outfall ran along the foot of the new bank which dammed off the old bed; the present Cross Bank Road along the Fisher Fleet runs on top of the bank itself. [11]

The North End in 1830, before the re-routing of the River Ouse and creation of the Docks: St Nicholas' Chapel is easily seen between St Ann Street and Pilot Street, which are linked by North Street. "London Wharf", running north from North Street, later became North Place.

1886 OS map of the North End.

pub gave place to dry land under the level crossing. John H Pratt (1859-1941) in his *Recollections* reported the fishermen's displeasure even after the earlier dock was built:

The Alexandra Dock was built on marsh land covered by water when the tides were high. The Fisher Fleet crossed this marsh and entered the river not far from the present Dock Gates.[12] The fishermen bitterly opposed this alteration and later threatened a riot when the Fisher Fleet was again curtailed to make the Bentinck Dock."[13]

Secondly, the docks brought increased freight traffic through the streets. British and overseas sailors passed in and out through the dock gates and frequented the North End.[14] In 1902 Kelly's *Norfolk Directory* reported 120 British and 209 overseas sailing and steam ships coming into the port. Labouring and portering work on the docks also brought in new faces from elsewhere in the town, including Vaughan Williams' Mr Leatherday's brother John, who for a while was dock gatekeeper. The late Jeanne Wheeler, who lived in Devonshire's Yard in the early 1930s, recalled the dockers leaving the docks in the evenings onto St Ann's Fort, with the fishermen coming up North Street from the opposite direction from their boats. She also recalled sailors from overseas, ill-fed on board ship, scavenging among the refuse bins in the yards after dark.[15] On the plus side casual work on the docks would prove a blessing to fishermen when catches were poor, while dockers and sailors brought extra trade to the North End's many pubs and shops. As mature men in the 1870s and 80s the 1905 singers will already have known a bustle in the streets unfamiliar to earlier generations.

In 1873 the St Nicholas Ironworks opened at the top of Pilot Street to expand the business of Frederick Savage, an agricultural engineer best known today for the revolution he brought to fairground rides, the famous gallopers driven by a central engine. Again, new job opportunities brought new faces, some of whom would soon be living in an enlarged North End. By the mid-1880s Loke

Then came the Docks railway, to bring efficient land transport to the new dock. The railway crossed Pilot Street to link the dock with the main railway system. In 1883 its success brought the inner Bentinck Dock, lying in the old river bed itself, north east of the Alexandra Dock beyond the cross bank.

This brought two major changes to the North End. Firstly, the extended docks now crossed the line of the old Fisher Fleet where the boats sheltered. The Gaywood River's course through the North End was diverted, leaving only a short stretch at its old mouth to act as the anchorage. The boats now lay well away from the fishermen's houses. The old Fishers Bridge beside the *Tilden Smith*

Road had been laid out running inland from the docks end of Pilot Street, with small streets of terraced houses developing on either side: Sir Lewis, Cresswell and Burkitt Streets to the north and Lansdowne, Birchwood and George Streets to the south.[16] In due course some of the fishermen would be living there alongside the new workers. The electoral registers of the early 1900s show fishermen moving from the yards into the new houses: two-up, two-down and each with its own toilet.[17] But curiously they also show movement the other way, whether because rents were higher or even because the tenants missed the enclosed community feeling in the old yards. Nevertheless, many men from the old fishing families set up home here. Vaughan Williams' singer Mr Carter himself ended his days with his adopted daughter Lottie's family in Sir Lewis Street, while his son Tom's family lived nearby in Cresswell Street.[18]

This was the wider North End into which Vaughan Williams was brought in January 1905 and which his singers knew in later life: still a tight community in essence but by no means as isolated as it had been fifty years earlier.

The life of the fishermen

In his 1910 lecture Vaughan Williams said he was taken into "some of the worst slums he had ever been into in his life. He was there very forcibly reminded of the fact that the appeal of the folksong was to the ear and not the nose …"

It is important not to form an impression of poverty-stricken fishing families living in dirty hovels from his use of the word "slum". Many of the fishermen indeed owned their own boats, a considerable capital outlay at some point in the family history, but their occupation is subject to the caprice of wind and weather and the level of fish stocks. At the time of Vaughan Williams' visit stormy weather had kept the boats at home: no catch and no income. Intermittent poverty did not prevent cleanliness; later eyewitnesses always emphasise the scrupulously maintained standards not just in the houses but in the shared maintenance of the communal facilities. The late Frank Castleton emphasised this strongly in his

Harry Southgate's shop and St Ann Street in 1959. The Southgates had been established on the "St Ann's Fort" corner for many years when this picture was taken. Harry's shop and post office continued into the 1970s, the last of the old North End provisions shops to go. The painted signs show that the Southgates had a thriving trade in the docks as well.
Picture Norfolk.

book. "The passages were tarred about three feet up and then white-washed. Their houses inside with their sparse furniture and uncovered tables and chairs would be scrubbed white and the wooden floor sanded."[19]

However, some issues the yard tenants could not address. Surveys taken after the 1930 Slum Clearance Act indicated damp and defective plaster in many cases, while narrow courtyards and dark and even narrower access passages were seen to contravene the new regulations. Many cottages in the yards of the North End and other parts of Lynn were flattened as a result.

The fishing operation in Lynn was not small: in December 1902 there were 45 fishing boats registered at the port of Lynn under the merchant Shipping Act 1894, employing 112 men and boys, as against 51 merchant vessels.[20] The catch at that time included sole, cod and smelt, with vast quantities of shrimps, mussels and cockles. The atmosphere was remarked on by the contemporary John H Pratt:

Fish, cockles and mussels were thus brought up into North End, resulting in unsavoury smells which barred many people from walking this way up to the Estuary river bank.[21]

When times were hard, self-help was resorted to: wild-fowling on the marshes and catching eels and small fry to supplement the larder. A boat might even be taken to the place in the Wash where the dredgers dropped silt from the docks. Coal could be found in this silt, dropped from coal ships during unloading. Mr Carter's daughter remembered: "When we had a hard winter and coal was short and we were short of money he (her father) used to go down the bank . . . and get quarter or half a peck of mussels. We'd have them perhaps two or three nights for tea . . . we'd burn the shells with coal dust on the fire. They used to smell and make a lot of dirt but they'd throw the heat out ever so much!"[22]

Fishermen's wives sold some of the fresh catch from a bowl on a stool at the front door and other members of the family did a variety of jobs to earn their keep. Censuses show daughters of 11 or 12 working at the brush factory, the jam factory and the sack factory; older girls went into service and little brothers often started off as errand boys before they were old enough to fish. Staple provisions were available for sale in Pilot Street and North Street, where there were a baker and butcher and shops which aimed to sell everything from food provisions to paraffin, candles and kindling, and most of these would have run a "slate" system for deferred payment.[23]

Fishermen's pubs and singing

In February 1908 a particularly vivid picture of the many North End pubs appeared in the Brewster's Court Report in the local paper. The future of the licence of the *Fisherman's Arms* in Pilot Street was in question and discussion of whether the pub was really necessary revealed how many alternative hostelries were available nearby. The *Grampus* and the *Earl of Richmond* lay in one direction in Pilot Street with the *Dog and Duck*, the *Fisherman's Return* and the *Tilden Smith* in the other. North Street could offer the *Norfolk Arms*, the *Black Joke* and the *Dock Tavern*, with the *Victoria* "on the Loke Road on the other side of the railway".[24]

An interesting exchange between the authorities then took place:

The *Fisherman's Arms* is used by that class of persons who call themselves fishermen?

Yes.

They are clanny?

Yes.

They like their own people and their own house?

Yes.

The landlord, Edward Benefer, revealed that the *Earl of Richmond* and the *Dog and Duck* were kept by fishermen, that "maybe some" fishermen used the *Grampus* while some used the *Dock Tavern*, although its landlord was not himself a fisherman. William Bailey was then called upon, a customer of some 25 years standing and probably a nephew of Vaughan Williams' Mr Bayley.[25] William had his own special seat in the pub and a special pint pot. He maintained that 40-50 fishermen at a time could be seen there, despite the assertion of PC Hunt, who had been in to count heads, that he only found four or five. "I don't think he saw us all," maintained William: "he didn't look round the corners." How reliable a witness William Bailey was may therefore be open to question, but an interesting sidelight was his describing it as "a skippers' house" where fishermen would meet to make arrangements for going to sea.

Over the years The *Tilden Smith*, by the docks railway level crossing, the first pub encountered by the fishermen on their way home from the Fleet, has claimed a strong association with their singing. Vaughan Williams never said or noted that he collected in any pubs in King's Lynn.[26] Apart from his days at the King's Lynn Union he doesn't say in his notebooks exactly *where* he heard the fishermen sing, while the single glimpse of him at work in Lynn shows him in the singer's own home.[27] Furthermore, only the year before Vaughan Williams' visit, the *Tilden Smith* had lost its music licence— apparently from insufficient use!

On Monday 29 February 1904, Joseph Barker said that he had held a music licence since 1892 and sought renewal. He had never had any trouble and had a nice music room and ladies were not permitted. The Chief-constable said that on the previous Saturday night there were about fourteen persons in the room and by about nine o'clock only five or six.

Sergeant Rayner said that the licence was not much used in the house and there was no music when he visited on the Saturday night. There were other music licenses in the vicinity. Licence refused.[28]

The 1908 Brewster's Court report quoted above shows that fishermen also gathered in other pubs. Singing at the *Fisherman's Arms* could be implied by Tom Howard's recollection of seeing men coming out of it at about 2 pm on a Sunday (closing time), when they would walk "up the middle of Pilot Street, unsteady on their feet, singing happily, but when they reached their front doors, the wife would open the door and the singing would stop!"[29]

Frank Castleton describes a competition in the *Fisherman's Arms* at which the winner would be the singer of the longest song. Young Frank sat through a 96-verse version of what he calls *Lord Bacon* before asking his father if he could go home please! This seems to have been a version of *Lord Bateman* to judge from the opening verse he quotes:

Lord Bacon was, he was, a noble lord of high degree
He shipped his-self aboard a vessel for some foreign parts he would go see.
He sailed east, he sailed west, 'til he came to proud Turkey;
There he was captured and made a prisoner 'til his poor life was most weary…

Singing was not limited to leisure hours, as interviews recorded by Mike Herring in 1967 in the North End make clear.[30] Fisherman Bill Chase recalled that Tom Barker, almost certainly Mr Harper's brother-in-law, or possibly the latter's son of the same name, played his fiddle "down the bank", presumably a reference to the Cross Bank bordering the Fisher Fleet anchorage, and in answer to the question "Where did they do the singing?" replied simply, "Anytime". Of a fisherman by the name of Bowman he remarked, "He was always singing. Not at concerts, and that, you know, when he was doing anything. He was always singing." Mr Bowman's daughter, asked "Did he sing while he was working?" she replied, "Oh yes, when he was down in

Singing in a North End pub.
Anne Roberts.

Cottages in True's Yard: with Timo Van Pelt (left) and Sam Southgate (right): fisherman, pilot and as a sailor "rounded the Horn"! The Southgates were also shopkeepers in the North End: Ernie Southgate's ship's chandlery is now part of the Fisherfolk Museum.
This picture shows the deep tarred band below the whitewash, attested by Frank Castleton as typical of the North End cottages.
True's Yard.

fishing he used to."[31] Reference is also made in the True's Yard files to older people and women singing while they were mending the nets.[32]

Crucially it was in this community that Alfred Huddle introduced Vaughan Williams to Duggie Carter (James Carter), who had a rich store of songs himself and was also the key to meeting and hearing the other singers. More about those singers in the next chapter.

Vaughan Williams' work in Lynn was assisted by the weather. There had been a massive storm and flood at New Year and many of the boats were in port. The *Lynn Advertiser* of 7 January 1905 reported the storm, which sounds like a classic East Coast surge of the kind experienced in 1953 and 2013.

Late on Friday night and early on Saturday morning an exceptionally heavy gale was experienced in Lynn and the country round. The wind blew from the north westerly direction with great velocity, and a hoarding erected near the new library on the London Road was blown down, taking with it a portion of the iron fencing which encloses the Greyfriars field. The tide in the Ouse rose with great rapidity, the water coming up with considerable force. The Common Staith and the South quays, King Staith Square, quickly became flooded, the water being no less than 3 feet deep near the quay corner of Globe Lane. In the Ouse the S.S.Cam broke away from its moorings and several smaller craft were carried away and in some instances sunk. [33]

No wonder the fishermen were hard at work the following week retrieving their boats and gear and getting back to sea to make up for the time they'd lost because of the bad weather. Nonetheless, by 14 January

Vaughan Williams had been able to collect 78 songs and tunes, some of which he'd never come across before. He was delighted with them, especially with the first song (James) Duggie Carter sang to him: 'The Captain's Apprentice'. Several others became favourites which he used many times. He returned the following year to seek out Mr Carter to hear more, but only for one day.

The Revd Alfred Huddle, Mr Carter and Mr Anderson

The Revd Alfred Huddle's close acquaintance with the first singers Vaughan Williams met, Duggie Carter and Joe Anderson, was explained by reminiscences of Mr Carter's adopted daughter, Lottie Westfield. She stated that in later life "he got to going to church; he got in with a Reverend Huddle I think the parson's name was … I can picture him now, he was only a little man. And Mr Joe Anderson, he was another fisherman, him and Mr Carter . . . used to go to church and in the finish they were confirmed."[34]

Alfred Huddle's own life and background may well have helped him to be accepted by the North Enders. Whereas members of the clergy were often sons of middle- or upper-class families, Mr Huddle, born in 1863 in Bath, was the son of a saddler. By 1881, when he was 17 and the family had moved to Portsmouth, Alfred himself was also following that trade. His call to the ministry was made possible by the Revd William Ayerst's establishment of Ayerst Hall in Cambridge, specifically to help men from poorer backgrounds to advance their education. He took his BA in 1888 and his MA in 1892. From 1897 to 1901 he served at Buckhurst Hill in Essex before taking up his curacy in King's Lynn.[35] The 1904 Kelly's Directory shows him living in Tuesday Market Place and the Register of Electors implies his home was along the north side of the market place, in one half of what is popularly called the Witch's Heart house.

Even though it is no longer in regular use, St Nicholas' Chapel is still regarded as the fishermen's chapel. Things had not been quite so during the 19th century, when concern was voiced over the low attendance,

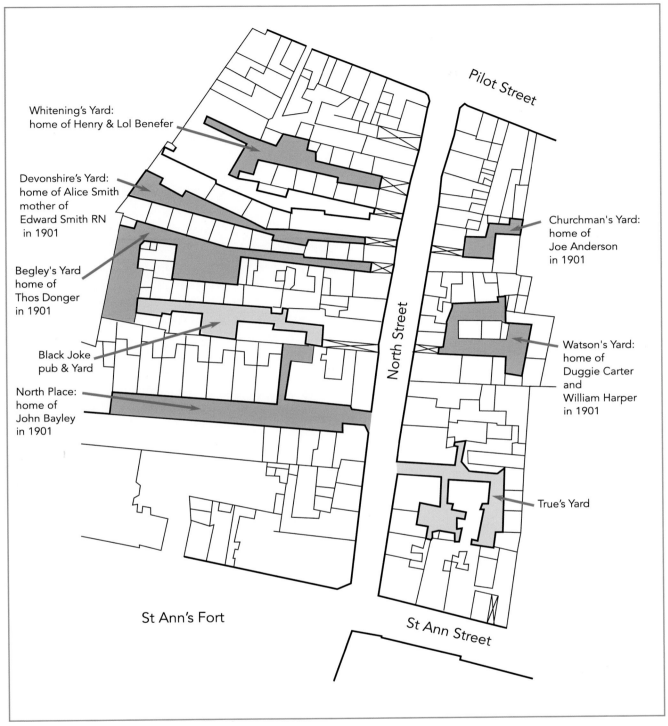

Whitening's Yard:
home of Henry & Lol Benefer

Devonshire's Yard:
home of Alice Smith
mother of
Edward Smith RN
in 1901

Begley's Yard
home of
Thos Donger
in 1901

Black Joke
pub & Yard

North Place:
home of
John Bayley
in 1901

Pilot Street

Churchman's Yard:
home of
Joe Anderson
in 1901

North Street

Watson's Yard:
home of
Duggie Carter
and
William Harper
in 1901

True's Yard

St Ann's Fort

St Ann Street

Map of North Street showing singers' homes: it shows that nearly all the singers lived in yards off the same street.

due partly to the system of privately owned pews which discouraged those not so entitled.[36] The result was a major mission week initiative in 1897. This led to a number of later confirmations[37] but if Duggie Carter's and Joe Anderson's confirmations were prompted by association with Alfred Huddle, they cannot have been influenced also by the mission, at least directly, as it took place long before his arrival in 1901. In 1907 he moved on to the parish of Trowse with Lakenham near Norwich, leaving in 1910 for an incumbency in the Ilketshall parishes in Suffolk, where he stayed until 1935. There is a glimpse of him on coastal defence with the

*Group photograph—
Revd Alfred Huddle,
curate of St Nicholas' and
RVW's "clergyman" met
by chance, with his
friends—singers
"Duggie" Carter
(standing) and Joe
Anderson.*

Ralph Vaughan Williams
Society.

5th Suffolk Regiment during the First World War, presumably as chaplain.

Huddle completed his service in the ministry at Hasketon near Woodbridge, in Suffolk, from which he resigned in 1941, but remained in Suffolk until his death in 1946, aged 83.

He was not necessarily personally responsible for introducing Vaughan Williams to all his North End singers, although he may well have helped with access to the Union workhouse, the next port of call after meeting Carter and Anderson. Vaughan Williams seems to have spent part of each of his next three days partly in the North End and partly in the Union.

In 1946 it was also claimed that he had been accompanied in the North End by John H Pratt (1859-1941), a local businessman who knew the North End well.[38] His *Reminiscences* have been quoted already but they make no reference to music in the North End nor to Vaughan Williams.[39]

Notes

1 Lucy Broadwood's diaries, Surrey History Centre.

2 *Lynn Advertiser,* 23 September 1910.

3 *Lynn News and Advertiser,* 25 July 1952.

4 Letter from Ralph Vaughan Williams to Ralph Wedgwood January 15th 1905 in the British Library database number 050115 VML189.

5 Williams, U.V. (1964) *Ralph Vaughan Williams,* London: OUP, p.72.

6 This scrapbook is held by the Vaughan Williams Memorial Library at Cecil Sharp House. The librarian at the time, Malcolm Taylor, said in an email to Alan Helsdon in April 2014 that the scrapbook's ownership was not certain. It could have belonged to RVW, but his view was that it could have been Lucy Broadwood's, judging by some of the handwriting including the sheet referred to above.

7 Plan of King's Lynn from actual survey 1830, John Wood surveyor, 53 Threadneedle St., London.

8 St Nicholas' Chapel was never allowed to become independent and is now vested in the Churches Conservation Trust and is the largest chapel of ease in the country. Its registers were the source of much of the information which helped to identify the singers.

9 McCarron, T. *Women in the North End,* lecture at True's Yard Fisherfolk Museum, 20 February 2014.

10 Three "excavators" recorded as resident in North Street in 1851 may well have been working on the project.

11 Parker, A. and Howling, B. (2004) *King's Lynn: A History & Celebration.* Salisbury:The Francis Frith Collection for Ottaker's p.67.

12 i.e. the lock gates leading out into the main river.

13 Pratt, J.H. *Recollections,* manuscript in King's Lynn Library local collection.

14 That is: non-resident seamen. Even in the 1840s there were merchant seamen living in the North End, often related to fishing families.

15 Personal 1930s reminiscence by Jeanne Wheeler.

16 A fascinating record of the development of this area based on Council minutes and other sources was compiled by D Winifred Tuck. Bound copy of her notes in King's Lynn Library.

17 Electoral registers in King's Lynn Town Hall archives.

18 Taped reminiscences of Carter family made in 1976 by Elizabeth James.

19 Castleton, F. (1988) *Fisher's End Part 2.* King's Lynn: True's Yard Publications, p.16.

20 Kelly's *Norfolk Directory,*1904.

21 Ibid. 13.

22 From Carter family tape made in 1976 by Elizabeth James at Lynn Museum.

23 Kelly's *Norfolk Directory,* 1904 and 1930s reminiscence from Jeanne Wheeler.

24 *Lynn Advertiser,* 14 February 1908.

25 John Bayley had a brother of that name but he had almost certainly died by 1908. This William Bailey was probably the son of Mr Bayley's brother Robert and was living in Devonshire's Yard in 1901. There were other young William Baileys drinking by 1908 but not old enough to have been doing so for 25 years!

26 On other collecting expeditions he notes when he has heard a song in a pub, who sang it and if they played an instrument to accompany it.

27 See later section, The Collector, the Singer and the Dumplings p.163.

28 From norfolkpubs.co.uk website reproduced from the local press.

29 Notes by Tom Howard in Howard family file at True's Yard.

30 See Appendix 1 p.242.

31 Date probably the 1920s or so; Mr Bowman worked frequently during the winter at the Saddlebow sugar beet factory and was killed in an accident there in 1933.

32 Reminiscences of the late Maggie Carter: notes at True's Yard Fisherfolk Museum.

33 *Lynn News,* 7 January, 1905.

34 Carter family tape made in 1976 for an exhibition at Lynn Museum.

35 The early life of the Revd Alfred Huddle was researched by Alan Helsdon from contemporary editions of Crockford's Clerical Directory and other sources.

36 Although latterday Northenders recall singing as boys in the choir at St Nicholas' Chapel, many earlier Northenders would have attended the Primitive and Wesleyan Methodist chapels and Sunday schools in Pilot Street. Both closed in 1932 when Methodist congregations united. The Primitive Methodist Chapel is now a replacement door and window showroom; the Wesleyan Chapel gave place to the Pilot Cinema (now demolished) in 1938.

37 *Lynn Advertiser,* 22 October 1897 and January 1898.

38 *Lynn News and Advertiser,* 14 May 1946.

39 See also p.164.

A Good Week's Work

'I boldly went up to one of them and said, 'Do any of you sing?'
Kate Lee, first secretary of the Folk Song Society

According to Vaughan Williams' field notebook, this is how his week's collecting went.[1] No wonder he was so pleased with the number and quality of the songs he heard. Twenty singers gave him songs on his two visits to West Norfolk. The first week's collecting in 1905 is on pages 43 to 260 of the notebook and his return visit in 1906 on pages 465 to 479. It's worth noting that Vaughan Williams, then aged 32, often overestimates the age of his singers!

1905

January 7th

Tilney All Saints:

Mr.J.Whitby, Sexton, of Tilney All Saints, near King's Lynn, aged about 50.

> Lord Bateman
> It Was One Morning
> Bold Carter

Tilney St Lawrence:

Stephen Poll, a labourer from Tilney St Lawrence aged about 80. He learnt the dances at Lynn Fair and he used to fiddle for dances. The old country dances made more money for him because each couple as they reached the top of the set gave him a penny.

> The Foxhunt
> Trip to the Cottage (dance)
> Gipsies in the Wood (dance)
> Low Backed Car (dance)
> Ladies' Triumph (dance)

January 8th

Tilney All Saints:

Mr J. Whitby:

> Lord Lovell
> The Red Barn
> The Streams of Lovely Nancy
> As I was a Walking
> Green Bushes
> The Yorkshire Bite (Lincolnshire Farmer)
> Young Jockie

January 9th

King's Lynn:

Mr Carter, fisherman aged about 70 at North End

> The Deeds of Napoleon
> The Captain's Apprentice
> Ward the Pirate
> As I was a Walking one Mid Summer's Morning
> The Dragoon and the Lady

Mr Anderson, fisherman aged about 70 of Lynn

> The Basket of Eggs
> The Yorkshire Farmer
> John Reilly
> Van Dieman's Land (or Young Henry the Poacher)
> Erin's Lovely Home
> The Sheffield Apprentice

Mr Crisp, sailor at the Lynn Union

> The Dream of Napoleon

Mr Leatherday, sailor, at the Lynn Union

> On Board a '98

Mr Woods, sailor, Lynn Union

> Napoleon's Farewell (this is doubtful because he was very hoarse. RVW)

Mr Leatherday (ditto Lynn Union)

> Spurn Point

Mr Crisp (ditto)

> The Princess Royal
> The Loss of the Ramillies

opposite: A North End yard..
Anne Roberts.

January 10th

King's Lynn:

Mr Chesson (ditto Lynn Union)
  Erin's Lovely Home
  Raven's Feather
Leatherday (ditto)
  Creeping Jane
Cooper (ditto)
  The Irish Girl
Elmer (ditto)
  It's of an Old Lord
Unknown singer (ditto)
  Hares in the Plantation
Mr Anderson
  The Bold Robber
  A Bold Young Sailor
  The Nobleman and the Thresherman (Jolly Threshermen)
  As I was a Walking (Handfuls of Roses)
Mr Carter
  The Blacksmith (with variant from J. Bayley January 11th)

January 10th and 11th

King's Lynn:

Mrs Betty Howard aged about 70 of King's Lynn
  Ratcliffe Highway
  Our Anchor's Weighed
  Sheffield Apprentice

January 11th

King's Lynn:

Crisp at Lynn Union
  The Cumberland's Crew
Mr Leatherday and Mr West at Lynn Union
  The Robin's Petition (Leatherday sang the tune and West the words)
Mr Crisp (ditto)
  The Maids of Australia
Crisp And Leatherday at Lynn Union
  Spanish Ladies
Mrs Larley (? Lolly) Benefer
  Barbary Allen
  The Farmer's Daughter

Typical fishing smack.
Anne Roberts..

Elizabeth of King's Lynn
    It's of a Shopkeeper
    The Three Butchers
Mr John Bayley of King's Lynn
    I went to Betsy

January 12th
    Sheringham:
B Jackson at the level crossing
    Come Nancy will you Marry Me?
Mr Emery at the Crown Inn Sheringham
    Near Scarborough Town

January 13th
    King's Lynn:
Mr Smith, sailor, of King's Lynn
    Bold Princess Royal
Mr Anderson
    The Bold Princess Royal
    Young Indian Lass

January 13th and 14th
    King's Lynn:
Mr Harper of King's Lynn
    Paul Jones or The American Frigate
    Fair Flora (a Welsh song)
    Just as the Tide was Flowing
    Oxford City
    Poor Mary
    Captain Markee
    Edward Gayen

Mr Donger ex sailor and sailmaker of Lynn
    Hills of Caledonia (John Raeburn)
    Pat Reilly
    Glencoe
    Spanish Ladies
    Come All you Young Sailors
    Come All you Gallant Poachers
    Banks of Claudy

January 14th
Mr Harper
    Betsy and William
Mr Carter
    The Golden Glove
Mr Harper
    My Bonny Boy
1906

September 1st
    King's Lynn:
Mr Elmer in Lynn Union
    Lord Bateman
    The 14th Day of February (not Bold
    Princess Royal)
    Kilkenny
    Bold Robber (doubtful – RVW)
Leatherday Lynn Union:
    Three Butchers
Mr Crisp
    Spanish Ladies

Mr Carter

    A Sailor was riding Along

Mr Donger

    Chanty – Heave Away

    Shenandoah

    Erin's Lovely Home

Vaughan Williams did not keep a diary, so we rely on his notebooks and his recollections when he was giving lectures later, through letters or through stories related to Ursula Vaughan Williams and included in her biography of him. So many questions are unanswered.

On the day he went to Sheringham, in the heart of what was fashionably called Poppyland at the time, could it be that his wife Adeline came up for the day? Or maybe they were already considering taking rooms there. Adeline found accommodation in Sheringham in 1917 and at the end of the Great War they lived there for two years in rented rooms, while she was nursing her brother Hervey, who was suffering from TB. Or could it be because when the first secretary of the Folk Song Society, Kate Lee, went to Wells next the Sea, and was told by one of the old fishermen she approached on the quayside that 'she had better go to Sheringham or Cromer, she would hear some songs as is worth hearing, on the beach there.'[2]

There is another mystery about the week's collecting. Did he note down everything he heard, or did he select only what Lucy Broadwood called 'genuine old ballads'? Many of the London lectures and discussions of 1903 and 1904 were about how to distinguish a genuine folk song from a less worthy successor. In Vaughan Williams' King's Lynn collection we find no working songs, comic songs, or music hall songs. Yet there was a music hall in the North End near the docks (you can still see the faint outline of 'music hall' on the wall of what was until recently the King's Lynn winter night shelter) and local people must have taken a fancy to some of the songs they heard there. Was this material which Vaughan Williams filtered out in the pursuit of the better tunes?

Fine tunes were certainly his quarry in this hunt for folk songs. Writing in the *Folk Song Society Journal*, Vol. II, he said that these melodies were part of a 'precious heritage'. He believed 'some rare old ballad or an exquisitely beautiful melody, is worthy within its smaller compass, of a place beside the finest compositions of the greatest composers.' Or was it that the singers sang him their showpieces, discounting their work songs and maybe more risqué pieces, because he was asking for 'genuine old ballads'. Kate Lee's experience with the four old fishermen in Wells a few years earlier is illuminating:

> I boldly went up to one of them and said, 'Do any of you sing?' 'Do any of us sing?' was the startled reply, as they were generally only asked about the weather and the boats and the departed glory of the town since the railway came to spoil the shipping, 'Sing! No, none of us sings.' 'Oh,' I said, 'don't you sing when you go out to fish?' 'Oh yes, of course we sings then.' 'What sort of songs?' 'Oh, all sorts of songs but none as you would care to hear. [3]

It is important to remember that at the time there has a sharp class divide between the collectors and the singers, but this serves to emphasise Vaughan Williams' success in bridging the gap. It is tantalising, and maybe we shall be able to turn up some of the answers one day. For now, we can only be grateful that he came and that his chance meeting with the Revd Alfred Huddle led to such a rewarding week.

The Singers and The Songs

Full identification of Vaughan Williams' 1905 contacts in King's Lynn has been a major research project, and some may well remain uncertain. The information in the collector's notebooks is mostly limited to a surname, title, and sometimes an initial or occasionally a forename noted in full. Sometimes he was given or estimated an age and often he recorded the singer's occupation. Inmates at the Union were specified as such. Only for Mr Carter do we have the benefit of direct information from descendants, recorded in 1976.

The family files archived at True's Yard Fisherfolk Museum and the genealogical facilities now available via the internet, along with the parish registers of St Nicholas' Chapel and of the parish church itself, have made it possible to compile extensive family trees for most of the names. While recognising that these may yet be incomplete, it has been possible to establish for most of the singers the most likely candidate and, in the event of there being more than one, which by reason of age is the most likely choice.

The 1901 census, used with the registers of electors for the early 1900s, made it possible to establish with some accuracy where most of the singers lived, in conjunction with the superbly detailed 25 inch Ordnance Survey maps of the mid-1880s. It cannot be emphasised too strongly that census returns provide only a snapshot at ten-year intervals; sometimes addresses and secondary occupations changed frequently. If someone is styled a "lodger" or a "visitor" in someone else's house, we have no way of knowing if that was a short- or long-term arrangement nor, in the latter case, why that person was there. This caution should be borne in mind with regard to some of the details in the biographies which follow. Terminology is sometimes

incorrect, e.g. William Harper appears as "son-in-law" in the household of his stepfather William Senter, instead of stepson; presumably William Senter wasn't sure how to describe the acquisition of a son by marriage! It also became clear that at that time people did not set the same store by exact ages that we do today and considerable discrepancies appear not just between censuses but between those and the marriage registers, with reference to indisputably the same persons.

For the singers in the King's Lynn Union workhouse we had the surviving, though sadly incomplete, workhouse records kept at the Norfolk Archive Centre, notably those of admissions, medical treatment and deaths, while the availability of the 1911 census made it possible to pick up the forenames, ages and former occupations of inmates not yet admitted in 1901.

Not all the sixteen King's Lynn contributors to Vaughan Williams' collection were fishermen. Of the nine North End singers, only Messrs Carter, Anderson, Bayley and Harper are known to have been fishermen themselves. Mrs Howard and Mrs Benefer were fishermen's wives and Elizabeth, who may perhaps have been

The Northenders.
Anne Roberts..

Joseph Pennell The River At Lynn, 1904.

Bayley's daughter, can fairly safely be said to have come from a fishing family. There were interesting links between them, either through their families or where they lived. The other two North End men were not fishermen: Mr Smith was a sailor albeit from a fishing family, and Mr Donger was a sailmaker and former seaman.

Of the seven singers at the workhouse, Mr Crisp and Mr Chesson had been merchant seamen; both of the men who may have been Mr Woods, had gone to sea. Vaughan Williams noted that Mr Leatherday was a sailor and his apparent preference for sea songs and his reference to one of his songs being a "Royal Navy" song suggest the same although his census record indicates that perhaps for most of his life, he, like Mr Elmer, was a labourer. Mr Cooper's and Mr West's occupations remain uncertain but are thought to have

been land-based; Mr West's life appears to have included some time in the army. None are known to have come from the North End, but Mr Chesson appears to have had strong family links there.

As far as is practical, the singers are dealt with in chronological order according to Vaughan Williams' notes. For clarity it has proved more helpful to list the North End singers first as a group, followed by the singers in the workhouse and finally the two at Sheringham.

The Singers in the North End

Here too the collector's notebook order has been varied for the purposes of clarity. The four fishermen, Messrs Carter, Anderson, Bayley and Harper, are examined first, followed by the women, Mrs Howard, Mrs Benefer, and Elizabeth, and then, the sailor, Mr Smith and sailmaker Mr Donger.

Notes

1   Kennedy, M. (1964) *The Works of Ralph Vaughan Williams* Appendix II. London: OUP p.647.

2   *Folk Song Society Journal*, (1899) Vol. I, p.9.

3   Ibid.

James 'Duggie' Carter

*"I never knew him with anything but a blue gansey and a peaked cap…'Where's my gansey?"
he used to say. "Where's my gansey, Lottie?"*

Memories of Mr Carter's daughter Lottie

A window onto Vaughan Williams' first singer, James Carter, opened in 1976 when an opportunity arose to record on tape, for Lynn Museum, a conversation with his daughter Elizabeth (Lizzie) Tilson, his adopted daughter Lottie Westfield and granddaughter Florrie Reid. As a result, he has become better known by the nickname "Duggie" Carter by which Lottie referred to him, further cemented by the naming of Duggie Carter Court off Hextable Road in the North End.

He was born c1844, the son of Thomas Carter and his wife Sarah Bouch, and grew up to become a fisherman like his father. His daughter maintained that, when the Ouse waters were released into their new channel in 1852, they took Duggie with them in a boat. He was so young at the time that it seems hard to believe; his granddaughter Florrie Reid, who had been told the story as a child by her father, was unsure whether he had been talking of *her* grandfather, Duggie Carter, or his own. His daughter Lizzie, however, insisted that it had been Duggie.

In 1865 Duggie married Alice Harper and by 1881 they were living in Watson's Yard off North Street, still his address in 1905, with three children: William, at 14 already a fisher boy, 12-year-old Rachel and 11-month-old Thomas (Florrie's father). Rachel perhaps died young as in 1976 Lottie and Lizzie recalled the final total as "Bill, but you never knew him", then Tom, Eddie, Elizabeth (Lizzie, born 1885) and James (Jim). The household was completed by their great-niece Lottie (Charlotte Norris, born 1892) whose mother had died. Her

grandmother was Duggie's sister Sarah Norris (née Carter); Lizzie recalled that her mother took Lottie in when she was fifteen months old.

Alice died aged 61 in 1904, only a few months before Duggie met Vaughan Williams.[1] Lottie said that Lizzie had been on the point of getting married when her mother died and "that held her back for about a month. After the month was over, she got married and I took over looking after him [Duggie] and the boy named Jim." Lizzie's wedding, not found in the parish registers, therefore perhaps took place in the first weeks of December, but on 2 December the funeral of Duggie's 87-year-old mother, Sarah Carter, took place at St Nicholas'. According to the burial register she died in the workhouse presumably in late November. In 1901 she had been living separately in Watson's Yard with his two unmarried sisters, Eliza and Pleasance, both in their mid-forties. In 1907 they too entered the Union and their 1911 census entries suggest they were not capable of independent living without their mother. They were there for many years; Pleasance died in 1920 and Eliza in 1939.

Duggie remained for the rest of his life with Lottie, who "never knew him with anything but a blue ganzy and a peaked cap … 'Where's my ganzy?' he used to say,

James "Duggie" Carter, the first of the fishermen to sing to RVW.
True's Yard.

opposite: Norfolk fishing boat.
Anne Roberts.

Elizabeth "Lizzie" Carter, Duggie Carter's daughter.
True's Yard.

'Where's my ganzy, Lottie?' He always had a peaked cap, never anything else, and a pair of blue trousers." A few years after 1905 they moved out of the North End to 13 Dilke Street, which no longer exists, near St John's Church, where Lottie married Frank Westfield, a carpenter, "at eight o'clock in the morning. There was me and my father – as I called him – and my sister Alice and brother Frank", i.e. her Norris siblings. They were still in Dilke Street at the 1911 census, when the enumerator recorded Duggie as "wife's uncle" and "labourer on dock". The latter agrees with what Lottie herself said of his later years; casual dock work was not unknown among older fishermen although the work itself was not light.

Within a few years, however, they were back in the North End at 4 Sir Lewis Street, one of the "new" Loke Road terraces. His family believed that he died soon after the First World War aged about 80, having been admitted to hospital but dying before he could be operated on; Hardwick Cemetery register however, while agreeing with the death in hospital, gives a burial date of 7 January 1915.

Watson's Yard, off North Street. Duggie Carter was living here in 1905.
True's Yard.

James "Duggie" Carter sang 7 songs in 1905:

> The Blacksmith
> The Captain's Apprentice
> Deeds of Napoleon
> The Dragoon and the Lady
> As I was a Walking One Midsummer's Morning
> The Golden Glove

In 1906 Vaughan Williams visited him again and collected 2 more songs:

> A Sailor Was Riding Along
> Ward the Pirate

Mr Carter has the distinction of being the man who astonished Vaughan Williams with his rendition of *The Captain's Apprentice*, which according to Ursula Vaughan Williams remained "always one of his favourites". Edgar Samuels' in-depth study of Mr Carter's 1905 songs maintained of *The Captain's Apprentice*, "This is the most intriguing song of the whole group and possibly of all the songs that RVW collected. The melody was one that was to have a profound effect on RVW and, along with *Dives* and *Lazarus* and *Bushes and Briars* was one of the most important folk songs in RVW's life."[2]

His granddaughter Florrie Reid remembered his singing at family evenings, especially on Sundays. Sometimes there would be singing and music until the young ones went to bed and then the adults would play cards. Lottie said, "They (the context is Duggie and Joe Anderson) used to go somewhere and sing these songs but I can't remember the songs he used to sing at all. I remember he used to say a recitation called *The Apprentice Boy At Sea*. I thought it was a recitation but apparently it's a song." Lizzie then remarked "I can remember that he sang *The Dark-Eyed Sailor*," and then Lottie continued, "The apprentice boy in this song, I remember they were cruel to this here boy and in the finish they lashed him to the rigging, see, and when he come down, after he'd been up there for so long… they threw water over him. Well, then there was this other song I can remember a few words: 'The dark-eyed sailor has been my downfall.' 'All you young fellows take warning by me, Never trust a sailor an inch above your knee'. Lottie seems to have run two songs together:

"You see, that's the sort of words that was in this song, that I can remember. It was a good few years ago: I'm eighty-four you see..." Interestingly, the *Dark Eyed Sailor* was not one of the songs Vaughan Williams noted in the North End, even though it has remained a great favourite with East Anglian singers.

The Captain's Apprentice

James Carter at the North End January 9th 1905

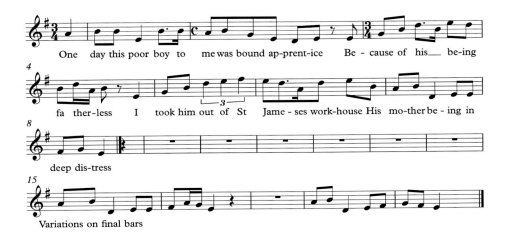

One day this poor boy to me was bound ap-prent-ice Be - cause of his__ be-ing

fa ther-less I took him out of St Jame - ses work-house His mo-ther be - ing in

deep dis-tress

Variations on final bars

The Captain's Apprentice

One day this poor boy to me was bound apprentice
Because of his being fatherless;
I took him out of St James's workhouse
His mother being in deep distress.

One day this poor boy unto me offended
But nothing to him I did say
Up to the mainmast shroud I sent him
And there I kept him all that long day.

All with my garling-spikk I misused him
So shamefully I can't deny;
All with my marlin spike I gagged him
Because I could not bear his cry.

His face and hands to me expanded
His legs and thighs to me likewise
And by my barbarous cruel entreatment
The very next day this poor boy died.

I asked my men if they'd release (?) me
If I'd give them golden store.
Out of my cabin straightway they hauled me
A prisoner brought me on Bristol shore.

And now in Newdigate I am confined
The writ of death I do deserve;
If I had been ruled by my servants
This poor boy's life might have been preserved.

You captains all throughout this nation
Hear a voice and a warning take by me.
Take special care of your apprentice
While you are on the raging sea.

The words of this song were noted in full by Vaughan Williams. It is the song from this week of collecting which had the most lasting effect on his music, often quoted in part. It is the opening theme of the Norfolk Rhapsody No 1, composed when he had just returned, full of enthusiasm, from his week in King's Lynn. It is still considered to be one of the most extraordinary songs he had collected. He also arranged it with piano accompaniment and it was published by Novello in 1908, interestingly without the more savage verses about the abuse of the poor captain's apprentice which were part of the original song. The tune is related to 'Oxford City', which was sung by his cousin Mr Harper later in the visit.

In the *Folk Song Society Journal* of 1906 Vaughan Williams writes: "Mr Carter belongs to a colony of fishermen who inhabit the 'North End' at King's Lynn. They possibly have a Norse ancestry – the wild character of this remarkable tune points to such a stock. This song was also sung to me by Mr Bayley, also a fisherman, who substituted 'gasket' for 'garling-spikk' in verse 2. The words are evidently local. 'St James's Workhouse' is King's Lynn Union.

Frank Kidson's note: Garling-spikk is most likely 'Marling spike' a small steel instrument for unpicking rope. The ballad was probably called forth by a particularly brutal case of ill treatment, similar to that narrated in it, which occurred some twenty or thirty years ago. There were tales of the mistreatment of apprentices with warnings to cruel captains and others who were in a position to abuse their young charges. In King's Lynn, the mistreatment of young Robert Eastick of King's Lynn had been reported in the local papers. The captain of the ship, Captain Johnson William Doyle was tried for cruelty towards young Robert, who was said to come from St James' workhouse in Lynn. There were broadside songs of other cases of captains mistreating their apprentices, including one in London, where "Captain Mills was confined at Newgate for the murder of Thomas Brown, his apprentice boy", according to a broadsheet published around 1800. There was also a record of an apprentice being killed off Minorca by the captain of the Loyal Britain. These are earlier cases and may well have led to the song being written; but the local case would have given an added force to the story for the King's Lynn fishing community.

For a full comparison read the study by Elizabeth James which clarifies that the song is much older than the 1857 Eastick case.[3]

The Deeds of Napoleon

Mr Carter at the North End, January 9th 1905

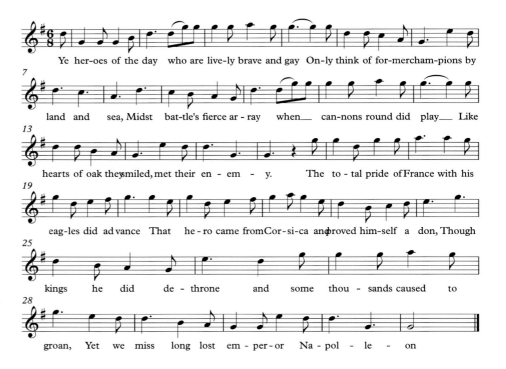

Ye her-oes of the day who are live-ly brave and gay On-ly think of for-mer cham-pions by land and sea, Midst bat-tle's fierce ar - ray when__ can-nons round did play__ Like hearts of oak they smiled, met their en - em - y. The to - tal pride of France with his eag-les did ad vance That he - ro came from Cor-si-ca and proved him-self a don, Though kings he did de - throne and some thou - sands caused to groan, Yet we miss long lost em - per - or Na - pol - le - on

The Deeds of Napoleon

Ye heroes of the day who are lively brave and gay
Only think of former champions by land and sea
Midst the battle's fierce array when cannons round did play
Like hearts of oak they smiled and met their enemy;
The total pride of France with his eagles did advance
That hero came from Corsica and proved himself a don
Though kings he did dethrone and some thousands caused to groan
Yes we miss the long lost emperor Napoleon.

Duncan, Jarvis and Lord Howe long the ocean they did plough
They fought the French, the Spaniards and the Danish fleet
When the crimson gore did flow then true courage they did show
They fought with desperation and were never beat;
The French they cried Mon Dieu while their decks to pieces flew
The Spaniards did surrender the Danish fleet was quite undone
Bold Boney fought on land an Emperor so grand
And his soldiers cried Long life to Napoleon!

Then the Norfolk hero bold he was never bribed by gold
Great honour to Lord Nelson, now a long time dead
To Copenhagen and the Nile he led them rank and file
But alas, at Trafalgar he fell and bled;
When Captain Hardy he did his duty so free
And Collingwood he acted like a true Britannia's son
He made a dreadful crash and their enemies did thrash
But I must tell the deeds of bold Napoleon.

Then Boney in a rage did his enemies engage
'Twas on the Peninsula he declared a war
He manoeuvred his men like the bold council of ten
When he went to Valenciennes and Vittoria
Then at Bazacco Hill, where the blood would turn a mill
From whence to Egypt he did go, but soon away did run,
To France he went again and rose a powerful train
Now "Come my lads to Moscow!" cried Napoleon.

O'er the Alps so wild he led his men and smiled
Over hills and lofty mountains and a barren plain,
When Moscow was in view, they their trumpets loudly blew,
But soon it turned their joy to grief and pain;
For Boney in a maze saw all Moscow in a blaze
Then his gallant army vanished like the snow before the sun
To France he went near craz'd and another army raised
Now "Come to death or glory!" cried Napoleon.

Then he away from France with his army did advance
He made the Dutch and Germans before him to fly
And then at Quartre Bras he loosed the dogs of war
When many thousand Prussians did fall and die;
And then at Waterloo many thousands he slew
Causing many a mother to weep for her son,
Many a maid shed a tear for her lover so dear
Who had died in the battles of Napoleon.

Bonaparte franchissant le Grand Saint-Bernard by Jacques-Louis David. Google Art Project.

Though so bravely he fought he at Waterloo was caught
He was taken to St Helena where he pined and died
Long time he there did lay till Soult came this way
To beg the bones of Bonaparte the Frenchman's pride;
Oh bring him back again twill ease the Frenchman's pain
And in a tomb of marble we will lay him with his son
We will decorate his tomb with the glories he has won
And in letters of bright gold inscribe "Napoleon."

Broadside printed by William Pratt, printer, 82 Digbeth, Birmingham. From the collection in the Bodleian Library.

In completing a version of this song collected shortly before he came to Norfolk, RVW used a text by Barr of Leeds of around 1850, which is almost identical. Henry Burstow sang the song to him at Horsham in Sussex in 22 December 1904, just over a couple of weeks before he heard it from Mr Carter in Lynn.

He notes in the *Journal of the Folk Song Society* that the middle cadence of the tune is distinctly Aeolian in character. Frank Kidson adds that the words must have been written before the second funeral of Napoleon. "I suspect that all the ballads with Napoleon as their hero have emanated from an Irish source, or from that large party of Englishmen who, originally holding the opinions of Thomas Paine, drifted, themselves and their successors into Chartists."

*Study of Napeolean
Benjamin Robert
Haydon.*
Yale Center for British Art.

Ward the Pirate

Mr Carter King's Lynn Jan 9th 1905

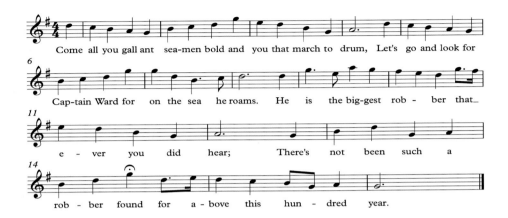

Come all you gallant sea-men bold and you that march to drum, Let's go and look for Cap-tain Ward for on the sea he roams. He is the big-gest rob - ber that ever you did hear; There's not been such a rob - ber found for a - bove this hun - dred year.

Ward the Pirate

Come all you gallant seamen bold and you that march to drum
Let's go and search for Captain Ward, for on the sea he roams,
He is the biggest robber that ever you did hear
There's not been such a robber found for above this hundred year.

A ship was sailing from the east and going to the west
Loaded with silks and satins and velvets of the best
But meeting there with Captain Ward it proved hard to maintain
He robbed them of all their wealth and bid them tell their king.

Captain Ward wrote a letter to our King on the fourteenth day of February
To know of him if he might come in and all his company
To know of him if he might come in old England to behold
And for his pardon he would give five hundred tons of gold.

Oh then the king provided a ship of noble fame,
She's called the *Royal Rainbow* perhaps you've heard her name
She was as well provided for as any ship could be
Full thirteen hundred men on board to bear her company.

Oh then this gallant *Rainbow* came crossing o'er the main
Saying, "Yonder lies bold Captain Ward, and here we must remain."
"I'm here, I'm here," cries Captain Ward, "my name I'll not deny
But if you are one of the king's fine ships you are welcome to pass by."

"Oh no," says gallant *Rainbow*, "It grieves our king full sore
That his rich merchant ships can't pass as they have done before."
"Come on, come on," says Captain Ward, "I value you not a pin,
For if you've got brass for an outward show then I have steel within."

Oh then the gallant *Rainbow* she fired, she fired in vain,
Till six and thirty of their men all on the deck were slain.
"Fight on, fight on.," says Captain Ward, "this sport well pleases me,
For if you fight this month and more your master I shall be."

It was eight o'clock in the morning when they began to fight
And so they did continue there till nine o'clock at night
"Go home, go home," says Captain Ward, "and tell your king from
me,
If he reigns king all on the land, Ward will reign king at sea."

Captain Ward was born in Faversham in Kent, working first as a fisherman, then joining the Royal Navy in Portsmouth. Then he became a highly successful pirate in the Mediterranean with a fleet and 500 men at his command. Ward died of the plague in Tunis in 1622. His exploits were excellent material for the ballad writers, even if, according to Roy Palmer, they sometimes got their facts askew. He says there never was a fight between Ward and a Navy ship called the *Rainbow*, so the story was probably written by 'some landlubber of a ballad writer'.[4] Nonetheless, it was a popular song and sung and reproduced for some 250 years.[5] Vaughan Williams noted the words from Mr Carter, including a verse from Mr Bayley. "Bayley describes this as 'The Master Song', he notes in his MSS. "He had won a silver watch from a cheap jack's singing match for singing it."

Captain Ward and the *Rainbow* is 287 p.145 in the *Child Collection of English and Scottish Ballads*. Frank Kidson noted in the *Folk Song Society Journal* Vol. II p.164 that this was a very old naval ballad and the words were printed by William Onley in the middle of the seventeenth century. It's also on broadsides by Catnach, Pitts and Such. It's in Halliwell's Vol. of the Percy Society 1841, and reprinted in *A Pedlar's Book of Ballads* in 1868. He says the event occurred in the reign of James I, and the first verse began:
Strike up ye lusty gallants
With music and sound of drum
For we have descried a rover
Upon the seas is come...

It appears in 19th century collections and was also heard by the collector Sabine Baring Gould. Vaughan Williams used the melody in the original version of the Norfolk Rhapsody No 1 and used it for his (now lost) military band suite in 1940. He arranged it for mixed chorus and a small orchestra in 1911 but this was never published. In 1907 he arranged it for voice after he had published *Folk Songs from the Eastern Counties*.[6] Clearly, he agreed with Mr Bayley that this was a master song!

Pirates by John Massey Wright.
Yale Center for British Art.

As I was a-Walking one Midsummer's Morning

Mr Carter, The North End, King's Lynn, January 10th 1905

As I was a-walk-ing one mid-sum-mers morning, one mid-sum-mer's mor- ning it hap-pened to be And there I did spy a___ beaut-i-ful dam-sel as I was a gang-ing all on the high-way.

As I was a-Walking one Midsummer's Morning

As I was a walking one mid summer's morning,
It happened to be a sunshiny day,
And there I espied a lovely young damsel,
As she was a walking along the highway.

I stepped up to her, I wished her good morning,
Oh where are you a-going so early this morn?
She answered, Kind Sir, I'm going to Croydon
That sweet pleasant place where I was born.

May I go with you, my fair pretty maiden,
For to bear you sweet company?
She turned herself round and smiling so sweetly
Kind Sir, you may do just as you please.

Now we had not been walking for scarcely one hour
Before this young couple's affectionates began
I said My fair maid, come sit down beside me
And then I will show you a sweet pleasant game.

She says My kind sir, I'm not given to gamble
But nevertheless I am willing to learn
The game that I will play, it must be all fours,
And then I will hold you three to one.

Then I picked up the cards, it being my turn to deal them,
Not knowing she had the deuce in her hand
Then she led off her ace and stole my jack from me,
Which made her high low jack and the game.

Then I picked up my hat and wished her good morning
I left her high low jack and the game
I said, "My fair maid, I will be over this way tomorrow
And then we will play the game over again."

Verse 1 as noted by RVW:
As I was a walking one midsummer's morning
One midsummer's morning it happened to be
And there I did spy a beautiful damsel
As I was a ganging all on the highway.

This seems to be a song known elsewhere as the *Game of All Fours*, or *All Fours*. Four versions were collected by Cecil Sharp between 1904 and 1908. George B Gardiner collected five variants, one in Surrey and four in Hampshire between 1905 and 1909. This version is from Mr William Randall at Hursley in Hampshire.

The Dragoon and the Lady

Sung by James Carter, at the North End, January 9th 1905

The Dragoon and the Lady

My father he's a knight and a knight of high renown
If I should wed a soldier it would bring his honour down.
It's your birth and my birth they never will agree
So take it as a warning bold dragoon, said she.

No warning, no warning, no warning will I take
I'd rather die than live for my own lover's sake
The lady heard these words and they made her heart to bleed
So to church they went together and married were with speed.

In going up to church and coming back again
The lady spied her father with seven armed men
Look yonder, cried the lady, we both shall be slain
For yonder comes my father with seven armed men.

There is no time to prittle, there is no time to prattle
The soldier being all armed, prepared for the battle
The soldier with his broadside sword he made their bones to rattle
The lady held the horse while the dragoon fought the battle.

O stay your hand, O stay your hand, the lady's father cried,
For you shall have my daughter and ten thousand pound beside
Fight on cried the lady, the portion is too small,
Fight on my bold dragoon and you shall have it all.

Come all you honoured ladies that have got gold in store
Pray not despise a soldier, although he may be poor
For they are men of honour, belonging to the Crown
Here's a health to Queen Victoria and her jolly light dragoon.

There are no words noted with this, but Cecil Sharp collected a version from Mrs Sage in Chew Stoke, Somerset on 1 April, 1907. He notes that Dragoon was always pronounced 'dragon' by country people with the accent on the first syllable. That would explain why RVW calls the song *The Dragon and the Lady* in his field notebook. The Revd Sabine Baring-Gould collected it on Dartmoor 'from an old moorman now dead' in 1878 and included fragments from another singer collected in 1892. Hammond collected it from Mrs Poole at Beaminster in June 1906. This version is from Sharp's collection.

Vaughan Williams had heard the song in December 1903 from Mr Garman in Ockley. He got one verse from him:

Says the Dragoon to the Lady it is time to give o'er
Says the lady to the Dragoon play me one tune more
For I like to hear your music, hear the tinkling stream,
But I like it much better love hear the nightingale sing.

The verse suggests it's related to *The Bold Grenadier*:

'Oh now,' says the soldier, 'it's time to give o'er.'
'Oh no,' says the lady, 'let's have one tune more.
For I do like your fiddle and the touch of your string
And I do like to see the flowers grow and hear the nightingales sing.'

Light Dragoons by Paul Sandby.
Yale Center for British Art.

The Blacksmith

Mr Carter King's Lynn January 10th 1905

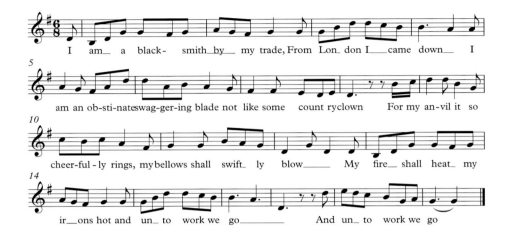

I am a black-smith by my trade, From Lon-don I came down I
am an ob-sti-nate swag-ger-ing blade not like some count ry clown For my an-vil it so
cheer-ful-ly rings, my bellows shall swift-ly blow My fire shall heat my
ir-ons hot and un-to work we go And un-to work we go

The Blacksmith

I am a blacksmith by my trade, from London I came down
I am an obstinate swaggering blade, not like some country clown.
For my anvil it so cheerfully rings, my bellows shall swiftly blow,
My fire shall heat my irons hot, and unto work we go,
And unto work we go.

There's Monday, Tuesday, Wednesday, these are the days we smithy,
There's Thursday, Friday, Saturday, and welcome Saturday night;
Then we receive our weekly wage and pay our alehouse score,
On Sunday we take our repose and on Monday we work once more.

Sometimes I've money in my purse, sometimes I am without,
But I am none the worse for that, can work for more, no doubt.
For my anvil it so cheerily rings, my bellows shall swiftly blow,
My fire shall heat my irons hot, and unto work we go.

These are the words noted from Mr
Carter by Vaughan Williams. Stave 4 is a
variation sung by Mr Bayley on 11 January.
Roy Palmer, in *English Country Songs*, says
he has not seen this song anywhere else.
Neither have I.

The Blacksmith.
British Library.

A Sailor was Riding Along

Mr Carter King's Lynn September 1st 1906

As a sail or was ri-ding a-long In the height of his glo-ry A sai-lor was ri-ding a-long As you shall hear my story He met with a char-ming young lass Asked her to go a-long with him, Some pleasures and pas-times to see, All in riding down to Ports-mouth.

A Sailor was Riding Along

As a sailor was riding along
All in the height of his glory
As a sailor was riding along,
As you shall hear my story,
He met with a charming lass
And he asked her to go along with him
Some pleasures and pastimes to see
All in riding down to Portsmouth.

She says, "Kind Sir, if I go along with you,
I am sure I must be married."
She said, "Kind Sir if I go along with you
I'm sure I must be carried."
She went with him straightway
And slept in his arms till next day
And she left him all the reckoning to pay
Riding down to Portsmouth.

It was early in the morning
She awoke and found him snoring.
Thus to herself she did say,
"He shall pay for his whoring
For the money he ain't spent on wine,
The rest of it shall be mine
And his gold watch too, I'll have besides
In riding down to Portsmouth."

Early in the morning he awoke
And found his lady missing
These words to himself did say,
"I have paid for my kissing
For she's robbed me of my gold watch and
purse,
And singed me which is ten times worse,
Sure I must have lain under a curse,
In riding down to Portsmouth"'

"Oh landlord, tell me what I have to pay,
That I may reward you,
Oh landlord, tell me what I have to pay,
That I may regard you;
And my horse I will leave here in pawn
Till back from the sea I do return,
And all such gallows ones I'll shun
In riding down to Portsmouth."

RVW did not note the words of this song from Mr Carter, but he did collect it again in Weobley in Herefordshire from a gipsy called Esther Smith, from her mother Mrs Whatton. Fred Hamer heard it from her daughter May Bradley in the 1960s.[7] Roy Palmer went to a broadside printed by William M'Call in Liverpool for a full version of the words. Grainger found the song in Lincolnshire.

This set of words is from a Harding broadside in the Bodleian collection Bod11760.

The Golden Glove

Mr Carter King's Lynn January 14th 1905

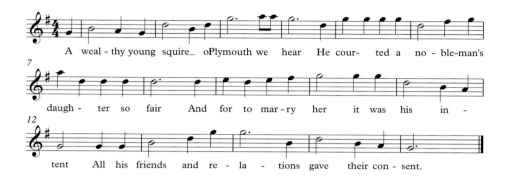

The Golden Glove

A wealthy young squire of Plymouth, we hear
He courted a rich nobleman's daughter so fair
And for to wed her it was his intent
And their friends and relations gave their consent.

The time was appointed for their wedding day
A young farmer was appointed to give her away
As soon as the lady this farmer did spy
It inflamed her heart, her heart she did cry.

She turned from the squire but nothing she said
Instead of being married, she took to her bed
For the thought of her farmer so ran in her mind
A way for to have him she quickly did find.

Coat, waistcoat and trousers she then did put on
And to hunting shed went with her dog and her gun
She hunted around where the farmer did dwell
Because in her heart Oh she loved him so well.

She oftentimes fired but nothing she killed
Till at length the young farmer came into the field
And for to discourse with him it was her intent
With her dog and her gun then to meet him she went

I thought you'd have been at the wedding, she cried
For to wait on the squire and give him his bride
Oh no sir, I would rather take a sword in my hand
By honour I would gain her whenever she command.

The lady was pleased when she heard him so bold
And gave him a glove that was covered in gold
And told him she found it when she was coming along
A-going a hunting with her dog and her gun.

The lady went home with a heart full of love
And gave out a notice that she'd lost a glove
And said whoever finds it and brings it to me
Whoever he is he my husband shall be.

The farmer was pleased when he heard of the news
With a heart full of love to the lady he goes
Saying Dear honoured lady, I've picked up your glove
And I hope you'll be pleased to grant to me your love.

It's already granted, I will be your bride
For I love the sweet breath of the farmer, she cried,
I'll be mistress of the dairy and in milking of the cow
While my jolly farmer goes whistling at plough.

And when they got married she told of the fun
How she went out a hunting with her dog and her gun
But now I have got him fast into a snare
I will love him for ever I vow and declare.

This was the version published in the *Journal of the Folk Song Society* No 21 p.30. It was widely distributed as a broadside ballad, and Lucy Broadwood said it was popular with the singers of the time. It was collected by Charlotte Burne in the late 19th century from a woman called Sally Withington in Shropshire. She said she had learned it during the 1820s from the singing of her mistress when she had been working as a maid on a local farm.[8] RVW had collected it before from Mrs Humphreys at Ingrave in Essex, April 1904 and from Mr Chenell at Kingsfold, December 1904, shortly before his visit to King's Lynn. Vaughan Williams did not note the text, so probably Mr Carter sang similar words to the versions previously collected. It also appears on broadsides from the 19th century.

Notes

1   Burial register, 21 October 1904.

2   Samuels, E. (1971) *Vaughan Williams and King's Lynn 1905*. Uppsala, Sweden: University of Uppsala, p.28.

3   James, E. (1999) The Death of Young Robert Eastick of King's Lynn in *English Folk Music Journal* Vol 7 No 5 pp 579-594.

4   Palmer, R. (1983) *Folk Songs Collected by Ralph Vaughan Williams*. London: .J.M.Dent and Sons Ltd., p.86.

5   Pitts' broadside of the song is reproduced in Shepard, L. (1962) *The History of Street Literature*. Newton Abbott: David and Charles, p.71.

6   Kennedy, M. (1964) *The Works of Ralph Vaughan Williams* Appendix I. London: OUP.

7   Ibid. 3, p.63.

8   Gregory, E.D. (2010) *The Late Victorian Folksong Revival*. Lanham, Maryland, USA: Scarecrow Press Inc., p.99.

Joe Anderson

"Now pay you attention to what I do say"

From Joe Anderson's song, 'The Saucy Bold Robber'

The famous picture of the Revd Alfred Huddle with two fishermen shows James Carter and Joe Anderson, the second singer he heard in King's Lynn.

Joseph Anderson, referred to by Lottie as Joe, was born c1834, second son of Thomas Anderson, fisherman. Joe and his brother Thomas both became fishermen but in 1851 their brothers John and James were plasterers. By 1861 Joe was running the *Black Joke* in North Street, a pub said to have been named, like the *Grampus* and the *Tilden Smith*, after a ship, and he and his first wife, Martha Allen, had a son also called Joseph, who was already a fisherman. *The Black Joke* was the name of several vessels but by the mid-19th century they seem to be no longer in existence, which might indicate the pub was a longstanding hostelry. One was a captured slave ship used later to suppress the trade and destroyed in 1832. Another was taken by the French in the Napoleonic wars.[1]

After Martha's death Joe married a widow called Mary Starling, who in 1861 had been living with her parents, her siblings and her baby John Starling. [2] In 1871 they lived almost next to the *Black Joke*. By 1881 Joe, Mary and John were living in Churchman's Yard off North Street, still Joe's home in 1905, not far from the Carters in Watson's Yard.[3] Three daughters had completed the household: Mary Ann, Agnes, and Rosanna, born in 1864, 1866 and 1874.

By 1901 Joe was a widower again, with only Rosanna still living at home until she married a fireman called William Alexander.

opposite: The basket of eggs.
Anne Roberts.

The wedding took place on 8 September 1904 at St Nicholas' Chapel, and Alfred Huddle officiated at the service.[4] The groom was the son of a blacksmith and probably not a North Ender, as his address was in Church Lane, presumably that close to All Saints' church in South Lynn. Joe still appeared next month at Churchman's Yard in the Register of Electors and was presumably living there alone in January 1905.[5] He died in April 1906; Alfred Huddle was still in the parish but he did not officiate at the funeral service. A Mr. T. Anderson was a subscriber to Mr Huddle's Testimonial in 1907; perhaps a link with Joe's brother Thomas' family.

Joe Anderson: The second fisherman to sing to RVW.
Ralph Vaughan Williams Society.

Churchman's Yard, North St.

Churchman's Yard, off North Street where Joe Anderson lived in 1905.
True's Yard.

Joe Anderson sang 12 songs:

As I Was A-Walking (Handfuls of Roses)
The Basket of Eggs
Bold Princess Royal
The Bold Robber
A Bold Young Sailor
Erin's Lovely Home
John Reilly
The Nobleman and the Thresherman
Sheffield Apprentice
The Yorkshire Farmer
Young Henry the Poacher
Young Indian Lass

Mr Anderson's total of twelve songs, all sung in 1905, is the highest any single singer reached. Vaughan Williams used three of them in his *Norfolk Rhapsodies I and II.*

The Basket of Eggs

Joe Anderson King's Lynn January 9th 1905

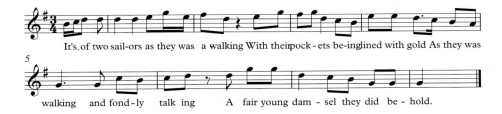

It's_of two sail-ors as they was a walking With their pock-ets be-ing lined with gold As they was walking and fond-ly talk ing A fair young dam - sel they did be - hold.

The Basket of Eggs

It's of two sailors as they was walking
with their pockets being lined with gold
As they was a walking and fondly talking
a fair young damsel they did behold.

With a little basket standing by her
but being tired she sat down to rest.
They said, "Pretty damsel may I carry your basket?"
The answer was "Kind sir, if you please"

But she say, "Young man I know nothing of you
of my basket of eggs I pray take care.
But if you should by chance out walk me
at the Half Way alehouse leave them there."

They walked on till they came to the half way alehouse,
they called for liquors of the best
"O landlord, landlord bring us some bacon,
for eggs we have and we will have a mess."

The landlord going to the basket
expecting eggs there for to find
"O sailor, sailor you are mistaken
instead of eggs we have a child."

One of them fell a weeping
but the other one says "Never mind
Here's one hundred pounds we will pay down fairly
to anyone that will take this child."

Little Nancy standing by the fire
all hearing what the sailors said
"O I will take it and kindly treat it
if you will first down the money pay."

"Are you the girl here they call Nancy
I danced with last Whitsuntide?"
"Oh yes, kind Sir, and I pleased your fancy.
Now the fiddler you must pay."

"We will go down to yonder valley
where the bonds of wedlock we will tie
We'll set bells ringing, sailors singing,
you'll enjoy your sweet happy bride."

RVW noted the words to this song from Joe Anderson. He also collected it in Somerset, and from the great Sussex singer Henry Burstow of Horsham at Leith Hill Place in December 1903. The tale also appears in broadsides. It was published in Vol. II p.46 of the *Folk Song Journal* along with two other versions. Vaughan Williams notes that it has 'some resemblance to tunes noted by me at King's Lynn, January 1905, and sung to the words *The Captain's Apprentice* and *Oxford City*. He collected a further version from Jake Willis in Hadleigh, Suffolk in September 1907.

The Yorkshire Farmer

Mr Anderson King's Lynn January 9th 1905

The Yorkshire Farmer
Good people attend and you shall hear
It's of an old farmer in Yorkshire did dwell
A Yorkshire boy he kept for his man
For to do his business his name was John.

With a fol, de lol, etc.

Early one morning he called for his man
For to go to the fair as you shall understand
Saying, 'Boy, the cow's in good order and her I can spare.'
Saying, 'Boy, the old cow you shall take to the fair.'

Away the boy went with the cow in a band
To go to the fair as you shall understand
As he was a going he met with three men
And he sold his old cow for six pounds ten.

Away they went to the alehouse to drink
Where the men paid the boy down his chink
There sat the old highwayman drinking of wine
Said he to himself 'All that money is mine.'

The boy unto the landlady did say,
'What am I do with my money, I pray?'
'Sew it up in your coat lining,' the landlady did say,
'For fear you should be robbed all on the highway.'

Now as John he was a walking home
This highwayman he followed him quite soon,
'Oh how far are you going?' the highwayman said,
'Four miles and further the poor boy replied.'

***

***

'Four miles and further the odds I don't know.'
So it's jump up behind and away they did go.

Then they rode till they came to a green shaded lane
'Oh now, little boy, I must tell you it plain,
Deliver up your money without any strife,
Or else this very minute I'll make an end of your life.'

When he found he had no time to dispute

***

From the lining of his coat he tore the money out
And amongst the long grass he scattered it about.

This highwayman he jumped from his horse
And little he thought it was to his loss,
For while he was gathering the money from the grass
To make him amends he rode off with his horse.

Oh he holloed and he shouted and bid him to stand
But the boy would not hear him and still galloped on.

***

***

Now as John as he was riding home
The servant was standing all in the front room
She runs to her master, says she, 'Here's a loss,'
Says she, 'The cow has turned into a hoss.'

When the saddlebag was opened, within was a hole,
They took sixty pounds in silver and gold,
Says the boy to his master, 'I hope you'll allow,
That master, dear master, I've well sold your cow.'

Sixteen-string Jack, the highwayman.
British Library.

These words, except for a variation in the first verse, were published in the second volume of the *Journal of the Folk Song Society*, where Vaughan Williams put Mr Anderson's version next to the one collected from Mr Whitby at Tilney All Saints the previous day. He says he's completed the words of the first by using the second, but there are still some lines missing, as indicated by the asterisks. He heard the song again from Hoppy Flack at Fowlmere in Cambridgeshire, in July 1907 and from Mr. Smith in Fowlmere a month later. The note by Frank Kidson says the song is usually known as the *Crafty Ploughboy*, or *The Highwayman Outwitted*, and under this title the words are found on a Pitt's broadside with the address of 14 Great Andrew St. They are also on later ballad sheets and are included in the *Pedlar's Pack of Ballads of 1868*. He says he has found a prose account of the event 'having just happened' in an old 18th century magazine, *The Universal Museum*, of February 1766. "It is quite possible," he says, "that the editor has for lack of copy dished up an old tale into a circumstantial account." He says the name of the shire involved varies, but the Yorkshire lad's sharpness is always given as a credit to his county. Cecil Sharp's note adds that the ballad's been sung to him in Somerset as the *Herefordshire Lad*.

Mr Anderson's version has two chorus lines on the end of each verse, Mr Whitby's does not, and the tunes are quite different.

Lucy Broadwood was sent a version of the song from Suffolk in 1893 which went under the title the *Yorkshire Bite*. It came from William Algar, aged 36, at Yaxley in November of that year. From the note on the manuscript, it looks as if he learned the song from Gilbert Woods, who died in about 1883 aged 87. The story was popular in East Anglia at the time. RVW did not note the words Mr Anderson sang, possibly because he knew of this version in Lucy Broadwood's collection. This is what Mr Algar sent: [6]

Sixteen-string Jack, the highwayman.
British Library.

Oh there was a farmer in Yorkshire did dwell
Had a Yorkshire boy he kept as his man
He did his business his name it was John

***

'Twas early one morning before it was day
He called to the boy and thus he did say
Why this very day take my cow to the fair
For she's in good order, I can her well spare.'

The boy he'd taken the cow and the bond
And he came to the fair, as we understand,
And he'd not been there but very little while
Before the boy he met with three men.
And he sold them his cow for six pound and ten
So away to the alehouse they went for to drink
And the farmer he paid the boy down all his chink.

And he called the landlady and thus he did say,
'Shall I do up my money come tell me I pray?'
'I'll sew it up in the coat-lining,' says she
'For fear on the road you robbed may be.'
And there sat a highwayman drinking o' wine
Oh thinks he to himself 'All the money is mine.'

The boy took his leave and away did he go
The highwayman followed him after also
And he soon overtook him all on the highway
'You are well overtaken, young man,' he did say.
'Get you up behind me,' the highwayman did cry.
'But how far are you going?' the boy did reply.
'Why I'm going three miles further for all that I know.'
The boy jumped up behind him and away they did go.

He rode till they came to a very dark lane
'Now,' said the highwayman, 'I must tell you plain
Deliver your money without any strife
Or else I shall surely take away your sweet life.'

The boy found there was no time to dispute
So he jumped off behind him without fear or doubt
And he rent the coat lining, the money drew out
And amongst the long grass it all scattered about.

The highwayman instantly lit (sic) off his horse
But little did think it was for his worse
The boy jumped up on horseback to ride away
The highwayman shouted and told him to stay
And still he would leave and kept on his way.
But when he got home his master said what a farce
What is my cow surely turned into a horse!

Oh master, oh master, your cow I have sold
And was robbed on the road by a highwayman bold
And the time he was putting the money into his purse,
To make it amends I came home with his horse
His master he laughed till his side he did hold
And he said,' for a boy you have been very bold.
And that's for the rogue you have served very right
And you have just given him a good Yorkshire bite.'

So they undone the pocket and soon they down told
Two hundred guineas in silver and gold
And that's for his courage and braveness severe
Three parts of the money he had for his share.
And now the highwayman has lost all his store
And he may go a robbing until he get more.

John Reilly

Joe Anderson King's Lynn January 9th 1905

John Reil-ly is my true love's name he lives down by the quay. He is as nice a young man as ev-er my eyes did see. My fa-ther he has ri-ches great and Reil-ly he was poor_ Be cause I loved my sai-lor dear he could not me en-dure.

John Reilly

John Reilly is my true love's name, he lives down by the quay.
He is as nice a young man as ever my eyes did see.
My father he has riches great and Reilly he was poor,
Because I loved my sailor dear he could not me endure.

My mother took me by the hand and these words to me did say
'If you are fond of Reilly you must leave this country,
For your father, he'll take his life and that without delay
So you must either go abroad or shun his company.'

'Oh mother dear don't be severe where must I send my love?
My heart lies in his breast, as constant as a dove.'
'Oh daughter dear I'm not severe, here is ten thousand pounds:
Send Reilly to America and purchase there some ground.'

Now when she got the money to Reilly she did run
Saying 'This very night to take your life my father charged his gun.
Here is ten thousand pounds in gold my mother gave to me
Sail over to Ameriky and I will follow thee.'

Oh when he got the money, next day he sailed away
When he stepped his foot on board these very words did say
'There is a token of your love I break it into two,
You have my hand and half my heart until I find her true.'

Less than twelve months after she was walking by the sea
Young Reilly he came back again to fetch his love away
The ship got wrecked, all hands were lost her father wept full sore
Young Reilly in his true love's arms lay drownded on the shore.

They found a letter in her breast and this is what it say
Saying 'Cruel were my parents that kept my love away
I hope this will a warning be to all young maids and
Never let the lad you love go to Ameriky.

The Shipwreck.
Anne Roberts.

Only a week before Vaughan Williams heard this song from Joe Anderson, he had taken it down from Mr and Mrs Truell of Gravesend, where he was out with his notebook on New Year's Eve. These are the words he noted from them. It was published in the *Folk Song Journal* Vol. II p.214, in which Frank Kidson added the note that he had seen the song on broadsides published by many printers and dated 1859. He said a version of the air was in the *Complete Petrie Collection* no 351, and in the first number of the Irish *Folk Song Society Journal* under the title *One Evening Fair*. Lucy Broadwood suggests a comparison with *Erin's Lovely Home*, collected by Cecil Sharp in Devon and published in the same journal. Vaughan Williams heard the song again at Acle in 1908 sung by Christopher Jay, and at the workhouse near Diss in 1911 sung by Mr Stephenson.

Young Henry the Poacher (Van Dieman's Land)

Mr Anderson, King's Lynn January 9th 1905

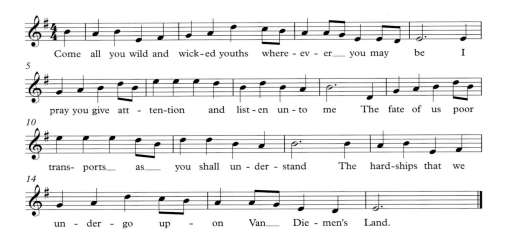

Come all you wild and wick-ed youths where-ev-er__ you may be I pray you give att-ten-tion and list-en un-to me The fate of us poor trans-ports__ as__ you shall un-der-stand The hard-ships that we un-der-go up-on Van__ Die-men's Land.

Young Henry the Poacher (Van Dieman's Land)

Come all you wild and wicked youths wherever you may be
I pray you give attention and listen unto me
The fate of us poor transports as you shall understand
The hardships that we undergo upon Van Diemen's land.

My parents reared me tenderly, good learning gave to me
Till by bad company was beguiled, which proved my destiny,
I was brought up in Warwickshire, near Southam town did dwell,
My name it is young Henry, in Harbourn known full well.

Me and five more went out one night into Squire Dunhill's park,
To see if we could get some game, the night it proved dark,
But to our great misfortune they trepanned us with speed
And sent us off to Warwick Gaol, which made our hearts to bleed.

It was at the March Assizes to the bar we did repair,
Like Job we stood with patience to hear our sentence there
There being some old offenders, which made our case go hard
My sentence was for fourteen years, then I was sent on board.

The ship that bore us from the land the Speedwell was her name
For full five months and upwards, boys, we ploughed the raging main,
Neither land not harbour could we see, indeed it is no lie,
Around us one black water, boys, above us one blue sky.

I often looked behind me towards my native shore,
That cottage of contentment that we shall see no more
Nor yet my own dear father, who tore his hoary hair,
Likewise my tender mother whose womb that did me bear.

The fifteenth of September, 'twas then we made the land,
At four o'clock we went on shore all chained hand in hand
To see our fellow sufferers, we felt I can't tell how,
Some chained unto a harrow and others to a plough.

No shoes or stockings they had on nor hat they had to wear
But a leathern frock and Lindsay drawers, their feet and hands were bare,
They chained them up by two and two like horses in a team
Their driver he stood over them with his Malacky cane.

Then I was marched to Sydney Town without any more delay,
Where a gentleman he bought me his book-keeper to be
I took this occupation, my master liked me well,
My joys were out of measure, I'm sure no-one can tell.

We had a female servant, Rosanna was her name,
For fourteen years a convict was, from Wolverhampton came
We often told our tales of love when we were blest at home,
But now we're rattling of our chains in foreign lands to roam.

This was a tune which impressed Vaughan Williams. He used it for the hymn *Oh God of Earth and Altar*, No 562 in the 1933 edition of the *English Hymnal* as the tune for G.K. Chesterton's text, and called it *King's Lynn*. It was chosen as one of the hymns for the re-burial of King Richard III in Leicester in 2015. The late John Jordan (1941-2012) came across it when he was the music director at St Margaret's in King's Lynn and he based his St Nicholas communion setting on it, written specially for the church as an alternative to his earlier St Margaret's setting.[7] In 1983 the tune was included in *Hymns Ancient and Modern* (New Standard) No 170, but unfortunately only as an alternative tune to the well known *The Church's one Foundation*, but it did ensure the availability of the tune as an alternative for other hymns in the book of the same metre.

Vaughan Williams heard the song from Mr Broomfield on 22 April 1904 at East Horndon in Essex. The song was sung in the 1950s by Harry Cox of Catfield.

Many versions of Henry's story were published on broadsides and relate to poaching cases in the courts at the time. Interestingly, Joe Anderson called his youngest daughter Rosanna. When he was about nine, a felon called Joseph Anderson was convicted of robbery and sentenced to seven years' transportation to Van Diemen's Land (modern day Tasmania) at Great Yarmouth Quarter Sessions. He did not sail until 1848 and was taken to Bermuda before being sent on to Van Dieman's Land. This man's family lived in Norwich and no connection has been found to the Lynn Andersons.[8] Maybe the coincidence of the name attracted him to this widely distributed song.

When the song was published in the *Folk Song Society Journal* Vol. II, Vaughan Williams noted that the full version of the words, 'which are of no great interest' are on a Such ballad sheet. He says the words of *The Gallant Poachers* in the *Folk Song*

A Government jail gang, Sydney, New South Wales.
National Library of Australia.

Society Journal Vol. I p.142, have much in common with them. Frank Kidson was more forthcoming about the words of the song. "The words of this ballad seem to have been very commonly known in country districts where poaching is a strong reality," he said. "It has been much printed on broadsides. I have copies by Such, Fortey and Bebbington of Manchester, in which last it is called *Young Henry's Downfall.*

To complete the song the burden:

'Young men all now beware

Lest you're drawn into a snare.'

Is to be appended to each verse and this is given in all the printed copies.

Kidson also notes that Young Henry's birthplace varies according to where the broadside was printed. He thought the ballad dated from 1835-40 and notes, "It is not so long ago that poaching had a penalty of seven and fourteen years' transportation attached." Fuller Maitland notes in the *Journal of the Folk Song Society* Vol. II that the tune seems nearly akin to *The Noble Lord*, a Sussex song. Roy Palmer believed the ballad appeared about 1830, perhaps in response to well publicised trials of poachers over the previous two years. One case at the 1829 Lent Assizes in Warwick involved eleven poachers being sentenced to death for shooting at the keepers on an MP's estate. The sentence was later commuted to transportation. As in the song, six were sentenced to fourteen years' transportation, and one of them was Henry White.

Erin's Lovely Home

Joe Anderson King's Lynn January 9th 1905

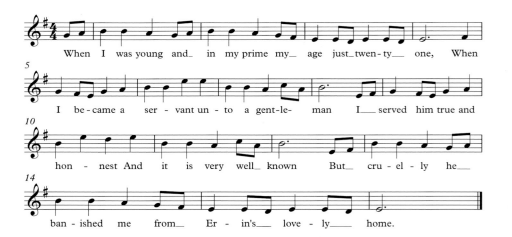

Erin's Lovely Home

When I was young and in my prime my age just twenty-one
When I became a servant unto a gentleman,
I served him true and honest, and it is very well known,
But cruelly he banished me from Erin's lovely home.

The reason he did banish me I mean to let you hear,
I own I loved his daughter, and she loved me so dear,
She had a heavy fortune, but riches I had none,
And that's the reason I must go from Erin's lovely home.

It was in her father's garden, all in the month of June,
When viewing of those flowers all in their youthful bloom,
She said 'My dearest William, if with me you'll come
We'll bid adieu to all our friends and Erin's lovely home.'

That very night I gave consent along with her to go
From her father's dwelling place, which proved my overthrow,
The night being bright, by the moonlight we both set off alone,
Thinking we'd get safe away from Erin's lovely home.

When we come to Belfast, by the break of day,
My true love she got ready our passage for to pay,
Five thousand pound she counted down, saying, 'This shall be your own,
And never mourn for those you've left in Erin's lovely home.'

But of her great misfortune I mean to let you hear,
It was a few hours after, her father did appear,
And marched me back to Omer Gaol in the county of Tyrone,
And there I was transported from Erin's lovely home.

When I heard my sentence, it grieved my heart full sore,
And parting from my true love, it grieved me ten times more
I had seven links on my chain and every link a year,
Before I can return again to the arms of my dear.

Before the rout came to the gaol to take us all away
My true love came to me and these words to me did say
'Bear up your heart don't be dismayed, I will not you disown,
Until I do return again to Erin's lovely home.

This is one of three versions of this song Vaughan Williams heard in King's Lynn. He did not make a note of any words, possibly because he had a broadside of the song in his collection and because it had been published in the Folk Song Journal. This version was printed by Such in London and says, 'Hawkers supplied'. So maybe a hawker headed for the King's Lynn Mart or fair and brought this with him. RVW also heard it in Ransbury from Mr Woolford in August 1904, and from Mr Smith in Salisbury in the same year. The song was published with full words in the *Folk Song Society Journal* Vol. I p.117 and in Sharp's *Folk Songs from Somerset*, as well as the *Journal of the Irish Folk Song Society* Vol. I p.11. Sharp reckoned the tune is related to four other songs which Vaughan Williams published after his Norfolk expedition.

Past and Present by T Blake Wirgman, 1883. The Graphic.

The Sheffield Apprentice

Joe Anderson, King'sLynn, January 9th 1905

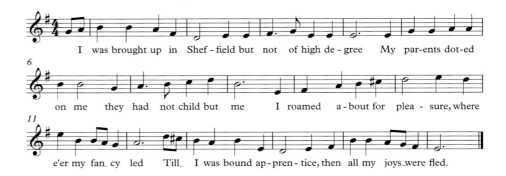

The Sheffield Apprentice

I was brought up in Sheffield, but not of high degree,
My parents doted on me, they had no child but me;
I roved about for pleasure, where'er my fancy led
Till I was bound apprentice, then all my joys were fled.

I did not like my master, he did not use me well,
I made a resolution not long with him to dwell,
A wealthy rich young lady from London met me there,
And offered me great wages to serve her for a year.

I had not been in London not one month, two or three,
Before my honoured mistress grew very fond of me
She said, 'I've gold, I've silver, I've houses and I've land
If you will marry me they'll be at your command.'

Oh no dear honoured mistress, I cannot wed you now,
For I have lately promised likewise a solemn vow,
To wed with dearest Polly, your handsome chambermaid,
Excuse me honoured mistress, she has my heart betrayed.'

She flew into a passion, and turned away from me,
Resolved within herself she would be revenged on me
The gold ring from her finger as she was passing by
She slipped it in my pocket and for it I must die.

For that before the justice, the justice I was brought,
And there before the justice I answered for my fault,
Long time I pleaded innocent but all that was in vain,
She swore so false against me that I was sent to gaol.

On the day of execution, all on that fatal day,
I prayed the people round me, "O pray come pity me,
Don't laugh at my downfall, for I bid this world adieu,
Farewell my dearest Polly, I died for love of you."

This song was also collected by Cecil Sharp and others and was published in Vol. I of the *Folk Song Society Journal* p.200. Vaughan Williams refers readers to the journal for the complete words. He did not note the words of the song as Joe Anderson sang it to him, but he had heard it before from Henry Burstow of Horsham, who sang it to him on 7 December 1903, and from Mr Pottipher at Ingrave on the 4 December 1903. He had a broadside of it in his collection. It was published by Novello in RVW's *Songs from the Eastern Counties* with these words. Cecil Sharp also collected it in Somerset in 1908.

In the introduction to *Songs from the Eastern Counties*, Vaughan Williams said:

The 15 melodies which are arranged in this volume are part of a much larger collection made in the Eastern Counties. It is not to be supposed that they are the exclusive property of the counties to which they are credited; all that is claimed for them is that they certainly are sung in these counties, and that most of the melodies have not as yet been discovered elsewhere. It will be noticed that which six songs from Essex and seven from Norfolk are given, there are only two from Cambridgeshire and none from Suffolk. This means, not that these two counties are less rich in folk songs than the others, but simply that time and opportunity have not yet been found to explore them. Nor do the songs collected from Essex and Norfolk represent an exhaustive search; all the Norfolk tunes come from King's Lynn and the neighbourhood, and the Essex songs from a small area near the town of Brentwood. It is to be hoped that an acquaintance with the melodies here given will incite others to explore those parts of East Anglia which are still unsearched.

I wish to take this opportunity of expressing my grateful thanks to the singers of these melodies, and to all those who helped in the work of collection.

The Sheffield Apprentice made a further appearance in his notebook, collected from Jim Austin, Little Shelford, Cambridgeshire, in 1907. This is *The Sheffield Apprentice* in Vaughan Williams' broadside collection, longer and with a touch of the broadside poet's licence:

I was brought up in Sheffield, but not of high degree,
My parents doted on me, having no child but me,
I roved about for pleasure where'er my fancy led
Till I was bound apprentice, then all my pleasure fled.

I did not like my master, he did not use me well,
I made a resolution not long with him to dwell,
Unknown to my parents I then did run away
And steered my course to London, oh cursed be this day.

And when I came to London, a lady met me there,
And offered me great wages to serve her for a year,
Deluded by her promises, with her I did agree,
To go with her to Holland, which proved my destiny.

I had not been in Holland passing half a year
Before my rich young mistress did love for me declare,
She said, 'My gold and silver, my houses and my land
If you consent to marry me will be at your command.'

I said, 'My loving mistress, I cannot wed you now
For I have lately promised and made solemn vow
To wed with lovely Polly, your pretty chambermaid,
Excuse me dearest mistress, she has my heart betrayed.

Then in an angry humour from me she flew away
Resolved for my presumption to make me dearly pay
She was so much perplexed she could not be my bride
She said she'd seek a project to take away my life.

As she was in the garden upon a summer's day
And viewing the flowers that were both fine and gay
A gold ring from her finger took as I was passing by
She slipt into my pocket and I for the same must die.

My mistress swore I'd robbed her and quickly I was brought
Before a grave old justice to answer for the fault
Long time I pleaded innocent, but every hope was vain,
She swore so false against me that I was sent to gaol.

Then at the next assizes I was condemned and cast
And presently the judge the awful sentence passed
From thence to execution he brought me to a tree
So God reward my mistress for she has wronged me.

All you that come to see me here before I die
Don't laugh at my downfall or smile at my destiny
Believe I'm quite innocent, to the world I bid adieu,
Farewell my pretty Polly, I die for love of you.

Frank Kidson notes that the words are Christie's *Traditional Ballad Airs* Vol II p.66 as noted down in the North of Scotland. Cecil Sharp says he's noted it twice in Somerset, one of them sung to the tune of *Erin's Lovely Home*.

The Hanged Man by Victor Hugo.
Metropolitan Museum of Art.

The Bold Robber

Mr Anderson, King's Lynn January 10th 1905

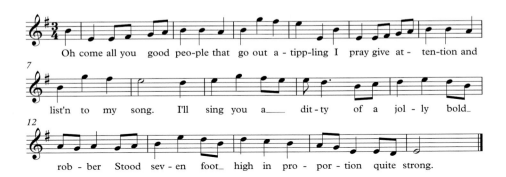

Oh come all you good peo-ple that go out a-tipp-ling I pray give at-ten-tion and list'n to my song. I'll sing you a___ dit-ty of a jol-ly bold_ rob-ber Stood sev-en foot_ high in pro-por-tion quite strong.

The Bold Robber

Oh come all you good people that go out a tippling
I pray give attention and list'n to my song
I'll sing you a ditty of a jolly bold robber
Stood seven feet high in proportion quite strong.

He robbed a lord and he robbed a lady
Five hundred bright guineas from each one of them
Till, as he was a-walking he met a young sailor
And bold as a lion he stepped up to him.

'Deliver your money my jolly young sailor,
You've plenty of bulk in your pocket I see.'
'Aye, aye,' says the sailor, 'I've plenty of money
But while I have life I have got none for thee.'

'I've just left my shipping and taken my money
I'm bound for old England my friends for to see.
I've ninety bright guineas my friends to make merry
So I pray, jolly robber, don't take them from me.'

Then the saucy bold robber struck the jolly young sailor
Such a blow on the head which brought him to the ground,
'Aye, aye,' says the sailor, 'you have struck me quite heavy
But I must endeavour to return it again.'

O then they both stripped, like lambkins they skipped,
They went life for life like to soldiers in field,
The ninety eighth meeting it was a completement,
And this jolly young sailor the robber near killed.

Says the jolly young sailor to the saucy bold robber,
'I hope you won't lay any blame on to me,
If I'd been a robber of ten hundred guineas,
I ne'er would have stopped a poor sailor like me.'

British Sailor by William Alexander, 1814.
New York Public Library.

The *Bold Robber* was published in *Songs of the Eastern Counties* by Novello. RVW took down the words. In the *Folk Song Society Journal* Vol. II p.166 Frank Kidson said he had never come across this ballad on a broadside or elsewhere. 'The tune is decidedly old and the song is one of the many narrative lyrics of highwayman exploits which formerly must have been sung around the firesides of most country inns.'

A Bold Young Sailor

Mr Anderson, King's Lynn January 10th 1905

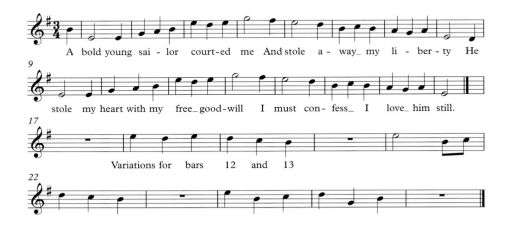

A bold young sai - lor court-ed me And stole a - way_ my li - ber - ty He

stole my heart with my free_ good-will I must con - fess_ I love_ him still.

Variations for bars 12 and 13

A Bold Young Sailor

A bold young sailor courted me
And stole away my liberty.
He stole my heart with my free goodwill
I must confess I love him still.

A grief to me I'll tell you why
Because she has more gold than I
Her gold will waste, her beauty blast,
Poor girl she'll come like me at last.

O once (I had no cause for woe) probably:
Oh once my apron strings were low
My love followed me through frost and snow
But (ah the changes time doth bring) But now my apron is to my chin
My love passes by and says nothing.

I wish I wish but it's all in vain
I wish I were (but free again) / I wish I were but a maid again
But free again I'll never be / But a maid again I'll never be
Till apples grow on an orange tree.

There is a bird in yonder tree
They say it's blind and cannot see
I wish it had been the same with me
Before I joined his company.

A brisk young sailor he courted me (or My true love once he courted me)
And stole away my liberty
He stole my heart with my free goodwill
I must confess I love him still.

This was published in the *Folk Song Journal* Vol. 1 p.252.

The note says, "This is like There is an Alehouse in Yonder Town", made up of stock verses which the collector has thought too frank in parts and hence inserted the lines in brackets. Clearly the words made little impression but the tune did - RVW used it in the *Norfolk Rhapsody No 1* as one of the soaring string themes of the piece. Frank Kidson notes that he's noted the ballad to other tunes. He says the subject of the ballad changes according to district: 'A rich young farmer' or 'A brisk young cropper'. No surprise that Mr Anderson sang of a bold young sailor!

The Nobleman and the Thresherman

Mr Anderson King's Lynn January 10th 1905

A no-ble man there lived in the vill-age of late There was a poor thresh-er-man his fam-il-y was great, He had got sev-en chil-dren and most of them were small He'd no-thing but hard la-bour for to main-tain them all.

The Nobleman and the Thresherman

A nobleman there lived in the village of late
There was a poor thresherman, his family was great,
He had got seven children and most of them were small
He'd nothing but hard labour for to maintain them all.

This nobleman he met with this poor man one day
And unto this poor thresherman these very words did say
'You are a poor thresherman, I know it to be true,
And how do you get your living as well as you do now?'

'Sometimes I do reap, and sometimes I do sow,
And sometimes I a-hedging and a-ditching too do go,
There's nothing goes amiss with me my harrow or my plough
And so I get a living by the sweat of my brow.

'When my day's work is done I go home late at night
All in my wife and family I take a great delight
My children they come round me with their prattle and their toys
And that is all the pleasure that a poor man enjoys.'

'My wife she is willing to join me in the yoke
We live like unto turtle doves and ne'er a one provoke
These times are very bad and we are very poor
But still we get our living and we keep cold from the door.'

'You are an honest fellow, you speak well of your wife,
And you shall both live happy all the last part of your life.
Here's forty acres of good land I freely give to thee
For to maintain your wife and self and your sweet family.

God bless all the farmers that take pity on poor men
I wish of them with all my heart their souls in Heaven may stand
And may those that are left behind a better pattern take
That they may follow after as quick as they can.

Man Threshing Wheat by Jean-François Millet, 1853.
Metropolitan Museum of Art, Harris Brisbane Dick Fund, 1927.

This song was included in Lucy Broadwood's *English County Songs* published in 1893, which RVW knew well. It was a broadside ballad which had gone into oral tradition in Sussex. Clearly Mr Anderson took a shine to it as well. E. David Gregory, in his book *The Late Victorian Folksong Revival* says 'it captures the pride and self-reliance of the rural worker but at the same time his sense of grievance about his landless condition and wages.'[9]

As I was a Walking Down by the Black Hospital - Handfuls of Roses

Mr Anderson

As I was a Walking Down by the Black Hospital—Handfuls of Roses

As I was a walking down by the black hospital
Dark was the morning, cold was the day,
Then who should I spy but one of my shipmates
Draped in a blanket far colder than clay.

He called for a candle to light him to bed
Likewise an old flannel to wrap round his head
His poor head was aching his poor heart was breaking,
For he was a young sailor cut down in his prime.

We'll beat the drums loudly, play the pipes merrily
Play the dead march as we carry him along
Take him to the churchyard and fire three volleys over him
There goes a young sailor cut down in his prime.

But now he is dead and laid in his coffin
Six jolly sailor boys march on each side
And each of them carries handfuls of roses
That no-one might smell him as we passed 'em by.

At the corner of the street there's two girls a-standing
Each to the other does whistle and sing
Here comes a young fellow whose money we squandered
Here comes a young sailor cut down in his prime.

On the top of his tombstone you'll see these words written
'All you young fellows take a warning by me
And never go courting those girls of the city
For these girls of the city were the ruin of me.'

'Never go courting flash girls of the city' was the moral of this story which appears in different versions around the country. RVW did not record the words of this song sung to him by Joe Anderson. The person struck down in their prime varies across the country from a young sailor to a trooper to a young girl. The late Cyril Tawney sang it as a navy song. James Reeves, in *The Everlasting Circle*, quotes two versions collected in 1906 in Dorset by Hammond and Gardiner. The first was sung by J. Curtis at Lyme Regis in March of that year; Gardiner heard it sung by 71-year-old Henry Adams at Basingstoke. Kidson says it is a version of the *Unfortunate Lad* (or *Rake*) and the words were published in the *Folk Song Journal* Vol.I p.254. When the song crossed the Atlantic it became *The Streets of Laredo*, a cowboy song. There are broadsides of the song published by Ross of Newcastle in 1876, and in Crosby's *Irish Musical Repository* in 1808.

Other versions make it clear that the young sailor was cut down in his prime by venereal disease, which was treated in London at the Lock Hospital. So maybe over time it makes the change from Lock to Black. *The Unfortunate Lad* includes the lines:
Had she but told me of it in time
I might have got salts and pills of white mercury
But now I'm cut down in the height of my prime.

The Lock Hospital was run by a charity founded in 1746 to treat syphilis, but didn't take male outpatients until 1862. Salts and pills of white mercury were thought to be a cure for venereal disease, so the song suggests that if the girl had warned him in time, the unfortunate lad might not have suffered from the disease. The handfuls or bunches of flowers are usually roses or lavender, 'not for to smell him as you pass him by'.

Joe Anderson's tune is a far more haunting one. He would probably have had a young sailor cut down, although RVW and A.L.Lloyd opted in the *Penguin Book of English Folk Songs* for the young girl cut down. In 1965 'Slinger' Woods of King's Lynn sang *A Young Sailor Cut Down* but to a different tune. It was on the 1965/6 recordings which include Bussle Smith, Slinger Woods and George Bone.

This version is Mr Curtis' except for the first line and the 'handfuls of roses'.

Lock Hospital, Hyde Park Corner by Thomas Shepherd.
Wellcome Collection.

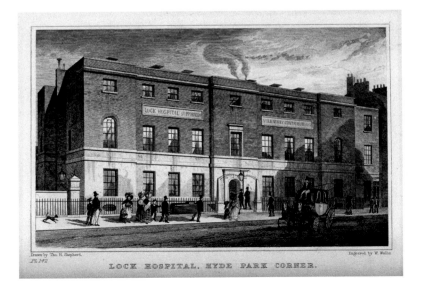

The Bold Princess Royal

Mr Anderson King's Lynn January 13th 1905

The Bold Princess Royal

On the fourteenth of February we sailed from the land
In the bold Princess Royal bound for Newfoundland;
We had forty brave seamen for our ship's company,
And boldly from the eastward to the westward sailed we.

We had not been sailing past days two or three
When a man from the foremast a sail he did see
She hove down upon us to see what we were
And under her foremast black colours she wore.

Now when this bold pirate she hove alongside
With a loud speaking-trumpet, 'Whence come you?' they cried.
Our captain being aft, boys, he answered him so:
'We've come from fair London and we're bound for Cairo.'

'Come haul down your topsails, your sternsails also,
For I have a letter to send home by you.'
'I'll not haul down my topsails nor heave my sails to,
But shall be in some harbour, not alongside of you.'

They fired shots after us but could not prevail,
The bold Princess Royal soon showed them her sail,
They drove us to windward but couldn't make us stay,
We hoisted our mainsail and then bore away.

'Thank God,' cried our captain 'the pirate is gone
Come down to your grog boys, come down everyone,
Come down to your grog boys and be of good cheer,
For while we have sea room, brave boys never fear.'

The Bold Princess Royal is a great favourite among East Anglian singers and the tale of her defiance caught the imagination of three of the singers in King's Lynn: Joe Anderson, Mr Crisp and Mr Smith. There are slight variations between them. This was the version of Mr Anderson's published in the Folk Music Journal No 2 p.170. RVW had first collected it from Charles Pottipher at Ingrave in April 1903. He refers to the *Folk Song Journal* Vol. I p.62 for the full words. Frank Kidson says he found two versions of the song and he says it's to be found on broadsides of the 1830s and 40s. Lucy Broadwood notes that the tune is related to *Sheepcrook and Black Dog* in her book *English County Songs*.

When the collector George Gardiner heard the song from William Randall in Hursley in 1905, he commented:

At daybreak on the June 21st, 1789, HM packet Princess Royal, nine days out from Falmouth on her way to New York (other accounts say Halifax) carrying mail, was accosted and pursued by a brig which was later identified as the French privateer Aventurier. At 7pm the Aventurier hoisted English colours and fired a shot, which the Princess Royal returned. After a further shot, the brig continued the pursuit. It was not until 3.30am on June 22 that the Aventurier resumed its attack, this time with a broadside and musket fire. The Princess Royal was outmanned, with a crew of 32 men and boys as opposed to the Aventurier's 85: and outgunned, too, with six cannon against the brig's sixteen. Nevertheless, the English ship gave a good account of herself, holding the privateer off for two hours, at the end of which time the Aventurier moved away and was obliged to return to Bordeaux for refitting, while the Princess Royal resumed her course, eventually arriving home on October 31st.

The doubt about this as a source of the song is that in every other version, the *Princess Royal* sets sail on the 14 February, and the story celebrates the speed of the ship, the courageous defiance of the crew and the seamanship which enables her to outrun and escape the pirate. 'We'll shake out our reef boys and for harbour we'll go!'

The Bold Princess Royal was sung to RVW at Horning in 1908, first in the village by an unidentified singer and then at Horning Ferry by Mr Barlow the same week. Both Robert and William Huw sang it to him at Southwold in 1910. The song remained in the repertoire of Norfolk and Suffolk singers well into the 1960s and 70s. Walter Pardon from Knapton, Sam Larner of Winterton, Harry Cox of Catfield sang it in Norfolk, and Bob Hart, Jumbo Brightwell and Bob Roberts sang it in Suffolk.

A packet ship by Thomas Chambers.
National Gallery of Art, Washington, USA.

Young Indian Lass

Joe Anderson King's Lynn January 13th 1905

As_ I was a-walk-ing on a far dis-tant shore I called at an ale house to spend half_ an hour And_ as I sat smo-king be - side me a glass By chance there came by a young In - di - an lass.

Young Indian Lass

As I was a walking on a far distant shore
I called at an ale-house to spend half an hour
As I sat smoking, beside me a glass,
By chance there came by a fair Indian lass.

She sat down beside me and squeezed my hand
She said, 'You're a stranger not out of this land
I have fine lodgings if with me you'll stay
My portion you shall have without more delay.

With a glass of good liquor she welcomed me in
'Kind sir, you are welcome to have any thing.'
But as I embraced her, this was her tone,
'You are a poor sailor and far from your home.'

We kissed and we tumbled in each other's arms
And all that long night I embraced her sweet charms,
With rural enjoyment the time passed away
I did not go to leave her till nine the next day.

This lovely young Indian on the place where she stood
I viewed her sweet features and found they were good
She was neat, tall and handsome, her age was sixteen,
She was born and brought up in a place near Orleans.

The day was appointed he was going away
All on the wide ocean to leave her to stay
She said, 'When you're over your own native land
Remember the Indian that squeezed your hand.

Early next morning we were going to sail
This lovely young Indian on the beach did bewail
I took off my handkerchief and wiped her eyes
'Do not go and leave me my sailor,' she cries.

We weighed our anchor, away then we flew
With a sweet and pleasant breeze and parted me from her view
But now I am over and taking my glass
So here's a health to the young Indian lass.

There were no words noted for this song, but RVW had a broadside of it in his collection. It was printed and published by Such. Vaughan Williams collected the song from Mr Woodford in August 1904 at Ramsbury. Jumbo Brightwell was recorded singing a version of it in the Blaxhall Ship in Suffolk in the 1960s. It was also in Walter Pardon's repertoire when he sang to Peter Bellamy in the 1970s.

Over the next few days after hearing Joe, Vaughan Williams was much occupied with collecting songs at the Union workhouse, dividing his time between this and further North End visits, to Mrs Howard, Mrs Benefer, "Elizabeth", and John Bayley, plus return visits to Duggie Carter and Joe Anderson. He then made his visit to Sheringham and on Friday, back in the town, he was introduced to Mr Harper, Mr Smith and Mr Donger. However, it will become apparent that there are interesting links between the four fishermen, Carter, Anderson, Bayley and Harper and it is therefore helpful to look at Messrs Bayley and Harper next in conjunction with Carter and Anderson.

Notes

1   Information from Wikipedia.

2   John and Charlotte Felgate: in 1845 a William Felgate had kept the *Fisherman's Arms*. Information from *White's Norfolk Directory* for 1845.

3   There were two North End yards by that name, the other being off St Ann Street.

4   St Nicholas' Chapel marriage register NRO PD39/106.

5   Curiously the next Electoral Register, drawn up in October 1905, suggests that by then he had moved across North Street to Devonshire's Yard. However when he died the parish register still gave his address as Churchman's Yard.

6   Letter is in the Full English database.

7   Personal recollection Elisabeth James.

8   Sources: Ancestry website, Australian convict transportation registers, the 1841 census. Contemporary criminal records show he and his brother had already been imprisoned for larceny the year before for stealing a pair of bellows from a yacht. He also took 30 shillings from a man near Yarmouth.

9   Gregory, E.D. (2010) *The Late Victorian Folksong Revival*. Lanham, Maryland, USA: The Scarecrow Press, Inc., pp.291-2.

John Bayley

"Bayley described 'Ward the Pirate' as a Master Song. He had won a silver watch from a cheap jack for singing it."

RVW's note with the song as sung by Carter and Bayley

Vaughan Williams' spelling of the surname is consistent in notebook and *Journal*, but no name spelt in that manner has surfaced in the official records anywhere in the town or at any time. This is the point however to recall the appearance of the name "Mr Bayley" on the list mentioned earlier and attributed to Lucy Broadwood's hand: "Bayley Hilda's Yard—Norfolk Street King's Lynn?".[1] If the reference pre-dates January 1905 there is no telling who supplied it or whether there is any link between this list and the letters to the *Morning Post* appealing for sources; however at least two names on the list refer to singers visited by Vaughan Williams a month before the October letter appeared. Most of the names relate to places in the south of England and some are known to have been visited over the next few years by other collectors. Two names immediately below Bayley's may relate to King's Lynn as they have no town cited: Mrs William Sandles "near the Chequers"; there was a pub of that name in South Lynn; and "Pegg? Philys Chapel Yard". Neither of these names have been found in official records although there certainly were several Peggs in the town *before* 1901, and indeed if they were no longer there or not known to Vaughan Williams' Lynn contacts in January 1905 it would explain why they remained unvisited!

If the contact details, however vague, were in Vaughan Williams' pocket in January 1905, it helps to explain why "John Bayley" in his notes has the distinctive spelling shared only by this list, a simpler explanation than a personal fancy of John himself, the rest of whose large family spelt it with an "i".[2] As this spelling appears in print in the *Journal* it has been retained here, but for John himself only, the rest of his family being styled "Bailey". Vaughan Williams' notebook says he was a fisherman.

"Hilda's" Yard must have referred to Hildon's Yard off the north side of Norfolk Street, which is not in the North End.[3] This is one of the main streets of the town centre and in 1905 was lined on both sides with many pubs, small shops and yards, full of cottages. The yards and pubs have gone, but it is still a street of small shops. However no connection has been established between John Bayley and Hildon's Yard before January 1905, although one of his daughters came to live there not long after.

The 1901 census reveals no one there with any obvious connection to the big North End Bailey family of which John Bayley can be shown to have been a member. He appears to have been the son of another John Bailey, Chelsea Pensioner, who was born c1790 at Middleton and whose wife Ann was born c1795 at South Wootton. The family moved around considerably before settling in Lynn, as their six known children were born in Middleton, (John himself in 1829), Ingoldisthorpe (1834 and 1836), and Sandbach in Cheshire (1838 and 1839) with only the youngest, Jacob, born in Lynn c1846, when even their mother was aged around 50. Nevertheless, both John Bayley and his eldest brother William became fishermen; sister Phoebe was a fish dealer, Robert a docks porter and Jacob a docks labourer.[4]

John Bayley married Catherine McCoy in August 1858, at St Nicholas' Chapel, after

opposite: Hildon's Yard.
Anne Roberts.

which they set up home in Pilot Street. John and Catherine both signed the register with a "mark" and were therefore presumably illiterate. Catherine's deceased father, William McCoy, was described as a shoemaker, as was the first witness, Reuben Lock, a close neighbour of Catherine's widowed mother Margaret McCoy.[5] His spidery hand wandered across the line in the register rather than along it, but the second witness wrote a beautiful regular hand which had perhaps been learned at St Nicholas' School in Pilot Street. This was Susannah Senter who with her mother Ann were also close neighbours of the McCoys in 1851. By 1861 they were living in North Street close to John Bayley's family and some years later she married the younger John's brother Robert. Further important links between 1905 singers and the Senter family will appear later.

John and Catherine had one surviving son, also a fisherman called John. Of their several daughters the third, Sarah, was thought at first sight possibly to provide the clue to Hildons Yard. In October 1905 she was registered as a householder there for the first time and seems to have remained

there for the rest of her life. Unfortunately, John's brother Robert had a daughter of the same name only five years younger so this point cannot be proved conclusively. She did not appear in the Register of Electors for 1905 itself, drawn up in October 1904. Women householders in the early 1900s were registered in a separate list from the men: they were able to vote in local elections only. John himself never appears in the voters' list, suggesting his homes did not reach the valuation qualification for unfurnished rented property set down in the 1884 Reform Act. At no time is John known to have been living with Sarah; she seems to have left home by 1881 and is never afterwards found at the same address as John and her siblings.

William Edwin Bailey, son of Sarah Bailey, born 18 February 1884 and baptised 28 March that year at St Nicholas' chapel, appears to have been her son. John Bayley certainly had a grandson of that name, who was part of his household in 1891 in North Place, off North Street. Still a fisherman in his early 60s, John now claimed to be a widower as he did at the next census in 1901.

That was not true. Catherine Bailey, fish

North Place: home of John Bayley and family. Rather bigger than the "yards" and almost a small street, alternatively known as "The Bone Yard": probably from its builder rather than any skeletal associations! True's Yard.

hawker, was living independently in 1891 in Brook's Yard, off Pilot Street, and also claiming to be widowed. Her identity is confirmed by her household: her youngest daughter Emily and her grandson Robert Panton, son of her eldest daughter Margaret. Her home qualified her to vote in the local elections and she was there in October 1900 when the 1901 Register was made up. By the census date in spring 1901 however the young people had left home and she was living as a boarder in Charles Anderson's house in North Street.[6] In 1908 her death in the workhouse is recorded in both its own register and that of St Nicholas'; the former notes that her burial was arranged "by friends" and the latter indicates that her previous address was Pilot Street, so she may once more have been living independently; her stay with Charles Anderson may not have been a long-term arrangement. This becomes an important consideration in a later section.[7]

John's own 1901 household consisted of his fisherman son John, who never married, a 43-year-old daughter Susan or Susanna(h)[8] also single and described as "general servant domestic", a widowed daughter Eliza and her small daughter Dolly, and two Bailey grandsons: 17-year-old William, presumably Sarah's son of that name, and 9-year-old Clarence. Clarence was born on 13 January 1892 and perhaps owed his unusual forename to the Duke of Clarence, once betrothed to the future Queen Mary before his unexpected death in 1892. No baptism record has been found to reveal which of the daughters, present or not, was his mother.[9] John's address was still North Place when he died in the summer of 1907.[10]

No later trace has been picked up of Eliza or Dolly, while the younger John died in hospital in July 1908 aged 44. In 1911 Clarence was still with Susanna in North Place: now aged 19 he was by then a fisherman and noted as the household head; Susanna was described as his aunt (fish hawker). William Bailey junior married Emma Penelope Carter (apparently no relation to Duggie) in 1906; by 1911 they were living in True's Yard. He was a fisherman.

John Bayley sang five songs, or parts of songs to Vaughan Williams:

The Captain's Apprentice
Ward the Pirate
The Blacksmith "Variation by J Bayley - Jan 11th" from rvw2/3/107 (Mr Carter's)
I went to Betsy; the only song Vaughan Williams noted from Mr Bayley alone.
Just as the Tide was Flowing "also sung by John Bayley - with variants"

It is noticeable that three of John Bayley's songs were more or less identical to three of Duggie Carter's, including the iconic *Captain's Apprentice*. His comment about *Ward the Pirate* quoted by Vaughan Williams in the *Journal* shows that he had been accustomed to singing it in public: "This song was also sung by Mr Bayley who described it as a "Master-song"... The original note in Vaughan Williams' notebook says: "Bayley describes this as "The [note definite article] Master Song". He had won a silver watch from a cheap-jack for singing it."[11]

I Went to Betsy

Mr Bayley King's Lynn January 11th 1905

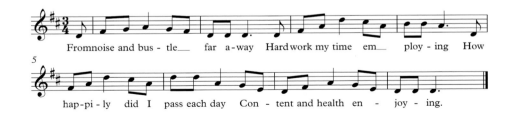

From noise and bus - tle___ far a - way Hard work my time em___ ploy - ing How hap-pi - ly did I pass each day Con - tent and health en - joy - ing.

I Went to Betsy

From noise and bustle far away,
Hard work my time employing,
How happily did I pass each day
Content and health enjoying;
The birds did sing and so did I
As I trudged o'er each acre,
I never knew what 'twas to sigh,
Till I saw Betsy Baker.

At church I met her dressed so neat
One Sunday in hot weather,
With love I found my heart did beat
As we sung psalms together,
So piously she hung her head
The while her voice did shake, eh!
I thought if ever I did wed
'Twould be with Betsy Baker.

From her side I could not budge
And sure I thought no harm on't,
My elbow then she gave a nudge
And bade me mind the serment;
When church was over out she walked
But I did overtake her.
Determined I would not be baulked
I spoke to Betsy Baker.

Her manners were genteel and cool
I found on conversation
She'd just come from boarding school
And finished her education.
But love made me speak out quite free
Says I, 'I've many an acre;
Will you give me your company?'
'I shan't', says Betsy Baker.

All my entreaties she did slight
And I was forced to leave her,
I got no sleep all that there night,
For love had brought a fever.
The doctor came, he smelt his cane
With long face like a Quaker,
Said he, 'Young man, pray, where's thy pain?'
Says I, 'Sir, Betsy Baker.'

Because I was not bad enough
He bolused and he pilled me,
And if I'd taken all his stuff
I think he must ha' killed me.
I put an end to all the strife,
'Twixt him and the undertaker
And what d'ye think was saved my life?
Why thoughts of Betsy Baker!

I then again to Betsy went
Once more with love attacked her,
But meantime she got acquainted
Wi' a ramping mad-play actor.
If she would have him, he did say,
A lady he would make her,
He gammoned her to run away
And I lost Betsy Baker.

I fretted very much to find
My hopes of love so undone,
And mother thought 'twould ease my mind
If I came up to London.
But though I strive another way,
My thoughts will ne'er forsake her,
I dream all night, and think all day,
Of cruel Betsy Baker.

When so many girls in folk song are called Betsy and this first line doesn't seem to appear anywhere, it's not clear which one Mr Bayley had in mind. But Betsy Baker, the story of a girl who ditches her lover for a 'ramping mad play actor', does have the line and the sentiment. It is on a broadside printed by T.Birt at the Seven Dials, and has the note that 'Country orders punctually attended to'. So maybe a ballad seller in Lynn brought it to Mr Bayley's attention.

No song comes up with this as a first line, so it must have been the part of a song that Mr Bayley remembered. None has offered an exact match. The Blackberry Fold is a possibility, a song which was found widely across southern England and was collected by E.J.Moeran. There's also a group of songs which belong to the 'cruel parents' group, which have the 'went to Betsy' line.

Bracebridge Hall, The Lovers, 1858.
Yale Center for British Art.

Notes

1   See p.49 n.6.

2   In fact John Bailey himself appears to have been illiterate, signing the St Nicholas' marriage register both as a bridegroom and later as a witness with a mark.

3   Norfolk Street runs parallel to and south of Austin Street, which is the southern edge of the North End. Norfolk Street was the main road out of town to Gaywood and Norwich.

4   These are all known to be children of John Bailey senior. There was another line of Baileys in the North End also descended from a Robert Bailey, also born in Middleton and perhaps the elder John's brother; several names appear in common between the two groups.

5   1851 census.

6   Son of Thomas Anderson and Catherine (nee Benefer): relationship of Thomas to Joe not known but perhaps a cousin; not his brother of that name. There were at that time two distinct Anderson lines of descent in the North End, descended from Thomas (born c1800) and Thomas (born 1810 and Joe's father): clearly related contemporaries but not brothers.

7   See later section, The Collector, the Singer and the Dumplings, p.163.

8   All three versions appear in records.

9   The coincidence of his birth early in the year of what is thought to mark Eliza's wedding may mean he was in fact her son and Dolly's elder brother.

10   Hardwick cemetery registers: John Bailey, aged 77, fisherman: died North Place; buried 10th June 1907.

11   The on-line Oxford dictionary defines "cheap-jack" as "A seller of cheap inferior goods, typically a hawker at a fair or market". Perhaps it wasn't a very reliable watch!

Mr. Harper

"N.B. Harper's brother said that the old songs were 'wonderful mellow'"
Vaughan Williams' note with his song Betsy and William

Vaughan Williams calls Mr. Harper a fisherman and comments that his brother[1] remarked that the "old songs" were "wonderful mellow". A number of Harper families have been traced, but all were descended from James Harper, born 1781 probably at Raynham, and his wife Ann Manning, whom he married in November 1803. Either Ann or perhaps her mother, may have been the Ann Manning "quack doctress", pictured by William White in his *Working Class Costume* published in 1818.[2]

Each of their four sons headed a Harper family in Lynn. Humphrey's daughter Alice married Duggie Carter in February 1865, but the rest of her family migrated to County Durham, where they entered the greengrocery trade. Charles' family seems to be associated with South Lynn in particular, although his son Henry also moved to County Durham, perhaps influenced by his uncle Humphrey's family, and married in Hartlepool in 1879.[3] James' family lived in Lynn but had no known connections with the North End or with fishing.

Only their brother, William, and his son of the same name followed the occupation of fisherman. William Harper senior married Elizabeth Rachel Bouch, daughter of Christopher Bouch and Rachel Manning, perhaps a relative of William's own mother Ann, in March 1830 and it is their son, William James, baptised in August that year, who was Vaughan Williams' "Mr Harper". William senior died in 1836 and later that year Elizabeth Harper married a widower, William Senter (1799-1864), an uncle of the

Susannah Senter who witnessed John Bayley's marriage and married his brother Robert.

The 1841 census showed William and Elizabeth Senter on their own with their new baby Esther, and young William Harper was with his grandmother, Rachel Bouch, together with William Senter's youngest surviving child from his first marriage, Hannah Senter. This may of course be an example of the census recording only a short term arrangement. By 1851 William, now 20 and a fisherman, was living with his mother and stepfather and his half-siblings Esther and Thomas (aged 7).[4]

In 1863 William married Sarah Anne Thomas. Sarah was not a North Ender but came from South Lynn, another maritime community, where her father Anthony Thomas was a mariner. Their son James, whose birthplace was listed as Middlesex by the 1871 census, was born well before the marriage and in 1861 had been living with his Thomas grandmother in South Lynn, described as "grandson (illeg)". No subsequent children have been identified. The family moved several times: from Chapel Yard in 1871 to 1 True's Yard by 1881; by 1901 William and Sarah were in Watson's Yard.

They were now near neighbours of Duggie Carter

Tom Senter, with his piccolo. Tom was William Harper's half-brother, and well-known in the North End as a talented—and largely self-taught—musician
True's Yard.

opposite: The gunship, Royal George, 1756.
Anne Roberts.

and it is interesting to note that William and Duggie were cousins, through their respective mothers; their grandmother Rachel Bouch, with whom William had been living in 1841, was living with Duggie's parents in 1861, styled "mother-in-law". At the same time, through his father, William was also cousin to Duggie's wife Alice Harper. This is a good illustration of how closely knit some of the North End families were.

After 1901 his movements are not known. He disappears from Watson's Yard and the Register of Electors after 1902-3. A William Harper, aged 78, died in the workhouse in November 1906, but he was not among the Union singers in January 1905. He may have arrived there for residential care no longer practical at home, perhaps from his son James' family home in Lansdowne Street, off Loke Road, where Sarah was living in 1911. She was ten years younger than William and outlived him until 1919. Their son James was not a fisherman; in 1911 he was a coal trimmer.[5] James usually uses his mother's maiden name Thomas, and a Mr Thomas subscribed to The Revd Alfred Huddle's testimonial.

In his noting of William Harper's songs Vaughan Williams remarks that his mother or possibly his brother said the old songs were "wonderful mellow". It is difficult to decide, even by handwriting comparisons, which it is. If he was indeed recalling something his late mother had said, it shows that Elizabeth Senter (formerly Harper) was herself familiar with "the old songs" and William may even have learned some of his songs by hearing her sing them at home. Even if the word is *brother*, William was not Elizabeth's only musical child.

William had no full brothers, but he did have a half-brother in Thomas Senter, some thirteen years younger than himself. In 1901 Thomas and his family were living in Burkitt Street off Loke Road, and he has also been identified as "old Tom Senter", who sang with a fiddle and was mentioned to Mike Herring in 1967 by George Edward "Bussle" Smith, one of the singers recorded in 1955 by the BBC at the *Tilden Smith*. Tom Senter's obituary in 1935 noted his playing the

concertina and "at the annual old folks tea at Lynn he always gave a solo".[6] He became well known as a self-taught musician, performing also on the accordion and piccolo, having joined the local temperance drum and fife band in 1917. The temperance apparently wore off as at his 89th birthday the newspaper reported "He enjoys his glass of beer and helps others to enjoy theirs by a tune on the piccolo which is the companion of his leisure hours."[7] It is noticeable that he did not contribute to Vaughan Williams' collection but the noting and attribution of his remark that the songs were "wonderful mellow" suggest strongly that he was present at the time.

William and Tom appear to have had another musician in the family, in their brother-in-law, a fish merchant called Thomas Barker. His wife, their sister and half-sister Esther Senter, died in 1901 but Thomas himself lived until 1914 at 1 Birchwood Street. In 1967 Bussle Smith referred to an "old Tom Barker" who played the fiddle, and this may well have been a reference to Thomas or perhaps to his son of the same name.

Mr Harper sang nine songs:

> Paul Jones or The American Frigate
> Betsy and William
> Captain Markee
> Edward Jorgen
> Fair Flora (a Welsh song)
> Just as the Tide was Flowing
> My Bonny Boy
> Oxford City
> Poor Mary

Like his cousin Duggie Carter and Joe Anderson, William Harper had an impressive catalogue of songs to draw on, of which one, *Oxford City*, was later included by Vaughan Williams in *The Penguin Book of English Folksongs*, published in 1959, which he edited jointly with A.L. Lloyd. The tune, to which he sang a set of words which Vaughan Williams noted in the book as not uncommon, bears a marked resemblance to his cousin's *Captain's Apprentice*. His large repertoire suggests that Mr Harper was a serious singer, as opposed to someone who just knew some old songs. His brother's wistful reference to "the old songs", the fact that the latter was "old Tom Senter" the musician and that their brother-in-law or nephew could have been "old Tom Barker" the fiddler, combine to make a powerful picture of music-making within one family.

Paul Jones or The American Frigate

Mr Harper King's Lynn Jan 12th & 14th 1905

An A-mer-i-can fri-gate call'd Ri-chard by name Mountedguns for-ty four from New New York she came, To cruise in the Chan-nel of old Eng-land's fame With a no-ble com-man-der Paul Jones was his name.

Paul Jones or The American Frigate

An American frigate, call'd the Rachael by name,
Mounted guns forty four from New York she came,
To cruise in the Channel of old England's fame,
With a noble commander, Paul Jones was his name.

We had not cruised long before two sails we espied,
A large forty-four and a twenty likewise,
Fifty bright shipping, well loaded with stores,
And the convoy stood in for the old Yorkshire shore.

'Bout the hour of twelve, we came alongside,
With a loud speaking trumpet, 'Whence come you?' he cried.
'Come answer me quickly, I hail you no more,
Or else a broadside into you I will pour.'

We fought them four glasses, four glasses so hot,
Till forty bold seamen lay dead on the spot,
And fifty-five more lay bleeding in gore,
While the thundering large cannons of Paul Jones did roar.

Our carpenter being frightened, to Paul Jones did say,
'Our ship she leaks water since fighting today.'
Paul Jones he made answer in the height of his pride,
'If we can do no better, we'll sink alongside.'

John Paul Jones.
Library of Congress.

109

Paul Jones he then smiled, and to his men did say,
'Let every man stand the best of his play.'
For broadside, for broadside they fought on the main,
Like true buckskin heroes we return'd it again.

The Ceraphus wore round our ship for to rake,
Which made the proud hearts of the English to sob,
The shot flew so hot, we could not stand it long,
Till the bold British colours from the English came down.

And now my brave boys we have taken a rich prize,
A large forty-four and a twenty likewise,
To help the poor mothers that have reason to weep
For the loss of their sons in the unfathomed deep.

Several broadside publishers picked up this song about a sea battle off the Yorkshire coast. Vaughan Williams did not note the words from Mr Harper, because he'd probably seen the broadside. These words are from a Disley broadside, titled simply *Paul Jones*.[8] A version called *Paul Jones the Pirate, a New Song* is in the Bodleian collection and dates from 1779.[9] The ship here is called the *Percy*, and she heads for the Yorkshire shore where she does battle with a forty-four under the command of "proud Richards" and wins not just the warship but a twenty a-gun ship and a convoy of "20 fine merchantmen loaded with store."

Fair Flora 'A Welsh Song'

Mr Harper King's Lynn January 13th & 14th 1905

Fair Flora (a Welsh song)
Come hither Fair Flora and sit down by me,
And we will be married when we can agree
No, no, says fair Flora, my time's not yet come
For to marry so early my age is too young.

I'll first go to service and there spend my time
And we will be married when I do return
Would you go to service to leave me to die
Come tell me fair Flora the reason for why.

Then it's good luck or bad luck for service she went
For to wait on a lady it was her intent
For to wait on a lady, a rich lady gay,
Which cloth-ed fair Flora with so costly array.

Then she'd not been in service past one month or two,
Before a letter been sent or to know how she'd do
But the answer was back again for to let him know
That she was advanced, and he was too low.

Then a little while after another been sent
With a line within it for to know her intent
But her answer was back again for to end all strife
Saying she never intended to make a poor shepherd's wife.

Then I'll go to my flocks and I'll bid them adieu
My work and my shears, I'll leave them with you
(My hook, crook and lapdog, I'll leave them behind
Once Flora, false Flora, has proved so unkind.)*

*taken from the end of the broadside version to complete the verse.

There was a broadside of this song in Lucy Broadwood's collection printed by Knight of Birmingham. Percy Grainger heard the song from William Clark in Barton upon Humber in Lincolnshire in July 1906. This is his version.

Lady in summer dress by William Alexander, 1814.
New York Public Library.

Just as the Tide was a-Flowing

Mr Harper King's Lynn January 13th & 14th 1905 also by Mr Bayley

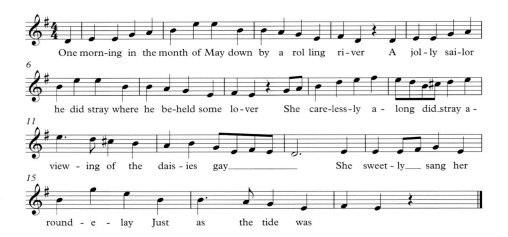

Just as the Tide was a-Flowing

One morning in the month of May
Down by a rolling river,
A jolly sailor he did stray
Where he beheld some lover.
She carelessly along did stray
Viewing of the daisies gay
She sweetly sang her roundelay
Just as the tide was flowing.

Her dress it was as white as milk
And jewels did adorn her,
Her shoes were of crimson silk
Just like some lady of honour.
Her cheeks were red, her eyes were brown,
Her hair in ringlets hanging down,
Her lovely brow without a frown
Just as the tide was flowing.

I made a bow and said, 'Fair maid,
How came you here so early?
My heart by you it is betrayed
And I could love you dearly;
I am a sailor come from sea
If you will accept my company
To walk and view the fishes play
Just as the tide is flowing.

Oh there it's we walked and there we talked
As we ganged down together,
The little lambs did skip and play
And pleasant was the weather.
Oh being weary we both sat down
Underneath a tree where branches hang
around
And what was done will ne'er be known
Just when the tide was flowing.

But as she lay upon the grass
Her colour it kept changing,
At last cried out this lovely lass,
''Ne'er let your mind be ranging.'
She gave me twenty pounds in store
Saying 'Meet me when you will, there's more
My jolly sailor I adore
Just as the tide is flowing.'

We both shook hands and off did steer
Jack Tar drinks rum and brandy
To keep his shipmates in good cheer
The lady's gold is handy.
It's to some public house we'll go
Where ale and wine and brandy flow
Success to the girl that will do so
Just when the tide is flowing.

Two verses of Mr Harper's version of this song were noted by Vaughan Williams (and his pen kept running out of ink!) but he would already have seen a set of words in Frank Kidson's *Traditional Tunes*. The version quoted there has a different tune, but was collected on the east Yorkshire coast by Kidson's collaborator Charles Lolley.[10] When the song was published in the *Journal of the Folk Song Society* Vol. II p.173 Kidson notes that it was on a ballad sheet by Barr of Leeds

and Hodges of London. It was also published on a Such broadside, and both sets of words are so close to that version that it seems to be the source. The verses which Mr Harper remembered are in italics. Mr Bayley also sang this song.

The song remained in the East Anglian repertoire for at least another 70 years and was sung by Walter Pardon of Knapton.

Oxford City

Mr Harper, King's Lynn Jan 14th 1905

In Oxford Ci-ty lived a la-dy And she was beau-ti-ful and fair O she was cour-ted by a sai-lor And he did love her as his dear.

Oxford City

In Oxford City lived a lady
And she was beautiful and fair,
Oh she was courted by a sailor,
And he did love her as his dear,

He said, 'My dear, let us get married,
Let us now no longer stay.
I'll work for you both late and early
If you my wedded bride will be.'

This girl she loved him, but at a distance;
She did not seem to be quite so fond.
He said, 'My dear, you seem to slight me
I'm sure you love some other man.'

He saw her dancing with some other,
A jealous thought came to his mind;
And to destroy his own true lover
He gave to her a glass of wine.

So soon she drank it, so soon she felt it
'Oh hold me fast, my dear,' said she
Is it that glass of wine you gave me
That takes my innocent life away?'

'That glass of wine which now I gave you
That glass of wine did strong poison hide,
So if you won't be my true lover
You'll never be no other man's bride.

'That glass of wine now which I gave you
Oh I have drinked of the same,' said he.
'So in each other's arms we'll die together
To warn young men of jealousy.'

'Oh hark, oh hark, the cocks are crowing
The daylight now will soon appear,
And into my cold grave I'm going,
And it's you Willie that's called me there.'

This tune is a variant of Vaughan Williams' favourite King's Lynn tune, that of 'The Captain's Apprentice.' On the MS he notes 'see marlin spike song'. He heard it earlier from Mrs Verrall at Horsham in December 1904.

The story of this song is found on broadsides published by Catnach and Such in London, Harkness in Preston and Jackson of Birmingham. When it was published in the *Penguin Book of English Folk Songs*, which RVW co-edited, it notes that the song was found in Sussex and Dorset, where Hammond also noted it. The text was completed by these sources.

Poor Mary

Mr Harper King's Lynn January 13th & 14th 1905

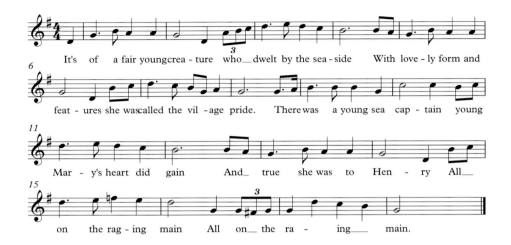

Poor Mary

It's of a fair young creature who dwelt by the sea side,
With lovely form and features she was called the village pride.
There was a young sea captain young Mary's heart did gain
And true was she to Henry while on the raging main.

It was in young Henry's absence a nobleman came
A-courting pretty Mary but she refused the same
'Your vows are vain for on the main there's one I love,' she cried
'Therefore begone, I love but one, and he is on the tide.'

Then mad with desperation the nobleman did say,
'To drove their separation I'll take her life away
'I'll watch her late and early and when alone,' he cried,
'I'll send her body floating along the silv'ry tide.'

The nobleman was walking one morn to take the air,
Down by the rolling ocean he met the lady fair.
Then said this artful villain, 'Consent to be my bride
You'll sink or swim far far from him who's on the silv'ry tide.'

With trembling limbs said Mary, 'My vows I'll never break
For Henry I love dearly and would die for his sweet sake.'
With his handkerchief he bound her arms and plung'd her over the side
And shrieking she went floating down the silv'ry tide.

It happened Mary's true love soon after came from sea,
Expecting to be happy and fix their wedding day.
'Oh we fear your love is kill'd,' her aged parents cried,
For she caused her own destruction in the silv'ry tide.'

Young Henry on his pillow he could take no rest
The thoughts of pretty Mary disturbed his breast,
He dreamt he was walking down by the ocean side
His true love he saw weeping by the silver tide.

With fright he aroused at midnight gloom went he,
To wander the sand bank o'er down by the raging sea.
As day break in the morning, poor Mary's corpse he espied
As to and fro it was rolling down by the silv'ry tide.

He knew it was young Mary by the ring on her hand,
He unbound the silk handkerchief, which put him to the stand,
The name of her murderer in full thereon he espied,
Which proved who ended Mary in the silv'ry tide.

The nobleman was taken and the gallows was his doom
For ending pretty Mary, who scarce attained her bloom.
Young Henry so dejected he wandered till he died
His last words were for Mary, who died on silv'ry tide.

No words were collected with this but Cecil Sharp heard it from Mrs Jane Gulliford in Combe Florey in Somerset in 1908 and it is also on a broadside called 'Poor Mary in the Silvery Tide.' Vaughan Williams noted when he wrote down the tune, 'Mr H. said I could take it up and down again just as you do in the music (i.e. when he was young). Vaughan Williams had heard the song before from Mrs Humphreys at Ingrave in April 1904 and from Broomfield at East Horndon in April 1904. It was printed in the *Folk Song Society Journal* Vol. I (4) p.216.

Captain Markee ('A man of war song')

Mr Harper King's Lynn January 13th & 14th 1905

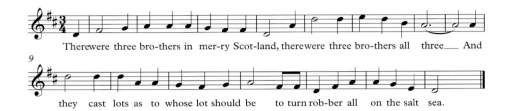

There were three bro-thers in mer-ry Scot-land, therewere three bro-thers all three___ And they cast lots as to whose lot should be to turn rob-ber all on the salt sea.

Captain Markee

There were three brothers in merry Scotland, there were three brothers all three,
And they did cast lots whose lot it should be to turn robber all on the salt sea.

The lot it fell to Captain Markee the youngest of all the three
To turn a Scotch robber all on the salt sea to maintain his two brothers and he.

They rov-ed they rov-ed all the winter's night till daylight did repair
They spied a rich merchant ship sailing far off and at length she began to draw near.

'O it's where are you bound,' says Captain Markee, 'O where are you sailing so high?'
'We be bound for Old England,' the ship's crew replied, 'if you will let us pass by.'

'Oh no, Oh no, ' says Captain Markee, 'Oh no that never can be
'For all your rich merchant goods we'll take away and your sailors all drownded shall be.'

'Bad news, bad news,' the ship's crew replied, bad news and a sorrowful sound,
For all the rich merchants goods you'll take away and 42 merry men drowned.'

They rov-ed they rov-ed this rich merchant ship for hours one two and three,
Till at length the salt water so fast flowed in and down to the bottom went she.

They lashed the sailormen back to back and threw them into the sea
(line missing)
'Some help, some help,' cries Captain Markee, ' and ?? we all could see
For you've the salt water and we've the money, now you've got to follow the sailors to sea.

This is similar to the ballad of Henry Martin, which was collected by both Frank Kidson in East Yorkshire and the Revd Sabine Baring-Gould in the West Country and was included in Sharp's 'Folk Songs for Schools.'. Vaughan Williams noted down the words of Captain Markee from Mr Harper, who called it a 'man'o war song'. The captain's decision to drown the sailors by lashing them together and throwing them overboard does not feature in other versions. In Traditional Tunes (published in 1891) Kidson prints two versions. He says Henry Martin was known among the fisherfolk of Flamborough, 'and with a little difficulty, by the judicious expenditure of tobacco, I was enabled to note down the following....' The other version he quotes was noted from William Cheetham of Horsforth who remembered some of the words and the tune from his boyhood. Mr Cheetham wrote to Kidson, 'To the best of my recollection, it ended by Master Henry being hanged 'to maintain his two brothers and he' and very properly, though sad. It must relate to buccaneering times, about a hundred and fifty or two hundred years ago. It was sung by a very old woman, a bobbin winder, in my mother's youth, about ninety years ago and my recollection of the air is from hearing it sixty years ago.' In verse 4, the challenge is more likely to be 'what makes you sail so nigh?' A sailing ship can steer closer to the wind when she is laden than when she has no cargo and sits higher in the water.

Edward Gayen

Mr Harper King's Lynn January 13th & 14th 1905

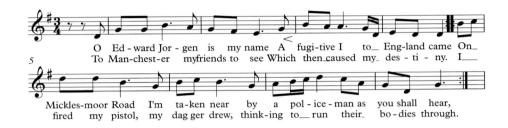

O Ed - ward Jor - gen is my name A fugi-tive I to_ Eng-land came On_
To Man-chest-er my friends to see Which then_caused my_ des - ti - ny. I_

Mickles-moor Road I'm ta-ken near by a pol-ice-man as you shall hear,
fired my pistol, my dag ger drew, think-ing to_ run their_ bo-dies through.

Edward Gayen

Edward Jorgen is my name, fugitive I to England came[11]
To Manchester my friends to see, which then caused my destiny.
On Micklesmoor Road I was taken near by policemen as you shall hear,
I fired my pistol, my dagger drew, thinking to run their bodies through.

The policemen there did boldly stand with all their truncheons in their hands
And with one blow they knocked me down they laid me bleeding on the ground.
Captured I was and I went along to the new buildings of iron strong
To Liverpool was committed there all for to take my trial there.

It's when my trial it does come on before a judge I was forced to stand
But never mind what they do say they can but take my life away.
Now in the court this young man stand his sweetheart came at his command
Tears from her eyes in streams did flow when she heard of his overthrow.

He says, 'My dearest I've done wrong, will you stay with me in prison strong?
'Yes, that I will while I have life, I wish I had been your wedded wife.'
I have robbed many dear heart for greed for which a great reward receive.'
Out of his pocket this watch he drew,' I robbed him of his money too.'

Roy Palmer says he's not seen any other version of this song, and it is one of Vaughan Williams' less legible notes, so sometimes it's difficult to be sure exactly what was being sung. Palmer says the words are sometimes garbled, and surmises that the song is 19th century and home made. It is in the *Journal of the Folk Song Society* Vol. III p.208, but there doesn't appear to be any broadside of this name. As far as we can make out, this is what RVW wrote down.

Betsy and William

Mr Harper, King's Lynn, January 14th 1905

Betsy and William

Young lovers all I pray draw near
Sad shocking news you soon shall hear
And when that you the same are told
It will make your very blood run cold.
Miss B.W. is my name
I have brought myself to grief and shame
By loveing (sic) him that loves not me
With sorrow now I plainly see

Mark well these words that will be said
By W.F. I was betrayed
By his false tongue I was beguiled
At length by him I was with child.
At rest with him I ne'er could be
Until he had his will of me
To his fond tales I did give way
And did from paths of virtue stray.

My grief is more than I can bear
I'm disregarded everywhere
Like a blooming flower I am cut down
And on me now my love does frown.
Of these false oaths he's sworn to me
That I his lawful wife should be
May I never prosper night nor day
If I deceive you, he would say.

But now the day is past and gone
But he had fixed to be married on
He scarcely speaks when we do meet
And strives to shun me in the street.
I did propose on Sunday night
To walk once more with my heart's delight
On the Humber banks, where billows roar
We parted there to meet no more.

Since he is false a watery grave
I have this night resolved to have
I'll plunge myself into the deep
And leave my friends behind to weep.
His word it was pledged to me
He ne'er will prosper nor happy be,
My ghost and my infant dear
Both shall haunt him everywhere

Dear, dear William, when this you see
Remember how you slighted me
Farewell vain world, false man adieu,
I drown myself for love of you.
As a token that I died for love
There will be seen a milk white dove
Over my watery tomb will fly
There you will find my body lie.

These cheeks of mine once blooming red
Must now be mingled with the dead
From thee deep waves to bed of clay
Where I must sleep till judgement day.
A joyful rising then I hope to have
When angels call me from the grave
Receive my soul, my God, from on high
For broken hearted I must die.

Grant me one favour, that's all I crave
Eight pretty maidens let me have
Dressed all in white, a comely show
To take me to the grave below.

Now all young girls I hope on earth
Will be warned by my untimely death,
Take care sweet maids when you are young
Of men's deluding, flatt'ring tongue.

This story of betrayal comes from the Humber. It was collected by Percy Grainger and also printed on many broadsides. The Yorkshire Garland Group has researched the song and found no record of the incident, but has found two Betsey Watsons and William Ellises in the records.

It was printed all over England by the broadside printers. The YGG say it is strange that what appears to be the seminal version by C. Mate of Dover was printed so far from where the event is alleged to have happened. The Mate broadside (Madden Collection 22 (Country printers 7), probably printed just after the event, is the only one to give background details.

This is where Vaughan Williams notes in his manuscript book that, 'Harper's brother/mother said that the old songs were 'wonderful mellow'.

Found Drowned by George Frederick Watts, 1867.
Watts Gallery.

My Bonny Boy

Mr Harper January 14th 1905

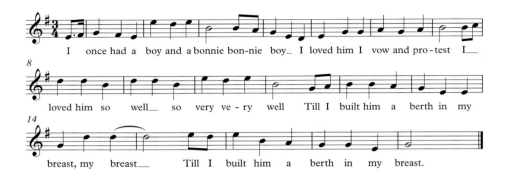

My Bonny Boy

I once loved a boy, a bonnie bonnie boy,
I loved him I'll vow and protest,
I loved him so well and so very very well,
That I built him a berth in my breast.

'Twas up the green valley and down the green grove
Like one that was troubled in mind
She whooped and she halloed and she played upon her pipe
But no bonnie boy could she find.

She look-ed up high and she look-ed down low
The sun did shine wonderful warm;
Whom did she spy but her bonnie bonnie boy,
So close in another girl's arms.

I pass-ed him by, on him ne'er cast an eye,
Though he stretched forth his lily white hand.
For I thought he'd been bound to love but one,
So I would not obey his command.

The girl that was loved of my little bonnie boy,
I am sure she is greatly to blame,
For many's the night he has robbed me of rest
But he never shall do it again.

My bonnie bonnie boy is gone over the sea
I fear I shan't see him again;
But were I to have him or were I to not,
I will think of him once now and then.

This song, according to Lucy Broadwood, goes back to the time of Charles II. In her 1893 book, *English County Songs*, her note says that the publisher Chappell refers to a similar ballad dating from Charles II's time called *My Bonnie Bird*, or *Cupid's Trepan*. The words she quotes are like those in *The New Cabinet of Love, songs sung at Vauxhall*. The song was published in the *Folk Song Journal II*. Vaughan Williams does not note the words he heard from Mr Harper other than the first verse. He noted in the *Journal of the Folk Song Society* that Mr Harper's words followed fairly closely those in Lucy Broadwood's book. Cecil Sharp collected the song two years later.

Heaven's Gate by T. Blake Wirgman, pub.1886.
The Graphic.

Notes

1 RVW's writing is hard to read here: it could be 'brother' or 'mother'. 'Brother' seems to make more sense given what we know about the family, as explained later.

2 The sketch included a pithy "Lies told faster than a horse can gallop. Ann Manning Lynn Regis." Ann may just have been a simple herbalist with rather bold expectations.

3 Moving to the industrial north-east, with which Lynn had a long-established coastal trade, was a noted phenomenon at that period when times were hard in Lynn.

4 Confusingly this enumerator described William Harper as William Senter's son-in-law instead of stepson as noted earlier.

5 A coal trimmer is a position in the engineering department of a coal fire ship which involves all coal handling tasks starting with the loading of coal into the ship and ending with the delivery of coal to the stoker.

6 *Lynn News and County Press,* 30 April 1935.

7 *Lynn News and County Press,* 27 September 1932.

8 Bodlian collection Bod 21041.

9 Ibid. Bod 8737.

10 Gregory, E.D. (2010) *The Late Victorian Folk Song Revival*. Lanham, Maryland, USA: Scarecrow Press, Inc., p.218.

11 The MS appears to say 'degit I to England came' here. Roy Palmer suggests 'and lately I to England came.' If Mr Harper said fugitive it might explain why Jorgen was pounced on by the police in Micklesmoor Road.

The Women Singers

"When I asked for a change of my guinea
She tipped me a verse of her song."

From 'Ratcliff Highway' sung by Betty Howard

After his initial sessions with Carter and Anderson, Vaughan Williams was not taken straight away to either Bayley or Harper, even setting aside his visits to the workhouse; he was introduced to two fisherwomen, Mrs Howard and Mrs Benefer. It may be that, despite being in their seventies, the men were occupied in the early part of the week in checking the aftermath of the stormy weather and its effects on the boats in the fleet.

Mrs Betty Howard

Howard is a strong Lynn fishing family name. Family tree compilation revealed three Mrs Elizabeth Howards living in the North End in 1905. Vaughan Williams maintained in his notes that Betty was aged around 70 and only one of the three was in her 70s, the others being very much younger. The most likely Elizabeth, or Betty, Howard therefore was baptised Elizabeth Senter in March 1827. Although Vaughan Williams noted no singers called Senter, this long-established fishing family has surfaced in connection both with Mr Bayley and Mr Harper. Like John Bayley's sister-in-law Susannah, Betty was a niece of William Harper's stepfather, William Senter. By 1851 she had married Thomas Howard,[1] a fisherman like his father. Like the four fishermen mentioned above at that time, they lived in or off North Street and were still there in 1871. They went on to have twelve children and all were still alive in 1911; it was no mean feat in the 19th century to have raised a family of twelve with no casualties. Six were still at home with their parents in 1881: four of the boys aged twelve and upwards were fishermen and no doubt those who had left home were also. Only two of the twelve were girls.

By 1901 however Elizabeth was a widow, living in North End Yard [2] with a four-year-old "boarder" called Julia Norton. Boarding the children of other families was frequent in the North End. Sometimes, as with the Carters and Lottie, one or both parents had died, but sometimes older couples with space to spare took in neighbouring children from families whose cottages were bursting at the seams.

Elizabeth described herself as 75 in 1901; she was still alive in 1911 but she and Julia, now aged 14 and described as her adopted daughter, had left the North End and were living in Purfleet Street in the town centre. Julia's name and the recording of the twelve children make clear that this is the same Elizabeth Howard, although she now told the census enumerator that she was 80 rather than 85!

Mrs Betty Howard sang 3 songs:

Homeward Bound
Ratcliff Highway
The Sheffield Apprentice

In the files maintained at True's Yard is an interesting list made by Maggie Castleton of songs she remembered being sung in the North End by men and songs sung by women. Maggie Castleton said that the women would sing while working; as a little girl she would wind the twine while her grandmother was "braiding" the nets and her grandfather would thread the net shuttles, and they would all sing the old

opposite: Girls cleaning mussels.
Anne Roberts.

songs. Reflecting a rather later date and with many songs from non-traditional sources, the women's song-titles exude a taste for sentimentality, but Mrs Howard's three songs show nothing of the kind! *The Sheffield Apprentice* had already come from Joe Anderson but the other two were totally different from what had gone before and very masculine in content: *Ratcliffe Highway*, set on a notoriously rough Stepney thoroughfare, is the popular old tale of a sailor's encounter with a waterfront pick-up and *Homeward Bound* is one of the few work songs in the collection. Did she learn them from the many menfolk in her household, or as one of the, usually elderly, women who occupied the side room in the pub, away from the men but probably not out of earshot?

The Gin Shop by George Cruickshank, 1829.

British Library.

Ratcliff Highway

Mrs Betty Howard Jan 10th & 11th at King's Lynn

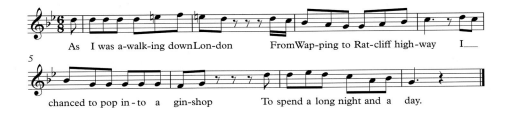

As I was a-walk-ing downLon-don   FromWap-ping to Rat-cliff high-way   I

chanced to pop in-to a   gin-shop   To spend a long night and a   day.

Ratcliff Highway

As I was a-walking down London,
Walking down Ratcliff Highway,
Mind you never step into a ginshop
To spend a long night and a day.

Old doxy come rolling up to me
As I had the money to sport.
A bottle of wine charged a guinea,
She quickly replied, 'That's your sort.'

The bottle of wine being finished
I allow four glasses coming on
When I asked for the change of my guinea
She tipped me a verse of a song.

The night being right in our favour,
So on board I quietly crept
I found a boat bound for Bedford
I got up on board of a ship.

These are Betty Howard's words collected by RVW. He noted in the *Journal of the Folk Song Society* Vol. II that 'it was impossible to take down the words of this song at all accurately, and at best they are fragmentary.' Perhaps Mrs Howard had a very strong Norfolk accent which he had difficulty understanding! The fuller version in *The Penguin book of English Folk Song*, by A.L. Lloyd and Vaughan Williams, is as follows:

As I was a walking down London
From Wapping to Ratcliffe Highway
I chanced to pop into ginshop
To spend a long night and a day.

A young doxy came rolling up to me
And asked if I'd money to sport,
Fort a bottle of wine changed a guinea,
And she quickly replied, 'That's the sort.'

When the bottle was put on the table
There was glasses for everyone,
When I asked for the change of my guinea,
She tipped me a verse of her song.

This lady flew into a passion
And put both her hands on her hip
Saying, 'Sailor, don't you know our fashion?
Do you think you're on board of your ship?'

'If this is your fashion to rob me
Such fashion I'll never abide
So launch out the change of my guinea
Or else I'll give you a broadside.'

A gold watch hung over the mantel
So the change of my guinea I take
And down the stairs I run nimbly
Saying, 'Darn my old boots, I'm well paid.'

The night being dark in my favour
To the river I quickly did creep
And I jumped in a boat bound for Deptford
And got safe on board of my ship.

So come all you bold young sailors
That ramble down Ratcliffe Highway,
If you chance to pop into a ginshop
Beware lads how long you do stay.

For the songs and the liquors invite you
And your heart will be all in a rage
If you give them a guinea for a bottle,
You can go to the devil for change.

RVW's note says Mrs Howard was about 70. He noted this song from her on 10 and 11 Jan 1905. Her words were incomplete, and when RVW and A.L.Lloyd decided to include the song in the *Penguin Book of English Folk Songs*, they supplemented the words with some from the Copper family sung in 1954, as well as a Catnach broadside, *Rolling Down Wapping*. This is their note on the song:

'In the first half of the nineteenth century, Ratcliffe Highway, Stepney, was the toughest thoroughfare in the East End of London. It was a place of sailors' lodging houses, sailors' pubs, sailors' ladies. Henry Mayhew has given us vivid descriptions of the Highway, with tall, brazen faced women dressed in gaudy colours, sly pimps and crimps, roaring sailors out for a good time, bearded foreign musicians from the fifteen dance halls of the locality, and the intrepid policemen of H Division walking through the throng in twos. The *Ratcliffe Highway* song may have been made for performances in ships' fo'c'sles, or it may have been made to impress the patrons of the *Eastern Music Hall*, the *British Queen*, the *Prussian Eagle* or another local public house licensed for music. In any case, it now has some ring of tradition and much of the ring of truth. Mrs Howard's text is supplemented from an unpublished version collected in Sussex in 1954 and kindly communicated by R. Copper, and from a broadside by Catnach.'[3] It was also published in volume II of the *Folk Song Society Journal* p.172.

Our Anchor's Weighed (Homeward Bound)

Mrs Betty Howard Jan 10th & 11th 1905 King's Lynn

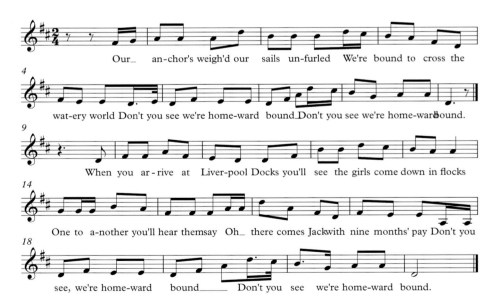

Homeward Bound

Our anchor's weighed, our sails unfurled,
We're bound to cross the watery world
Don't you see we're homeward bound,
Don't you see we're homeward bound.

When you arrive at Liverpool Docks
You'll see the girls come down in flocks,
One to another you'll hear them say,
'O there comes Jack with nine months' pay.'

Chorus
Don't you see, we're homeward bound,
Don't you see, we're homeward bound!

When we arrive at the 'Dog and Bell'
The very best liquor they do sell
In comes the landlord with a smile,
Saying, 'Drink my lads, it's worth your while.'

Now your money is well nigh spent
There's none to be borrowed, none to be spent,
In comes the landlord with a frown
'Get up my lad, let Bill sit down.'

This is one of the few sea shanties which Vaughan Williams heard in Lynn and it was sung to him by a woman. Most of the songs he noted were ballads, but this shanty had wide currency. In *Ships, Sea Songs and Shanties*, Captain W. B. Whall says it was sung the world over, with sailors adapting the first line to their home port. It was published in the *Folk Song Society Journal* Vol. III pp.214-5.

RVW noted these words from Mrs Howard. The tune of the first verse is slightly different from the rest.

A barque homeward bound.
British Library.

The Sheffield Apprentice

Mrs Betty Howard, King's Lynn January 10/11th 1905

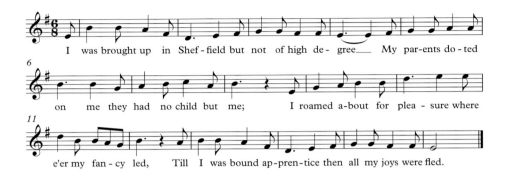

The Sheffield Apprentice

I was brought up in Sheffield, but not of high degree,
My parents doted on me, they had no child but me;
I roamed about for pleasure, where'er my fancy led
Till I was bound apprentice, then all my joys were fled.

I did not like my master, he did not use me well,
I made a resolution not long with him to dwell,
A wealthy rich young lady from London met me there,
And offered me great wages to serve her for a year.

I had not been in London not one month, two or three,
Before my honoured mistress grew very fond of me
She said, 'I've gold, I've silver, I've houses and I've land
If you will marry me they'll be at your command.'

Oh no dear honoured mistress, I cannot wed you now,
For I have lately promised likewise a solemn vow,
To wed with dearest Polly, your handsome chambermaid,
Excuse me honoured mistress, she has my heart betrayed.'

She flew into a passion, and turned away from me,
Resolved within herself she would be revenged on me
Her gold ring from her finger as she was passing by
She slipped it in my pocket and for it I must die.

For that before the justice, the justice I was brought,
And there before the justice I answered for my fault,
Long time I pleaded innocent but all that was in vain,
She swore so false against me that I was sent to gaol.

On the day of execution, all on that fatal day,
I prayed the people round me, 'O pray come pity me,
Don't laugh at my downfall, for I bid this world adieu,
Farewell my dearest Polly, I died for love of you.

RVW did not note down the words from Mrs Howard. He had heard the song a few days before from Mr Anderson. It was printed by several broadside publishers.

These were the words of the *Sheffield Apprentice* in Vaughan Williams' broadside collection.

For further notes, see Mr Anderson's version of the song (p.88).

I was brought up in Sheffield, but not of high degree,
My parents doted on me, having no child but me,
I roved about for pleasure where'ere my fancy led
Till I was bound apprentice, then all my pleasure fled.

I did not like my master, he did not use me well,
I made a resolution not long with him to dwell,
Unknown to my parents I then did run away
And steered my course to London, oh cursed be this day.

And when I came to London, a lady met me there,
And offered me great wages to serve her for a year,
Deluded by her promises, with her I did agree,
To go with her to Holland, which proved my destiny.

I had not been in Holland passing half a year
Before my rich young mistress did love for me declare,
She said, 'My gold and silver, my houses and my land
If you consent to marry me will be at your command.'

I said, 'My loving mistress, I cannot wed you now
For I have lately promised and made solemn vow
To wed with lovely Polly, your pretty chambermaid,
Excuse me dearest mistress, she has my heart betrayed.

Then in an angry humour from me she flew away
Resolved for my presumption to make me dearly pay
She was so much perplexed she could not be my bride
She said she'd seek a project to take away my life.

As she was in the garden upon a summer's day
And viewing the flowers that were both fine and gay
A gold ring from her finger took as I was passing by
She slipt into my pocket and I for the same must die.

My mistress swore I'd robbed her and quickly I was brought
Before a grave old justice to answer for the fault
Long time I pleaded innocent but every hope was vain,
She swore so false against me that I was sent to gaol.

Then at the next assizes I was condemned and cast
And presently the judge the awful sentence passed
From thence to execution, he brought me to a tree
So God reward my mistress for she has wronged me.

All you that come to see me here before I die
Don't laugh at my downfall or smile at my destiny
Believe I'm quite innocent, to the world I bid adieu,
Farewell my pretty Polly, I die for love of you.

Harriet "Lol" Benefer (née Bailey). A rare picture of a 1905 singer: one of the three female singers and a niece of John Bayley.
True's Yard.

Mrs Benefer

Like the Howards, the Benefers were a big North End fishing family and the name is still prominent today. Vaughan Williams' notes gave Mrs Benefer a first name which looks like "Larley". It may have been a nickname but underneath he has written an alternative with a query, which at first sight appeared to be "Lotty?". This was thought initially to identify her as Mrs Charlotte Ann Benefer, born around 1858 and wife of John Benefer, fisherman.[4]

Further research however suggested that the scribbled "Lotty" is really "Lolly", a not unlikely interpretation of Vaughan Williams' "Larley". Close examination showed a suggestion of two loops behind the cross-strokes of the double "t". "Larley" could have been the collector's phonetic rendering of what he heard as the name, later corrected, in the light of a perceived dialect lengthening of the first vowel, to "Lolly" and then to "Lotty" as a more likely name or vice versa.

What he may not have realised is that North End nicknames were notorious for their base on something other than a Christian name, e.g. "Duggie" for James Carter. With that possibility in mind, a much stronger contender for the role of "Mrs Larley Benefer" is in fact Harriet Ann "Lol" Benefer, born c1864 and a daughter of John Bayley's brother William Bailey.

Harriet's nickname appeared in print alongside her real name in the press report of a serious 1882 domestic brawl which resulted in the death of a neighbour and the imprisonment of her father, her mother, her elder sister and herself for manslaughter.[5]

On 8 March 1885 she married Henry Benefer, a cousin of Charlotte Benefer's husband. At the time of their marriage Henry lived in Lansdowne Terrace off Loke Road, but by 1901 the couple lived in Whitening's Yard off North Street. Henry was still a fisherman but later they kept a provisions shop on the corner of North Street and Pilot Street. In due course it was taken over by their son Tom. His son, Tom "Boots" Benefer, was well known as a samphire gatherer and seller.[6] Kelly's Directory gives "Mrs H Bennerfer" (sic) shopkeeper in 1922, although not in 1916; by 1928 Thomas' name appears instead. He seems to have been also the singer Tom Benefer who was recorded by the BBC at the *Tilden Smith* in 1955 and his sister Harriet (1889-1922) married her fellow singer "Bussle" Smith in 1911.[7]

The relationships raised by this possibility are extremely interesting. Harriet's father William was a brother of John Bayley, almost the next singer to be visited. In addition Harriet's sister Naomi married John Laws Norris, whose mother Sarah Norris was Duggie Carter's sister. Naomi's six children included Charlotte, known as Lottie, who was adopted by the Carters after Naomi died c1893-4 and whose reminiscences were recorded in 1976. The other Norris children lived with their grandmother Sarah Norris, only a few doors away in Watson's Yard from the Carters.

Mrs Benefer sang 2 songs:

Barb'ry Allen
The Farmer's Daughter

Mrs Benefer's two songs are both narrative ballads much more suited to passing the time while mending nets. The most likely set of words for *The Farmer's Daughter* (*The Banks of Sweet Dundee*) noticeably tells of a heroine who comes out spectacularly triumphant at the end, having littered the scene with defunct villains, which may have had a strong appeal to the feminine imagination.

Tom (Boots) Benefer and samphire cart in Pilot Street: Lol and Henry's grandson, whose samphire cart is now in the Fisherfolk Museum. The Fisherman's Arms to left of Tom's arm identifies the street: the jettied front beyond it was the Grampus pub. He is outside the family shop at the junction with North Street, where the dog is crossing the road.
True's Yard.

"T Benefer, grocer, confectioner and tobacconist": The shop on the corner of Pilot Street and North Street was kept by Lol and her husband Henry Benefer, later taken over by their son Tom, who was recorded singing in 1955 by the BBC.
True's Yard.

Barbary Allen

Larley Benefer at Lynn Jan 11th 1905

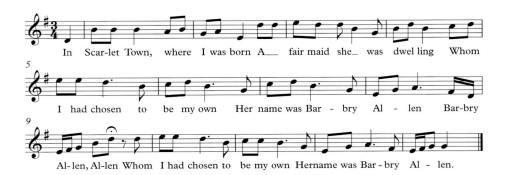

Barb'ry Allen

In Scarlet Town where I was born
There was a fair maid dwelling,
Whom I had chosen to be my own
And her name it was Barbara Allen.

All in the merry month of May
When green buds they are shooting
This young man on his death bed lay
For the love of Barbara Allen.

He sent his man unto her then
To the town where she was dwelling
'You must come to my master here
If your name be Barbara Allen.

'For death be printed in his face
And sorrows in him dwelling
And you must come to my master dear
For bonny Barbara Allen.'

'If death be printed in his face
And sorrows in him dwelling
Then little better shall he be
For bonny Barbara Allen.

So slowly, slowly she got up
And slowly she came to him
And all she said when she came there
'Young man, I think you're dying.'

He turned his face unto her then
'If you be Barbara Allen,
My dear, said he, come pity me,
As on my death bed I am lying.'

'If on your death bed sure you be
What is that to Barbara Allan?
I cannot keep you from your death
So farewell,' said Barbara Allen.

He turned his face unto the wall
And Death came creeping to him
Then 'Adieu, adieu, and adieu to all
And adieu to Barbara Allen'.

As she was walking on a day
She heard the bell a-ringing,
And it did seem to ring to her
'Unworthy Barbara Allen.'

She turned herself around about
And she spied the corpse a-coming
'Lay down, lay down the corpse of clay
That I may look upon him.'

And all the while she looked on
So loudly she lay laughing,
While all her friends cried out amain,
'Unworthy Barbara Allen.'

When he was dead and in his grave,
Then Death came creeping to she
'Oh mother, mother, make my bed
For his death hath quite undone me.

A cruel creature that I was
To slight him that loved me dearly,
I wish I had been a kinder maid
The time that he was nigh me.'

So this maid she then did die
And desired to be buried nigh him
And repented herself before she died
To she did ever deny him.

This was such a well-known song that Vaughan Williams did not note the words from Mrs Larley Benefer (sic) when she sang it to him on Jan 11th. It was already in Frank Kidson's *Traditional Tunes* of 1891, noted from singers in Yorkshire. The New and Old Song Ballad Company printed it and sold the broadsides for a ha'penny each. Child collected it in Scotland, Gardiner found it in Hampshire and Southampton. Kidson's note says that early forms of the song are on black letter broadsides. Samuel Pepys noted in his diary in 1665/6 that Mrs Knipp,

…"with whom I sang, and in perfect pleasure it was to hear her sing, especially her little Scotch song of Barbary Allen." In 1764 Goldsmith was 'sung to tears' when his old dairy maid sang it to him. Kidson says the ballad had two tunes, one published by Chappell and the other found in Scottish song collections. The Hammond brothers heard the song in Bridport Union in Dorset from Henry Way when they were cycling round the county between 1905 and 1908 in search of songs.

Which version of the words Mrs Benefer put to her tune we don't know, but some do use the name Barbary Allen or Ellen rather than the better-known Barbara Allen.

This is the ha'penny broadside version reproduced in Leslie Shepard's book, *The Broadside Ballad*.[8]

The Farmer's Daughter

Larley Benefer King's Lynn Januiary 11th 1905

The Farmer's Daughter

It's of a farmer's daughter, so beautiful I'm told.
Her father died and left her five hundred pounds in gold.
She lived with her uncle, the cause of all her woe,
But you soon shall hear, this maiden fair did prove his overthrow.

Her uncle had a ploughboy young Mary loved full well,
And in her uncle's garden their tales of love they'd tell;
But there was a wealthy squire who oft came her to see
But still she loved her ploughboy on the banks of sweet Dundee.

Her uncle and the squire rode out one summer's day
'Young William is in favour,' her uncle he did say;
'Indeed, 'tis my intention to tie him to a tree
Or else to bribe the press gang on the banks of sweet Dundee.'

The press gang came to William when he was all alone,
He boldly fought for liberty, but there were six to one.
The blood did flow in torrents. 'Pray kill me now,' said he
'I would rather die for Mary on the banks of sweet Dundee.'

This maid one day was walking, lamenting for her love,
She met the wealthy squire down in her uncle's grove.
He put his arms around her. 'Stand off, base man,' said she.
'You sent the only lad I love from the banks of sweet Dundee.'

He clasped his arms around her and tried to throw her down
Two pistols and a sword she spied beneath his morning gown.
Young Mary took the pistols and the sword he used so free
But she did fire and shot the squire on the banks of sweet Dundee.

Her uncle overheard the noise and hastened to the ground.
'Oh since you've killed the squire, I'll give you your death-wound.'
'Stand off!' then young Mary said, 'undaunted I will be.'
The trigger drew and her uncle slew on the banks of sweet Dundee.

The doctor soon was sent for, a man of noted skill,
Likewise came his lawyer for him to sign his will;
He left his gold to Mary who fought so manfully
And closed his eyes no more to rise on the banks of sweet Dundee.

Other singers called this the *Banks of Sweet Dundee*. Frank Kidson published it in *Traditional Tunes* in 1891, sung to him by Mr Benjamin Holgate of Leeds, but he says he heard it in Scotland, the North, other parts of Yorkshire and Berkshire. "Though sublime doggerel," he writes, "the song is even now a great favourite with the old folk who still remember it." He says it is also on a Catnach broadside. His tune is different from Mrs Benefer's. RVW collected it from George Sewell at Ingrave in April 1903. It was published in the *Folk Song Society Journal* Vol. I p.232.

"Elizabeth"

Elizabeth was the only singer to be identified by Vaughan Williams by her first name alone. It was initially assumed from that fact that she must therefore have been, unlike the other singers, very young. As she appears directly after Mrs Benefer, the first "Elizabeth" to be examined was a daughter of William Benefer, who had kept the *Fisherman's Arms* in Pilot Street and was the late cousin of the husbands of both Charlotte and Harriet Benefer. In 1905 she would have been living at the *Fisherman's Arms* with her mother and stepfather, who had succeeded her late father as landlord; she would have been aged 16 or 17.

However, in the collector's notebook it is clear that, while she follows Mrs Benefer, Mr Bayley seems to be slotted in between Elizabeth's two songs. A further possibility is that Elizabeth may have been John Bayley's widowed daughter, Eliza, part of his household in 1901. She would have been 35 in 1905, but if she was present when Vaughan Williams met her father, he may simply have heard her addressed by her first name, or a diminutive thereof, and realised later that he did not know her surname except that, as a widow, her name was not Bayley.

Elizabeth sang 2 songs:

It's of a Shopkeeper
The Three Butchers

Without knowing more about Elizabeth's background, even accepting that she may be one of the two persons suggested above, speculation about where she learned her songs is of little value. Elizabeth Benefer, growing up at the *Fisherman's Arms*, may well have heard men singing in the bar; we know virtually nothing about Eliza's life, not even her late husband's forename, while her surname is not easy to decipher sensibly in the 1901 census; and this identification rests only on her being John Bayley's daughter.

It's of a Shopkeeper

'Elizabeth' January 11th 1905

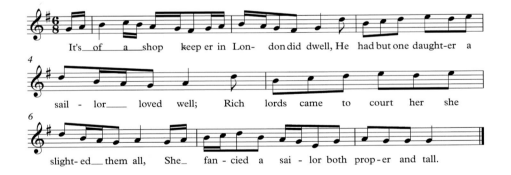

It's of a Shopkeeper

It's of a shopkeeper in London did dwell
He had but one daughter whom a sailor loved well…

There was a rich merchant in London did dwell
He had a fair daughter, none could her excel,
Rich lords came to court her, she slighted them all
And she fancied a sailor both proper and tall.

Till at length it was discovered by some men
To see a young sailor of late coming there,
'Hold, hold,' said her father, 'I'll soon them part,
And if they prove loyal it is not from my heart.'

He called down his daughter with an angry frown,
'Can't you get better matches of fame and reknown?
Can't you get better matches your arms to embrace,
Than to wed with a sailor, your friends in disgrace?',

'Dear honoured father, your pardon I crave,
There's none in this world but the sailor I'll have
That sailor is willing, and the lad I adore,
And indeed I'll go with him where loud cannons roar.'

'Dear daughter, with you I never will part
Since it is a young sailor that has gained you heart
Come do it in haste, and talk not of me,
And when it's all over we'll kindly agree.'

As this couple were walking down by the church door,
A press gang there met them, about half a score,
They took him prisoner and marched him away,
And instead of great mirth it was a sorrowful day.

The lady dressed up in a suit of men's clothes
And straight to the captain she instantly goes,
She yet as a sailor, it fell to her lot,
For to be put to lie in her lover's hammock.

As the lady and sailor were crossing the deep
Says the lady to the sailor, 'You sigh in your sleep.'
'I once had a sweetheart,' the sailor did say,
And by her cruel father I was sent away.'

'I am an astronomer, reared to my pen,
Astrologing books I peruse now and then
Come tell me your age, I'll look up your lot,
To know if you'll gain the fair lady or not.'

He told her his age and the day of his birth,
She says: 'You were born for great joy and mirth,
You shall have your sweetheart, in spite of them all,
And here is your Ellen, just at your call.'

This couple got married among the ship's crew,
You may say the young lady proved loyal and true,
They are now safely landed on Colombia's fair shore
And a fig for her father, he'll ne'er see her more.

Shopkeepers are rare heroes of songs, and whether Elizabeth's song was a version of the broadside 'The Pining Maid' or the young shopkeeper of Exeter we don't know. The first is a broadside in the Roxburghe Collection; the second in a book called the *Complete Pocket Song Book*, published in Massachusetts in 1905 with music by Mason. There is also the family of songs where the girl's father is variously an old lord, a rich merchant or a rich farmer. Mr Elmer sang of an old lord, so this could be Elizabeth's take

on the same tale, as the first line Vaughan
Williams gives seems to fit this set of songs.
This is the broadside ballad published 1867
by W. Birmingham, Dublin.

The Three Butchers

Sung by Elizabeth the same day King's Lynn January 1905

It's of three jo - vial but - chers as I've heard ma - ny say Were
go - ing to some mar - ket town their___ mo - ney for to___ pay.

The Three Butchers

It's of three jovial butchers as I've heard many say
They were going to some market town their money for to pay.

They rode together for a mile or two and a little more beside
Said Johnson unto Jipson, 'I heard a woman cry.'

Then 'Stop I won't' said Jipson, and 'Stop I won't,' said Ryde
Then,' Stop I will,' said Johnson, 'for I heard a woman cry'.

So Johnson he alighted and viewed the place all round
And saw a naked woman with her hair pinned to the ground.

'How came you here?' said Johnson, 'How came you here?' said he
'Two highwaymen have a-robbed me and that you plainly see.'

Then Johnson being a valiant man, a man of courage bold,
He took the coat from off his back to keep her from the cold.

And Johnson being a valiant man, a man of valiant mind,
He sat her up upon his horse and mounted up behind.

And as they rode along the road as fast as they could ride
She put her fingers to her lips and gave three piercing cries.

Out sprang ten bold highwaymen with weapons in their hands
They stepped up to young Johnson and boldly bid him stand.

'Then stand I will,' said Johnson,'as long as ever I can
For I never was in all my life afraid of any man.'

*From The Life and
adventures of Tom King:
the highwayman.*
British Library.

And Johnson being a valiant man he made those bullets fly
Till nine of them ten highwaymen all on the ground did lie.

Now this wicked woman standing by young Johnson did not mind
She took a knife all from his side and stabbed him from behind.

But the day it being a market day and people passing by
They saw this woman's dreadful deed and raised a hue and cry.

Then she was down to Newgates brought bound down in iron strong
For killing the finest butcher as ever the sun shine on.

This song was printed on broadsides going back many years. Cecil Sharp collected a version of it from Tom Symes of Bredon, Puckington, in 1903. Lucy Broadwood included a fuller version in *English Folk Songs and Carols* in 1906. Hammond found it in 1906 in Wareham in Dorset. RVW had already noted a version from Mr Crisp when he heard Elizabeth sing it. He'd also heard it from James Punt in East Horndon in Essex on 21 April 1904. These are the words from Hammond's version.

Notes

1   Baptised March 1831, the son of William and Mary Howard.

2   Then situated between Pilot Street and Loke Road; since the 1960s the link with Pilot Street has gone.

3   Lloyd, A. L. and Williams, V. R. (1959) *The Penguin Book of English Folksongs*. London: Penguin, p.121.

4   It is not impossible that her husband was the "old John Benefer" referred to as a singer by Bussle Smith in 1967, although this could equally well have been John's cousin of the same name (born 1855). However in 1901 he seems to have been living at St Germans and may never have come back to the North End.

5   *Lynn News and County Press,* 24 June and 1 July 1882.

6   Information from a letter from Tom Benefer's daughter Mrs Violet Topping in the family file at True's Yard.

7   There were two other Thomas Benefers of almost the same age but both were outside the town with their families by 1901 (Thomas W Benefer, son of John, at St Germans) and 1911 (Thomas E Benefer, son of Charles, at Magdalen "Fishing on the Ouse").

8   Shephard, L. (1962) *The Broadside Ballad: the development of the street ballad from traditional song to popular newspaper.* London: Herbert Jenkins p.148.

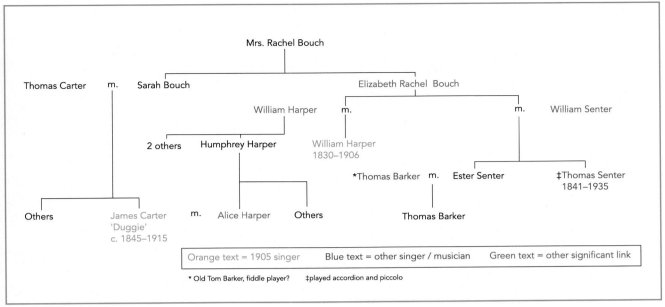

Fig. 1: family links between North End singers and musicians (Carter, Harper and Senter).

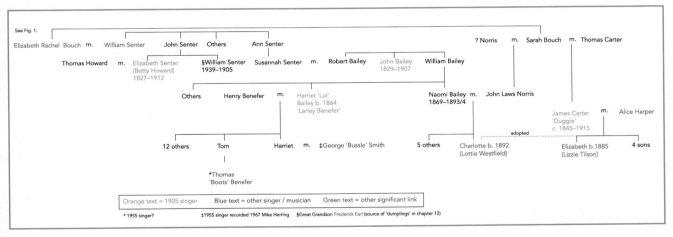

Fig. 2: family links between North End singers and musicians (Bailey, Benefer, Carter and Senter).

Mr Smith and Mr Donger

The remaining two North End singers, Mr Smith and Mr Donger, were identified respectively in Vaughan Williams' notebook as 'sailor' and 'a sailmaker'. Along with Mr Harper they were not only the last two North End singers to be introduced to him, but they were also the last of all the singers he heard in January 1905.

Because of his unusual surname and distinctive trade, Mr Donger was not difficult to track down and was a relative newcomer to the North End. As sailors are not often found in the fishing families, it was assumed for a long time that Mr Smith, whose lack even of an initial promised a difficult, if not impossible, search to find him, should be bracketed with Mr Donger as a possible outsider. He appeared not to be linked with the four men discussed above nor with the women. His single song was noted before a return visit to Joe Anderson, the day after the composer had made his visit to Sheringham.[1]

Mr Smith

The first line of enquiry was whether Mr Smith could have been a relative of fisherman George "Bussle" Smith, recorded by the BBC in 1955 at the *Tilden Smith* and interviewed by Mike Herring in 1967. Asked if his father, also George Smith, ever sang, he replied firmly that he sang "to himself but he never sing 'em in the pub. I learned some songs off o' him." However, Bussle was still living at home in 1905 and would have remembered if his father had sung, albeit one song, to Vaughan Williams, seeing that one of Mike Herring's aims was to track, if possible, what had happened to the singing tradition since 1905.

Bussle's grandfather, George William, was also considered, not least because, unlike the younger Smiths in North End

opposite: Mending sails.
Anne Roberts.

Begley's Yard, North St.

Begley's Yard, home of Thomas Donger the sailmaker.
True's Yard.

Yard, he and his wife lived in Begley's Yard, off North Street, also the home of Mr Donger. But it still seemed unlikely that Bussle knew nothing of the visit.

In any case, Mr Smith was a sailor, not a fisherman. All census and parish register entries which were studied for any of Bussle's big family referred to the menfolk as fishermen.[2] The fishermen would almost certainly never describe themselves as sailors, although many went on to serve at sea during the First World War and Bussle himself was for some time a member of the Naval Reserve.

Other potential sea-going Smiths, as listed in Kelly's Norfolk Directories[3] were examined, ranging from a master mariner living in the town centre who was called George William Smith but who had no known links with the North End, to Henry John Smith, a Trinity House pilot living in Pilot Street. He was in fact the son of a fisherman, but had died in 1903. Sailmaker William Osbert Smith was also considered, but proved never to have gone to sea, having entered his father's business as a young man and then succeeding him in later years. Research into him did prove useful in finding out about Mr Donger.

The cemetery registers show surprisingly few Smith mariners and none who fitted date-wise with this study. The only possibility seemed to be that Mr Smith met Vaughan Williams by chance when he was passing through Lynn and was then off to sea again. As the Dorset song *The Single Sailor* says, a single sailor is soon forgot:

'I've neither gold and I've neither crown,
But I'll sail the ocean all round and round,
I'll sail the ocean until I die
I don't care where my poor body lie.'[4]

Curiously, that proved to be not far from the truth when Mr Smith was finally found by chance in a fresh examination of the 1901 census. This identification carries a fair degree of certainty because this Smith was indeed a member of the big North End fishing family. The reason he had escaped notice was a longstanding assumption that if he was a North End Smith he would be found among the older family members alive in 1905. But Edward Smith was aged only 28 and serving in the Royal Navy. When Vaughan Williams encountered him, he must have been back on leave. It is nothing short of a miracle that when the 1901 census was taken he was at home with his widowed mother, a net maker called Alice Smith, and younger brother Henry, a ropemaker aged 15. They lived in Devonshire's Yard off North Street. This is the only Lynn census in which he appears as an adult; he does not feature in 1911 and in 1891 he was only 15.

The 1891 census does show that his father was James Smith, fisherman. He died in 1893 but his family tree shows that Edward was a great-grandson of George William Smith, born c.1803 believed to be an ancestor of Bussle Smith and of his grandparents[5], who lived just down the street in Begley's Yard. This would make him a second cousin of Bussle himself. Edward was not a casualty in the First World War and an Edward Smith, born in King's Lynn in the right year, appears in the 1921 census at Gillingham, near Chatham in Kent—not unlikely as a destination for an ex RN.

Mr Smith sang one song:

The Bold Princess Royal

The Bold Princess Royal

Mr Smith of Lynn (sailor) January 13th 1905

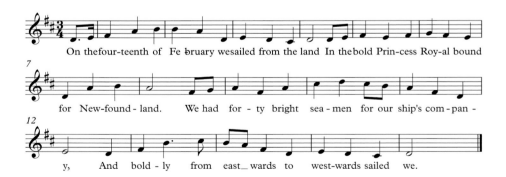

The Bold Princess Royal

On the 14th of February we sailed from the land
In the Bold Princess Royal bound for Newfoundland.
We had forty bright seamen for our ship's company
And boldly from the eastward to the westward sailed we.

We had not been sailing but two days or three
When a man from our masthead strange sails he did see.
They come boring down on us to see what we wore
And there 'neath her rigging black colours we saw.

'Oh no,' cries our captain, 'what shall we do now?
Here comes a bold pirate to rob us I know.'
'Oh no,' says our first mate, 'it shall never be so
For we'll shake out our reef boys, and for harbour we'll go.'

Then up spoke the pirate as he came alongside,
Through a loud-speaking trumpet, 'Whence come you?' he cried.
Our Captain being aft boys, he answered him so,
'We are come from fair London and we're bound for Cairo.'

'Then lower your tops'ls and lay your ship to,
For I have a message to send home by you.'
'Oh I'll lower my tops'ls and I'll heave my ship to,
But 'twill be in some harbour, not alongside of you.'

They chased us to windward all night and all day,
They chased us to leeward and made no headway.
They fired shots after us, but none could prevail,
And the bold Princess Royal soon showed 'em her tail.

'Thank God,' cried our captain when the pirate had gone,
'Go down to your grog boys, go down every one.
Go down to your grog boys and be of good cheer,
For while we have sea-room, my lads, never fear.'

This was the third version of the *Princess Royal* Vaughan Williams had heard in King's Lynn. Jo Anderson and Mr Crisp had sung it to him earlier in the week and in 1903 Mr Pottipher had sung it to him at Ingrave in Essex. This tune bears more similarity to the tune of *The Yellow Handkerchief*, sung in Suffolk by the great gipsy singer Phoebe Smith and others. For further notes on the song, see the notes with Joe Anderson's version. These words are those handed down from Bob Roberts.

Mr Donger

Vaughan Williams noted that Thomas Donger was a sailmaker and former sailor. Thomas Donger has not been traced in the census returns until his first appearance in Lynn in 1881 from which we can calculate that he was born in 1842 in 'Hodson', presumably Hoddesdon in Hertfordshire.

Thomas perhaps spent most of his younger days at sea, but he is known to have married at Wisbech in 1878. His wife, Charlotte Arms, was the daughter of a blacksmith at Walpole St Peter. There certainly was a sail and tent maker in Wisbech in 1876 by the name of Poppleton[6] and it is tempting to see this as where Thomas began his new career. In 1881 they were in King's Lynn, where all their two sons and four daughters were born. At this date they were not living in the North End but in Coburg Street, near St John's Church.

Thomas' business as "master sail, tent and marquee maker" employed three men and three boys and was based at 33A Norfolk Street. Kelly's 1883 Directory boasted an impressive advertisement for his products, including "tilts" for roundabouts, presumably a knock-on opportunity provided by the proximity of Frederick Savage's fairground engineering works. It seems Thomas was an entrepreneur: Kelly's Directory for 1888 shows him at 68 High Street, running the *Beaconsfield* restaurant and public house, in addition to his other business. The sailmaking business was still in

Norfolk Street and the home address was Blackfriars Road; Coburg Street runs into Blackfriars Road and if their home had been on the corner, it may be that it was still the same house.

Thereafter the firm vanishes from the directories during the 1890s. By 1901 the Dongers had left Blackfriars Road and had moved into what must have been a smaller house in Sir Lewis Street, one of the terraces off Loke Road. The house must have been very new, since as late as 1887 the OS map shows as yet very few houses in Sir Lewis Street.[7] Furthermore, Thomas was now 'employed' not an employer. By 1901 the family had moved into one of the cottages in Begley's Yard off North Street, and not only Thomas Donger but his son Thomas, also a sailmaker, were so described.

It raises the question of who employed them, since the directories do not show many sailmakers in Lynn. His fellow sailmaker William Osbert Smith had headed a long-running family business in St Ann's Street, which by 1896 had moved to 120 High Street and South Quay. A ship's chandler called Frederick Humphrey had appeared in St Ann's Street and it is tempting to see his premises, next to St Nicholas' graveyard, as perhaps William Smith's former site.[8] The Dongers could have been working for William Osbert Smith but in 1904 he closed his major business and moved to Lansdowne Street, where he worked 'on his own account'[9] until his death in 1912. He had no sons to carry on his business and was perhaps semi-retired. By 1900 Humphrey's business was also making sails and by 1904 he had expanded his directory entry to 'ship chandler, sailmaker, oil and colour merchant, sack and bag manufacturer'. It may be the Dongers were working for him.

In 1908 a business under Thomas Donger's name, described as "sail, tent and marquee maker; tarpaulins, sacks and bags, Tuesday Market Place" re-appeared in Kelly's Directory and was still there in 1912, perhaps in the premises behind the north side of Tuesday Market Place.[10] This may have been run by Thomas junior with his father, who was now in his sixties, semi-retired. Thomas senior was working 'on his

Mr Donger's advertisement from an 1883 Directory

T. W. DONGER,
33, NORFOLK STREET,
KING'S LYNN,
Sail, Tent, and Marquee Maker.

Waterproof Covers, Stack Cloths, Sacks, Bags, Tilts for Steam Roundabouts, Window Blinds, &c.

TENTS on Hire for FEASTS and GALAS.

Downham Market attended on Fridays; Wisbech Market on Saturdays.

own account' but his younger son Horace , who had been a young fisherman in 1901, was now also a sailmaker described as employed, perhaps in his brother's business. Thomas junior, still described as a sailmaker, was not at home and on census night was lodging at the *Rose and Crown* in Wisbech. There were no sail or tent makers listed in Wisbech in Kelly's at that time, but in 1883 Thomas senior had attended Downham and Wisbech markets weekly.

Sadly, with the coming of World War 1, young Thomas enlisted as a private in the Essex Regiment and was lost at sea in August 1915; his name is on the War Memorial in Tower Gardens in the town centre. His father's funeral took place only a few months later in December 1915.

Thomas Donger may have been well acquainted with the young sailor Edward Smith, who may have visited him when he was home from sea as well as his relations in Begley's Yard. Thomas had been a sailor when he was younger, and rope makers and sailmakers would have been well known to the fishermen as they fitted out their boats for work in the Wash.

Mr Donger sang 8 songs in 1905:
> Banks of Claudy
> Come All You Gallant Poachers
> Come All You Young Sailors
> Glencoe
> The Hills of Caledonia (John Raeburn)
> The Convict
> Pat Reilly
> Spanish Ladies

In 1906 he sang:
> Erin's Lovely Home
> Heave Away
> Shenandoah

Mr Donger was, like Carter, Anderson and Harper, one of the major suppliers of songs for Vaughan Williams in January 1905 and also one to whom he made a further visit in September 1906. His songs include several which may reflect his background as a former seafarer: they include four on board work songs, one of which (*Spanish Ladies*) was also sung in the Union by ex-mariner Mr Crisp and by Mr Leatherday who knew it was a Royal Navy song, although the collector noted that his words were very fragmentary. Thomas Donger's other work songs were *Heave Away*, and *Shenandoah*. He also knew songs which turn up elsewhere with maritime singers: *John Raeburn* (also sung by Mr Crisp) and *Erin's Lovely Home* whose words were found by Gale Huntington in old whaler logbooks.[11]

The Mart in 1900—the spread of canvas shows fairground needs which could be met by a firm like Mr Donger's.
True's Yard.

Hills of Caledonia

Mr Donger ex-sailor & sailmaker King's Lynn Jan 14th 1905

The Hills of Caledonia

My name it is John Raeburn, in Glasgow I was born,
The place of all my residence I'm forced to leave in scorn;
The place of all my residence I'm forced to go away
To leave the lovely hills and dales of Caledonia.

My character soon taken was and I was sent to gaol
My friends stood all around me, there was none that could me bail;
And then my old mother her old grey locks did tear
Saying, 'Son, o son, what have you done to be sent so far awa'?'

When we reached the gangway leading to the ship
The guard stood all around me for fear I'd make a break
The guard stood all around me for fear I'd break awa'
And try to regain the hills and dales of Caledonia.

There is a girl in Glasgow Town, a girl I love so well,
And if ever I return again along with her I'll dwell.
I'll quit all my night-walking and shun bad company
And bid farewell to the hills and dales of Caledonia.

This was also sung to Vaughan Williams by Mr Crisp earlier in his 1905 visit. He noted the words from him but did not do so from Mr Donger, maybe because they were similar. The two tunes are quite different: Mr Crisp's in 6/8, Mr Donger's in 2/4; Mr Crisp's is modal, Mr Donger's in a major key. But these words fit both, even though the two men must have learned them from different sources. Frank Kidson notes in the *Folk Song Journal* Vol. II that in Ford's *Vagabond Songs of Scotland* Vol. II 1901, the hero of the ballad was one James Raeburn, a baker, who was transported for theft (though innocent) some sixty years ago (i.e. around 1840). Kidson says he has several broadsides with the song under the title *Jamie Raeburn*. It had six verses.

Pat Reilly

Mr Donger, King's Lynn, January 13/14th 1905

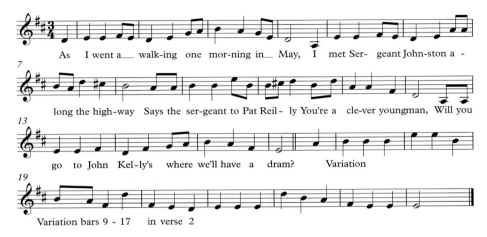

Pat Reilly

As I went a walking one morning in May
I met Sergeant Johnston along the highway
Says the sergeant to Pat Reilly, 'You're a clever young man.'
Will you go to John Kelly's where we'll have a dram.'

Then as we sat smoking and drinking our dram,
Says the sergeant to Pat Reilly, 'You're a handsome young man,
Oh would you list, take the shilling, and then come with me,
To the sweet county Longford, strange faces you'll see.'

Oh I took the shilling and the reckoning was paid
The ribbons were bought and we hoist the cockade,
Oh but early next morning sure we all had to stand
Up before our grand general with our hats in our hand.

He says to Pat Reilly, 'You are a shade rather low,
Unto some other regiment I'm afraid you must go.'
'Oh let me go where I will, sure I've got no-one to mourn,
For my mother is dead and will never return.'

My father got married and fetched a stepmother home,
She fairly denies me and does me disown,
Oh had my father a-been honest and learnt me my trade
I never would have listed nor hoist the cockade.

This song is on broadsides found in England, and in oral tradition in England, Canada and Australia. It's the story which attracted the attention of the Irish popular press, and the song has wide currency, according to Irish archives. The online Traditional Music Library has a similar set of words from Sam Henry's *North of Ireland collection*. Frank Kidson says the air is the same as that for *Green Bushes* in his book *Traditional Tunes*. Vaughan Williams did not note any words from Mr Donger.

Glencoe

Mr Donger, King's Lynn, January 13th & 14th 1905

As_ I was a-walk-ing one even-ing of late When Flo-ra's gay man-tle the fields dec-cor-ate, I__ care-less-ly wan-dered where I did not__ know On the banks of a foun-tain that lies in__ Glen-coe.

Glencoe

As I was a walking one evening of late
When Flora's gay mantle the fields decorate,
I carelessly wandered where I did not know
On the banks of a fountain that lies in Glencoe.

Like her whom the prize on Mount Ida was won
There approached me a lassie as bright as the sun
The ribbons and tartans around her did flow
That once graced McDonald, the pride of Glencoe.

With courage undaunted I to her drew nigh,
The red rose and lily on her cheek seem'd to vie;
I asked her name and how far she did go,
She answered me, 'Kind Sir, I'm bound for Glencoe.'

I says, 'My dear lassie, your enchanting smiles
And comely sweet features have my heart beguiled,
If your kind affections on me you'll bestow
You'll bless the happy hour we met at Glencoe.'

'Young man,' she made answer, 'your suit I disdain,
I once had a sweetheart, young Donald his name,
He went to the wars about ten years ago
And a maid I'll remain till he returns to Glencoe.'

'Perhaps your young Donald regards not your name
But has placed his affections on some foreign dame
And may have forgotten for ought that you know,
The lovely young lassie he left in Glencoe.'

'My Donald's true valour, when tried in the field,
Like his gallant ancestors, disdaining to yield,
The Spaniards and French he will soon overthrow
And in splendour return to my arms in Glencoe.'

'The power of the French, love, is hard to pull down,
They have caused many heroes to die of their wounds,
And with your own Donald it may happen so,
The man you love dearly perhaps is laid low.'

'My Donald can ne'er from his promise depart
For love, truth and honour are found in his heart.
And if I ne'er see him I single will go
And mourn for my Donald, the pride of Glencoe.'

Now finding her constant, I pulled out the glove
Which at parting she gave as a token of love;
She hung on my breast while tears down did flow,
Saying, 'Are you my Donald, returned to Glencoe?'

'Cheer up, my dear Flora, our sorrows are o'er,
While life does remain we shall never part more;
The rude storms of war at a distance may blow
While in peace and contentment I reside in Glencoe.'

A broadside printed by Walker of Durham and by Catnach gives this set of words as *Donald's Return to Glencoe*. Vaughan Williams notes in the *Folk Song Society Journal* that 'the words to this tune were unfortunately not noted.' We shall never know whether he did not note them, or Mr Donger could not remember them. Frank Kidson notes in the *Folk Song Society Journal* Vol. II p.171 that there is a version of the tune in the *Complete Petrie Collection*, and he had found versions in Yorkshire and Scotland. Gail Huntingdon found it in the ship *Catalpa*'s logbook of 1856 and the *Romulus*' logbook of 1851.[12]

GlenCoe photographed in 2016.
Brian Pocius.

Spanish Ladies

Mr Donger, King's Lynn, January 13th & 14th 1905

Fare- well and a-dieu to you Span-ish la-dies Fare-well and a-dieu, you
lad-ies of Spain For we've re-ceived or-ders to__ sail for old__
Eng-land But we hope ve-ry soon we shall see you a-gain.

Spanish Ladies

Farewell and adieu to you Spanish ladies,
Farewell and adieu to you ladies of Spain
For we've received orders to sail for old England
And I hope very shortly to see you again.

Chorus
We'll rant and we'll roar like true British sailors
We'll rant and we'll rave across the salt seas
'Till we strike soundings in the Channel of old England,
From Ushant to Scilly is thirty-four leagues.

We hove our ship to with the wind at sou'west boys,
We hove our ship to for to take soundings clear
In fifty five fathoms with a fine sandy bottom
We filled our maintops'l, up Channel did steer.

The first land we made was a point called the Deadman
Next Ramshead off Plymouth, Start, Portland and Wight,
We sailed then by Beachie, by Fairlee and Dungeness,
Then bore straight away for the South Foreland light.

Now the signal was made for the Grand Fleet to anchor,
We clew'd up our tops'ls stuck out tacks and sheets,
We stood by our stoppers, we brailed in our spankers,
And anchored ahead of the noblest of fleets.

Let every man here drink up his full bumper
Let every man here drink up his full bowl,
And let us be jolly and drown melancholy
Drink a health to each jovial and true hearted soul.

This song was found in the logbooks of Royal Navy ships as far back as the 18th century. Stan Hugill, in *Shanties from the Seven Seas*,[13] describes it as a 'famous old naval song'. He says it was a homeward-bound song sung at the capstan, and quotes the versions sung by his father. Vaughan Williams picked up three versions of *Spanish Ladies* in King's Lynn from Mr Donger, Mr Crisp and Mr Leatherday. He did not note the words, quite possibly because it was so widely known. Verse 4 describes how the sails were handled and secured when the ship came to anchor.

The barquentine "Waterwitch"
Anne Roberts.

Come All You Young Sailors

Mr Donger, King's Lynn, January 13th 1905

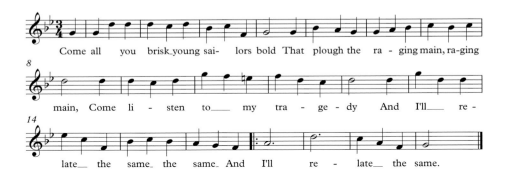

Come all you brisk young sai- lors bold That plough the ra - ging main, ra-ging main, Come li - sten to__ my tra - ge - dy And I'll__ re - late__ the same_ the same_ And I'll re - late__ the same.

Come All You Young Sailors

Come all you brisk young seamen bold
That plough the raging main
Come listen to my tragedy
And I'll relate the same.

Parted I was from my own true love
She's the girl that I adore,
And sent I was to the raging main
Where foaming billows roar.

To the East Indies we were bound
Our gallant ship to steer
And all the way we sailed out
I thought of Polly dear.

We had not sailed out very far
Before a storm did arise
The raging seas were mountains high
And so dismal were the skies.

Our captain being a valiant man
All on the deck doth stand.
"A full reward of fifty pounds
To the first that sees the shore!"

Our boatswain up aloft did go
On the main top so high
He looks around at either side
Neither light nor land did spy.

He being the foremost of the ship
A light he chanced to spy
"Bear off, my lads, before the wind,"
The boatswain he did cry.

The sailors tried to master the ship
The Scilly Rocks to clear
"On the ocean wide we must abide
Till daylight doth appear."

The very first time the gallant ship struck
So loud our captain cried
"The Lord have mercy on us all,
We in the deep shall die."

Out of eighty seamen bold
There was but four got on shore
Our gallant ship to pieces went
And never was seen no more.

And when the news to Plymouth came
Our gallant ship was lost
Caused many a fine young sailor bold
Then to lament this cause.

It's Polly, love, you must lament
For the loss of your sweetheart
It's the raging seas and stormy winds
Caused you and me to part.

This tune is very similar to the one sung by Bob Roberts as the tune for Henry Martin, the story of one of three brothers of merry Scotland who made a living by 'turning robber all on the salt sea.' Finding the words which Mr Donger had in mind has been tricky, but this song called *The Rocks of Scilly*, or *The Wreck off the Scillies* seems a good candidate. The treacherous rocky waters off the Scillies claimed the life of Sir Cloudesley Shovell, who came from Cockthorpe in North Norfolk. Shovell was aboard *HMS Association* when she struck the rocks off the Scillies and foundered on 22 October 1707. Although he floated ashore, one story is that he was killed for the sake of his emerald ring. Other versions of the story say he and his officers took to a barge which was lost in the storm. Most of his men were lost. Maybe the Norfolk connection would have had some influence on Mr Donger, but we can only guess.

These words were collected by Vaughan Williams, but there is no indication of where or when. F. Collinson also collected the song. Although Mr Donger didn't include the 'brisk' young sailor, the absence of any note of the words suggests that either he had forgotten them, or Vaughan Williams decided not to note them. Enigmatically, when he published it in the *Folk Song Society Journal* Vol. II p.172, he says 'The words of this song were not noted.' Cecil Sharp says he collected the tune in Somerset as the melody for Henry Martin.

The Sailors Farewell by George Elgar Hicks.

Come All You Gallant Poachers or Van Diemen's Land

Mr Donger, King's Lynn, January 13th-14th 1905

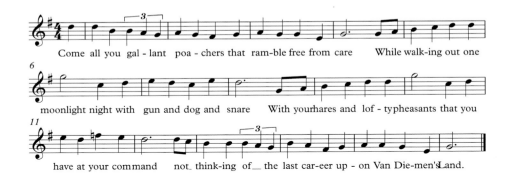

Come all you gal - lant poa - chers that ram-ble free from care   While walk-ing out one

moonlight night with gun and dog and snare   With your hares and lof - ty pheasants that you

have at your command   not think-ing of__ the last car-eer up - on Van Die-men's Land.

Come All You Gallant Poachers or Van Diemen's Land

Come all you gallant poachers that ramble void of care,
While walking out one moonlight night with gun and dog and snare,
With your hares and lofty pheasants that you have at your command
Not thinking of the last career upon Van Diemen's Land.

It's poor Tom Brown from Nottingham, Jack Williams and poor Joe,
They were three daring poachers, the country did well know,
At night they were trepanned by the keepers hid in sand:
Fourteen years transported boys upon Van Diemen's Land.

The very day we landed upon that fateful shore
The planters they stood round us full twenty score or more;
They ranked us up like horses and sold us out of hand
They roped us to the plough, brave boys, to plough Van Diemen's
Land.

The cottage that we lived in was built of clods and clay,
And rotten straw for bed, and we dare not say nay;
Our cots were fenced with fire, to slumber when we can,
To drive away wolves and tigers come by Van Diemen's Land.

There was a poor girl from Birmingham, Susan Simmons was her
name,
Fourteen years transported, you all have heard the same,
Our planter bought her freedom he married her out of hand,
She gave to us good usage upon Van Diemen's Land.

It's oft-times when I slumber I have a pleasant dream,
With my pretty girl I've been roving down by a sparkling stream,
In England I've been roving with her at my command,
But I wake broken hearted upon Van Diemen's Land.

Come all you daring poachers, give hearing to my song,
It is a bit of good advice although it is not long.
Lay aside your dogs and snares, to you I must speak plain,
For if you knew our hardships you'd never poach again.

The broadside publisher Catnach printed this ballad and it turns up all over the country, and it's the poachers who are clearly the heroes. Roy Palmer suggests it might go back as far as 1811/12 as it inspired a Luddite song of the period.[14] There were many later versions. In 1828 it was enacted by Parliament that that if three men were found in a wood after dark and one of them carried a gun or bludgeon, all were liable to be transported for 14 years. Roy Palmer's theory is that the ballad was written in 1829 or 30 in direct response to the first cases brought under the new Act. He considers Young Henry the Poacher to be a sequel to this. The late Jimmy McBeath, a Scots shepherd, was recorded by collector Alan Lomax singing it in 1951; Peter Kennedy recorded Harry Cox of Catfield in Norfolk singing it in 1953; Bill Leader recorded it from Walter Pardon of Knapton in 1975. Vaughan Williams heard it from Mr Broomfield in East Horndon in Essex in 1904 and Lucy Broadwood collected it in the 1890s, publishing in the *Folk Song Journal* in 1902. In *The Common Muse*[15] the Catnach version is sourced in Nottingham. However, it seems to have caught the imagination of Norfolk singers. All the versions are very similar. This is from RVW's 1904 Essex version and that of Walter Pardon.

Map of Van Diemen's Land from Views in Australia or New South Wales & Van Diemen's Land Delineated, in Fifty Views by Joseph Lycett, 1825.

historyarchive.org.

Banks of Claudy

Mr Donger, King's Lynn January 13th 1905

Banks of Claudy

'Twas on one summer's morning, all in the month of May,
Down by yon flow'ry garden where Betsey did stray;
I overheard a damsel in sorrow to complain
All for her absent lover who ploughs the raging main.

I went up to this fair maid and put her in surprise
I own she did not know me I being in disguise,
Says I, 'My charming creature, my joy and heart's delight,
How far do you travel this dark and rainy night?'

'The way, kind sir, to the Claudy, if you will kindly show,
Pity a maid distracted, for there I have to go;
I'm in search of a faithless young man, and Johnny is his name,
All on the banks of Claudy I'm told he does remain.'

'It's six weeks and better since your true love left the shore
He is cruising the wide ocean where foaming billows roar.
He is cruising the wide ocean for honour and for gain,
I was told his ship was wrecked off the coast of Spain.'

When she heard the dreadful news she fell into despair
To wringing of her hands and tearing of her hair;
'Since he is gone and left me, no man on earth I'll take,
And in some lonely valley I'll wander for his sake.'

His heart was filled with joy, he could no longer stand,
He flew into her arms, saying 'Betsey I'm the man,
I am the faithless young man who you thought was slain,
And since we are met on Claudy's bank, we'll never part again.'

The *Banks of Claudy*, according to Frank Kidson in *Traditional Tunes*[16], was to be found in *The Ancient Music of Ireland* in 1840 and in *Christie's Ballad Airs*. Kidson noted down the song from a girl in Dumfriesshire to a different tune from Mr Donger's. But the words he used, supplemented from a London broadside, are similar to versions found elsewhere. The song is part of the Copper family's repertoire at Rottingdean in Sussex, and when Vaughan Williams was in King's Lynn the Coppers were also active members of the Folk Song Society, introduced by its first secretary, Kate Lee. Their version was printed in the *Folk Song Society Journal* Vol. I, p.19.

This is Kidson's version.

The Convict

Mr Donger, King's Lynn January 13th 1905

A con-stant girl was heard to cry And wipe the tears from out her eye Saying the cruel laws of our Grac- ious Queen They have trans-port-ed my Sham-rock Green.

The Convict

The constant girl was heard to cry
And drop a tear from her tender eye
The cruel laws of our Gracious Queen
They have transported my Shamrock Green.

The sun was fair, the clouds advanced,
When a convict came to the Isle of France
Around his leg he wore a ring and chain
And his country was of the Shamrock Green.

The coastguard waited upon the beach
Till the convict's boat came within his reach
The convict's ring did shine and spark
That it softened the veins of the coastguard's heart.

Then the coastguard launched his little boat
That on the ocean with him to float,
The birds at night take their silent rest
But the convict here has a wounded breast.

Then the coastguard came to the Isle of France
Towards him the convict did advance
When the tears from his eyes did fall like rain
'Young man, I hear you're of the Shamrock Green.'

'I am a Shamrock,' the convict cried,
'That has been tossed on the ocean wide.
For being unruly, I do declare,
And was doomed a transport for seven years.

'When six of them are gone and past,
We were sailing home to make the last;
When the stormy winds did blow and roar
Which cast me upon a foreign shore.'

Then the coastguard played a noble part
And with brandy cheered the convict's heart
Although the night is so far advanced
You shall find a friend in the Isle of France.

Then a speedy letter went to the Queen
About the dreadful shipwreck of the Shamrock Green
Then a reprieve was sent by the next post
To the absent convict they thought was lost.

'God bless the coastguard,' the convict cried
'Who saved my life from the ocean wide
I will drink his health in a flowing glass
And good success to the Isle of France.'

And now I'm landed once more on shore
And with my Polly I do adore
In spite of laws and our gracious Queen
I have got married to my Shamrock Green.

In 1935 Lilias Rider Haggard, the daughter of the famous author and politician, published *I Walked by Night* the history of the king of the Norfolk poachers, Frederick Rolfe.[17] She included songs he sang and wrote down for her and they include this one, *The Convict Shamrock Green*. His own comment on the ballads in *I Walked by Night* puts them back into the first half of the 19th century, because he learned them from his mother and grandmother and reckoned they had been written 100 years before. He remembered other old people singing these songs as well. "They were the songs that were sung at Harvest Homes, and some of them were rather rude and vulgar, or would be thought so now, but the words of a song in them days was little thought on, if the musick were new."

Frederick Rolfe's story is told in Charlotte Paton's book, *The King of the Norfolk Poachers*.[18]

The song appears on broadsides by several different printers. Howse of Worcester, Harding and Firth. This Firth[19] version in the Bodleian online collection gives the more coherent tale than Fred Rolfe's under the title of the *Isle of France*.[20]

Heave Away

Mr Donger, King's Lynn September 1st 1906

Heave Away

As I walked out one summer's morn down by the Salthouse Docks
Heave away, my Johnnie, heave away, away!

I met an emigrant Irish girl conversing with Tapscott
And away, my bully boys, we're all bound to go!

'Good mornin', Mr Tapscott Sir,' 'Good morn, me gal,' says he.
'Oh it's have you got a packet ship all bound for Amerikee?'

'Oh yes I have got a packet ship, I have got one or two.
I've got the Jinny Walker and I've got the Kangaroo.

'I've got the Jinny Walker and today she does set sail,
With five and fifty emigrants and a thousand bags of meal.'

The day was fine when we set sail, but night was barely come,
An' every lubber never ceased to wish himself at home.

That night as we was sailing through the Channel of St James,
A dirty nor'west wind came up and druv us back again.

We snugged her down an' we laid her to, with reefed main tops'l set,
It was no joke, I tell you, 'cos our bunks and clothes wuz wet.

It cleared up fine at break o' day and we set sail once more
An' every son-of-gun was glad when we reached Amerikee's shore.

Bad luck to them Irish sailor boys, bad luck to them I say,
For they all got drunk, broke into me bunk, and stole me clothes
(meal) away.

This is unusual in Vaughan Williams' haul of songs from King's Lynn because it's associated with the operation of bigger sailing ships. It is a true shanty, a song used to co-ordinate the efforts of a gang of men to work the ship, especially hauling and heaving the gear. Stan Hugill says this is a genuine brake-windlass shanty. 'The work was too heavy for one movement up and one movement down; so the windlass brakes were dragged down from the top position to the level of a man's waist and then pushed down to knee-level in a second movement… This naturally timed the song, and it seems that shanties needed for this kind of work were usually sung in 2/4 or 6/8 time.'[21]

Hugill gives several versions, which are associated with the operations of the Tapscott American Packets, which took tens of thousands of emigrants to America and Australia in the 19th century. The Tapscotts were described as 'systematic villains.'[22] One of the requirements was taking yellow meal to eat on the journey.

This is the Hugill version which fits most happily with Mr Donger's tune.

Shenandoah

Mr Donger, King's Lynn September 1st 1906

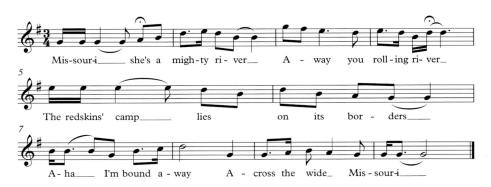

Shenandoah

Missouri she's a mighty river
Away, you rolling river,

The redskin camp lies on its borders
Aha, I'm bound away 'cross the wide Missouri.

The white man loved the Indian maiden
With notions his canoe was laden.

'Oh Shenandoah, I love your daughter,
I'll take her 'cross yon rolling water.'

The chief disdained the trader's dollars
'My daughter never shall you follow.'

At last there came a Yankee skipper
He winked his eye, and he tipped his flipper.

He sold the chief that fire water
And 'cross the river stole his daughter.

'Oh Shenandoah, I long to hear you
Across that wide and rolling river.'

This was widely printed in books of national song and community song books. Captain W.B. Whall, master mariner, makes it the first in his collection called *Ships, Sea Songs and Shanties*, which was published in 1912. This is his note on the song:

The seaman of today knows nothing of this old song but the tune and one line, 'Oh Shenandoah, I love your daughter.' There must be some merit in it to have lasted so long, even in a debased form.

Originally it was a song, not a shanty, and had nothing to do with salt water, for the 'wide Missouri' is … nowhere near the sea. It is given here as a good specimen of the American sea song of which there used to be a number. It must be some fifty years since it was sung as a song. It probably came from the American or Canadian voyageurs, who were great singers…

In the early days of America, rivers and canals were the chief trade and passenger routes and boatmen were an important class. Shenandoah was a celebrated Indian chief in American history, and several towns in the States are named after him. Besides being sung at sea, this song figured in old public school collections. When very young I heard a Harrow boy sing it. That must be nearly fifty years ago. (That would be in the 1860s).

Stan Hugill describes it as one of the most popular capstan or windlass shanties. He says no two shantymen ever sang the same pronunciation of Shenandoah.[23]

Erin's Lovely Home

Mr Donger September 6th 1906

Erin's Lovely Home

All you that are at liberty, I hope you will draw near,
For a sad and dismal story I mean to let you hear.
Now in a foreign country I languish, sigh and moan,
When I think on the days I spent in Erin's lovely home.

When I was young and in my bloom, my age was twenty-one,
I had become a servant unto a gentleman
I served him true and honest and very well it's known
With cruelty he banished me from my native home.

The reason that he banished me I mean to let you know
It's true I loved his daughter and she loved me also;
She had a handsome fortune but I alas I had none,
That is the reason I must go from Erin's lovely home.

'Twas in her father's garden all in the month of June
While viewing the flowers all in their youth and bloom,
She said, 'My dearest Willie if you with me will roam,
We'll bid adieu to all our friends in Erin's lovely home.'

That very night I gave consent, it proved my o'erthrow
And from her father's dwelling along with her to go,
The night being bright with moonlight we both set off alone
And thought that we would get off from Erin's lovely home.

When we came to Belfast it was the break of day
'My love,' she says, 'we will prepare our passage to pay.'
Five hundred pounds she counted down, saying 'This is all your own,
So never fret for those you left in Erin's lovely home.'

But to my great misfortune as you shall quickly hear,
'Twas in a few hours after her father did appear
He marched me off to Omagh in the county of Tyrone
For which I was transported from Erin's lovely home.

When I received my sentence it grieved my heart full sore
To leave my love behind me it grieved ten times more
There's seven links upon my chain and every link a sore
Before I can return unto my native home.

When the rout came to the gaol to take us all away
My true love she came to me and this to me did say
'Cheer up, you hear, don't be dismayed, I won't you disown,
Until you do return to Erin's lovely home.'

These words are from a broadside called
A new song called Erin's Lovely Home. It was
the third version of the song that RVW heard
in King's Lynn. Mr Chesson and Jo Anderson
also sang it. It obviously went down well with
the Northenders. For further information,
see the note with Mr Chesson's version
(pp.196-197).

The Lovers by N. Currier.
Library of Congress.

The Collector, the Singer and the Dumplings

For many years after 1905 Vaughan Williams' visit remained, by and large, unknown in the town, despite his reference to it in his lecture in 1910,[24] which had been picked up and reported fully by the *Lynn Advertiser* on Friday 23rd September 1910. As his cousin Gwen Raverat observed, at that time he was not a 'great man'; in 1905 his greatness was yet to come and he was still making his way in the world of collecting and composing.

Reference to the visit in the *Radio Times* in 1946 stirred some curiosity, not to say incredulity, in the *Lynn Advertiser*:

Lynn listeners to "serious music" were no doubt intrigued by the "Radio Times" note on the famous composer Vaughan Williams, whose Norfolk Rhapsody No 1 in E minor was performed by the BBC Symphony Orchestra on Saturday evening. In explanation of this work it was stated "some forty years ago Vaughan Williams went to live in King's Lynn and there he made friends with the country people and took down from their singing a number of folk tunes which might otherwise have been forgotten. It is on these tunes that his three Norfolk Rhapsodies are founded." This old association with the town will be unknown to the majority, even of older residents. Does anyone recall the eminent composer's residence at Lynn, of which his musical genius was able to take such advantage? Whether the burgesses of Lynn include themselves with the category of "country folk" is a point it is not proposed to enlarge upon or argue here![25]

The item brought the following reply, to which is owed the single glimpse we have of him at work in the North End:

Following a reference in the Town feature column to Vaughan Williams' visit, in which the correspondent viewed the whole collecting story with some scepticism, Mr F.W. Earl of 16 North End Yard wrote in to say:

An old aunt of mine, who lived and died in the North End, was fond of relating the story of how, in her younger days, a strange gentleman came to her mother's house just at the time dinner was being prepared, and the dumplings put in the saucepan to boil the allotted time. This gentleman persuaded her father to sing for him one of the old songs and while he was singing it Dr Vaughan Williams was taking it down. Her father was rewarded with, I believe, a shilling. But by the time the eminent composer bid them farewell, the dumplings, alas, had boiled an hour and a half.

Years later the late Mr John H Pratt mentioned to me the composer's search for folk-tunes in Lynn, stating that he had accompanied Dr Vaughan Williams on his round of the North End of the town, when the great musician visited the fisher folk and encouraged them to sing for him, making notes of all he heard. This also confirmed the reminiscences related by my aunt.[26]

Mr Earl did not recall Mr Pratt mentioning any visit to other parts of the town.

It was hoped that identification of Mr Earl's aunt would also identify the singer of whom this story was told. However, despite long investigation of Frederick Earl's family connections, no suitable woman has come to light whose surname matches any of those noted by Vaughan Williams. It is possible, of course, that she was a "courtesy" aunt: a distant cousin or even unrelated at all.

Nevertheless, examination of the singers themselves, despite their large number, can point the way to some extent. The seven workhouse singers, plus Mrs Howard, Mrs Benefer and Elizabeth, can be eliminated straightaway. So can the widowers, as the composer came "to her mother's house", who presumably was cooking the dumplings: this eliminates Duggie Carter and Joe Anderson. William Harper was not a widower, but he appears to have had only a son and no daughter. Thomas Donger was at home and had four daughters, but only one was still at home in 1901, aged 11, and would hardly qualify as the "old aunt" of someone only ten years younger than herself. Moreover, neither she nor her sisters "lived and died" in the North End as all were born before the Dongers moved to the Begley's Yard and three, if not four, married away from the town. The family seems to have had no earlier connections with this area.

John Bayley, despite telling two separate census enumerators that he was widowed, certainly had a living wife and several daughters, but spread, at various times, over two or more addresses. The very fact that the aunt specified that the collector came "to her *mother's* house", while the story focused entirely on her father might perhaps be seen as fitting the Bayley situation. In 1901 Catherine Bailey was recorded by the census living with Charles Anderson and his family in North Street, but this may have been only a temporary arrangement and there is no evidence that she was still with him in 1905. She could well have moved back to Pilot Street, as her 1908 burial entry in the parish register gives that address as well as the workhouse, which might imply she had not been in the Union very long. Whatever had led to the Baileys' separate living arrangements, it is not impossible that John was visiting and dining with Catherine when Vaughan Williams tracked him down.

Although he is credited with five songs, the collector only wrote down the melody for one (*"persuaded her father to sing for him one of the old songs"*). In the Earl story the composer was in the house for an hour and a half which could be accounted for by discussion and singing snatches of John's other four songs. If John's daughter Eliza was the "Elizabeth" noted earlier she may have been present, as her songs were recorded either side of John's; the inclusion of her own songs would lengthen the time.

Frederick Earl's mother Leah Love Earl never married nor did his father appear on the record of his baptism but there was a Bailey link to be found in his family. His great-grandfather on his mother's side was William Frederick Senter, brother of

Susannah, the wife of John Bayley's brother Robert. John Bayley and his daughters were only connected to the Senter-Earl line by marriage but in a close community might well have been considered "aunts". If Eliza was "Elizabeth" she must have been present but the daughter telling the story need not have been there at all.

This story also introduces "the late Mr John H Pratt" and his claim to have accompanied Vaughan Williams in the North End, about which nothing further is known. John Pratt (1859-1941) was a businessman, partner in the ironmongers' firm of Plowright, Pratt and Harbage in Norfolk Street. He lived in Tower Street in the town centre and is remembered particularly for an association with St Margaret's Church (King's Lynn Minster), of which he was at the time of his death a churchwarden.[27] In 1930 in his *Recollections*, quoted earlier, he says that his family had a long association with St Nicholas' Chapel. The work also shows that he knew the North End very well and had great affection for it. In the 1881 census the census shows him living at his grandfather's house in King Street, from which attendance at St Nicholas' Chapel would be logical.

No reference is made to music in his obituary or to any association with Vaughan Williams, but he is known himself to have been musical and was a member of the choir at the parish church. He is not, however, among those whose help in his collecting is acknowledged by Vaughan Williams in the *Folk Song Journal*, where he did include his thanks to Huddle, Carter and Anderson.[28] One possibility is that he met Vaughan Williams, perhaps through the chapel and Alfred Huddle, and took an interest in what he was doing.

Notes

1   See chapters *King's Lynn Union Workhouse* and *The Day Trip to Sheringham* (pp.167-225).

2   The few exceptions found were not sailors.

3   Kindly researched by Peter Salt.

4   Ed. Brocklebank, J. and Kindersley, B. (1948) *A Dorset Book of Folk Songs*. London: EFDSS, p.8.

5   There is a slight query over this as the St Nicholas' marriage register and the banns book give George William's father as Joseph. However George William Senior b.1803 did have a son George born in the right year and a search has revealed no trace at all of Joseph Smith, fisherman, in the right generation. This seems to be a genuine anomaly in the registers, unless Joseph was George William senior's nickname.

6   *Kelly's Cambridgeshire Directory 1876.*

7   The terraces south of Loke Road seem to have been built first.

8   The tall frontage, faced with dark red brick, survived until the 1980s, when it gave way to housing.

9   i.e. not an employer.

10 i.e. behind the Revd Alfred Huddle's house.

11 Huntington, G. (1970) *Songs the Whalemen Sang*. New York: Dover Publications, pp.105 & 199.

12 Ibid. p.113.

13 Hugill, S.(1961) *Shanties from the Seven Seas*. London: Routledge and Keegan Paul, pp.385-386.

14 Palmer, R. (1979) *Everyman's Book of Country Songs*. London: J.M. Dent & Sons, pp.98 & 101.

15 de Sola Pinto, V. and. Rodway A.E (1957) *The Common Muse*. London: Chatto and Windus.

16 Kidson,F. (1891 re-published 1970) *Traditional Tunes*. Wakefield: S.R.Publishers, p.88.

17 Rider Haggard, L. (ed) (1935) *I Walked by Night: Being the Life and History of the King of the Norfolk Poachers by Himself*. Woodbridge: Boydell Press Ltd /Waveney Publications, p.74.

18 Paton, C. (2009) *The King of the Norfolk Poachers*. Ipswich: Old Pond Publishing.

19 Bodleian Online collection 25476.gif

20 The Isle of France was Mauritius.

21 Hugill, S. (1961) *Shanties from the Seven Seas*. London: Routledge and Kegan Paul, p.303.

22 Coleman, T. (1974) *A passage to America*. London: Harmondsworth.

23 Ibid. 21, p.172.

24 See chapter *King's Lynn: The Unexpected Treasure House of Song* (pp.39-49)

25 *Lynn News and Advertiser*, 30 April 1946.

26 Ibid.,14 May 1946.

27 Ibid. Obituary, 19 December 1944. See also n.25.

28 JFSS/1906/8/142

King's Lynn Union Workhouse

"I spent many happy mornings… listening to their almost inexhaustible stock of splendid tunes."

RVW talk on BBC Radio March 27th, 1940

The composer's visits in the North End were interspersed throughout the week with those made to the Union workhouse. The building still stands in Extons Road, on the parish boundary between the parishes of All Saints South Lynn and St John. In 1905 its chaplain was the Revd Arthur Herbert Hayes, Rector of the latter parish and also a Guardian, in which capacity he was "involved in entertainment" at the Union.[1] This workhouse was built in 1856 to replace a much older building, which stood in St Margaret's parish.

The older building had begun life as St James' Chapel, a subsidiary chapel of ease of the priory and parish church, like St Nicholas', and dated in part from the 12th century. Disused by the 16th century, in 1682 its remaining parts were converted, reputedly by the Lynn architect Henry Bell, into "a Workhouse or Hospitall", said to have held 100 persons. The more stringent regime of the 1834 Poor Law Amendment Act required this ancient building to house 200 people with a mere £750 budget for the necessary structural alterations.

The nave had long gone, so a massive crossing tower, resting on 12th century pillars, had been largely unbuttressed on the western side for at least three centuries. Ongoing discussion of longstanding settlement and cracks where the buttresses met the walls came to a sudden end when on 20 August 1854 the tower collapsed.[2] The press reported only two fatalities: the clock repairer who was climbing it to find out why the clock had stopped unexpectedly—probably through movement—

and the only inmate reputedly left in the building because he refused to leave his bed when "On Sunday morning,… pieces of mortar fell now and then in the sleeping room and having a shrewd suspicion something was about to happen, he [another of the inmates] advised his companions to go with him into the front yard for safety, which they did."

They had been noticing unpleasant cracking noises in the walls and floor for some time.[3] The communal rooms on the lower floor were now evacuated because the chaplain noticed the tower doorway parting company with its wall. Luckily most of the young inmates were at church and others housed in the side wings were not endangered during the collapse.

A single transept wall remains from this building, behind London Road Methodist Church which was raised on the site in 1858. The reference to "St James Workhouse" in Duggie Carter's *The Captain's Apprentice* has not gone unnoticed but, although the *Lynn Advertiser* reported in 1857 an incident uncannily similar to the plot of the song, further research revealed that the song was in existence long before that date and known in other areas, sometimes with a different name assigned to the workhouse.[4]

The replacement workhouse on its new site was designed by architects Medland

St James' Workhouse, built 1856, also known as King's Lynn Union: This is the workhouse visited by RVW.

Colin James.

opposite: A sailor ashore.
Anne Roberts.

and Maberley at a cost of £14,000 and in 1904 still housed 200 people. It had its own chapel over the dining room, with stained oak benches to hold 250 people. "This chapel impressed the eminent Dr Richardson, who inspected the hospital and other institutions in the early [18]60s, as 'one of the most beautiful I have ever entered in any building, much less a workhouse'".[5] It was to this building that Vaughan Williams secured an introduction in January 1905.

The official discontinuation after the 1834 Poor Law Amendment Act of "outdoor" parish relief, a cash handout to buy food, frequently forced destitute families to become workhouse inmates. In his book *Vintage King's Lynn* published in 1976, Michael Winton claimed, "scores of able-bodied fishermen had to spend a part of the winter in the workhouse" when times were hard, presumably discharging themselves when improved catches seemed likely.[6]

By 1905 the rules had relaxed, not least to ease the pressure on space, and temporary relief in hard times in the form of "meal tickets" was coming back into increasing use. The workhouse which Vaughan Williams found was seen much more as the last resort of the old and infirm, such as Mr Carter's mother Sarah and her two daughters, who for whatever reason were no longer able to support themselves, or who had been rendered incapacitated by accident or illness. The inmates attracted more official sympathy than they had in 1834, when amazement would have greeted this news item, which appeared in the *Lynn Advertiser*, while Vaughan Williams was actually in King's Lynn:

> At the Workhouse on Wednesday 11th [January]... inmates [were] given a substantial meat tea by Miss Pope and her brothers [Messrs H & A Pope] in the dining hall which was tastefully decorated by the master and matron and the officers of the house.... At 7pm an entertainment was commenced and an interesting and amusing programme was gone through to the evident delight of those for whom it was arranged, and a large audience from the town and neighbourhood.[7]

Vaughan Williams was at work there and his singers would have attended and enjoyed this event; the latter part of it seems to have been open to the public!

When workhouses ceased to function, the building continued to provide the Hospital's care of the elderly department.[8] But in the minds of that age group it never quite lost its association with the workhouse stigma and as late as the 1970s patients were for that reason often deeply distressed at being admitted to it. At that date one might still be shown in an outhouse the stone crusher on which vagrants had once had to perform for a set time in return for a bed.[9] After the Queen Elizabeth Hospital united all departments on a new site in Gaywood, St James' was retained by the hospital authorities, used for administrative purposes and out-patient clinics only.

The Workhouse Singers

As the first of the workhouse visits directly followed Vaughan Williams' initial sessions with Carter and Anderson, it is tempting to see the germ of the idea coming from Duggie Carter himself, whose mother had died in the workhouse only a month before. The Revd Alfred Huddle might have offered to secure the necessary introduction, perhaps via his superior, the Revd Robert Gordon Roe, incumbent of the parish, who was a Guardian, or his fellow cleric, the Revd Arthur Hayes, rector of All Saints' South Lynn. Vaughan Williams himself may have already been considering it, having noted seven out of a total of 245 songs in workhouses in 1903/4.

The men he met in the workhouse were not necessarily linked with the northern part of the town nor with fishing. Only Mr Chesson appears to have had definite links with the North End. Churchman Chesson, who appears to have been his apparent kinsman and contemporary, was married to Duggie Carter's brother-in-law's sister.[10] It is not impossible that Duggie thought of John Chesson but John seems never to have lived —or therefore sung—in the North End. In any case he was not among the first workhouse singers heard by the collector. The over-60s there were not expected to work but enforced leisure outside the home environment must have been tedious; those who had been accustomed to sing at work and elsewhere might naturally have continued to do so to entertain themselves and others in the day room.

Mr Crisp

The first workhouse performer was almost certainly Charles Crisp, already in the Union and described as aged 64 in the 1901 census. He was a former able seaman with the merchant service; "Ret seaman" had been written in above his census entry. Other census references vary his date of birth between 1837 and 1841 but uncertainty of age leading to discrepancies between census returns is not uncommon, occurring frequently among many of the 1905 singers. His birthplace varies also between Gaywood and King's Lynn.[11]

He probably spent a large part of his life away from Lynn. According to the United Kingdom Merchant Navy Seamen Records he was on military service between 1853 and 1857.[12] In 1861 he was among those listed in the census on board "various vessels"; he is stated to be an ordinary seaman, here aged 20, on board the *Ceres*.[13]

He was first admitted to the workhouse in May 1899, when he claimed to be a Unitarian;[14] thereafter he moved out and in again a number of times before 1905, now always as a member of the Church of England. In November 1906 he featured in the punishment book for having been "Allowed out on leave; was entrusted with two overcoats to bring to the workhouse; instead of doing so he stole them by selling one and trying to sell the other." He was arrested on suspicion and charged by the Master of the workhouse, being sentenced to one month's hard labour. He was still resident in the Union at the 1911 census, as "Charles Robert Crisp, formerly a mariner, merchant service", born in Gaywood and aged 70 according to the record, emphasising the vagueness over his date of birth.

His name in the composer's notebooks was for a long time read as "Crist" and on some pages this does appear to be what Vaughan Williams wrote. However, in at least one instance close inspection shows an upright stroke, easily read as a "t", which is in fact the long stroke of a "p", with a small loop behind, while in 1901 the names of Crisp and a later singer, Mr Elmer, occur in the Union census together,[15] and in fact they seem to have been present together whenever they sang to the composer.

Mr Crisp sang 6 songs in 1905:

The Cumberland's Crew
Dream of Napoleon
Erin's Lovely Home
The Loss of the Ramillies
The Maids of Australia
The Princess Royal
Spanish Ladies, with Mr Leatherday

In 1906 he added:

Spanish Ladies

Mr Crisp's large repertoire strongly reflects his maritime career: songs about ships—*Bold Princess Royal*, *Loss of the Ramillies*, *The Cumberland's Crew*, *Spanish Ladies* (to which he added another version in 1906) and two songs which also turn up in the repertoire of the ex-seaman Donger: *John Raeburn* and *Erin's Lovely Home*.

The Dream of Napoleon

Mr Crisp, King's Lynn Union, January 9th 1905

The Dream of Napoleon

One night sad and languid I went to my bed,
But I scarce had reclined on my pillow,
When a vision surprising came into my head:
Methought I was traversing the billow.
One night as my vessel dashed over the deep
I beheld a rude rock that was craggy and steep
The rock where the willows now seemed to weep
O'er the grave of the once famed Napoleon.

Methought that my vessel drew near to the land
I beheld clad in green this bold figure;
With the trumpet of fame clasped firm in his hand
On his brow there was valour and vigour.
'O stranger,' he cried, 'hast thou ventured to me
From the land of thy fathers who boast they are free?
If so a tale I'll tell unto thee
Concerning the once famed Napoleon.

Remember that year so immortal,' he cried,
'When I crossed the rude Alps famed in story
With the legions of France, for her sons were my pride,
And I led them to honour and glory.
On the plains of Marengo I tyranny hurled
And wherever my banner the eagle unfurled,
'Twas the standard of freedom all over the world
And the signal for fame,' cried Napoleon.

'Like a soldier I've been in the heat and the cold,
As I marched to the trumpet and cymbal,
But by dark deeds of treachery I have been sold,
While monarchs before me have trembled.
Now rulers and princes their station demean
And like scorpions spit forth their venom and spleen,
But liberty soon o'er the world shall be seen,'
As I woke from my dream, cried Napoleon.

RVW collected this song with the words of three verses. He had heard it two weeks or so before he came to Norfolk from Henry Burstow at Leith Hill. Roy Palmer says the ballad was printed in the 1830s but possibly dates from an earlier song, as the Battle of Marengo was in 1800. It was in the *Folk Song Journal* Vol. III p.162 and adds verses from a broadside printed by Harkness of Preston.[16]

Napoleon's reputation changed over the years—something of a hero at the start, but an enemy later. This song survived for more than a century and, in the 1970s, Norfolk fisherman Sam Larner was recorded singing it (*A Garland for Sam*, Topic 12T244, 1974). Gail Huntingdon in *Songs the Whalemen Sang* gives the same words from the *Cortes'* logbook 1847.

The Bold Princess Royal

Mr Crisp, King's Lynn Union, January 9th 1905

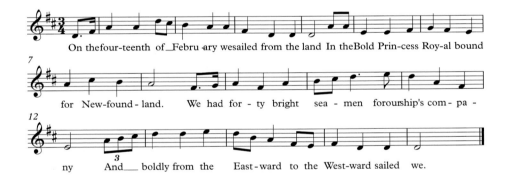

On the four-teenth of February we sailed from the land In the Bold Prin-cess Roy-al bound for New-found-land. We had for-ty bright sea-men for our ship's com-pa-ny And boldly from the East-ward to the West-ward sailed we.

The Bold Princess Royal
On the fourteenth of February we sailed from the land
In the Bold Princess Royal bound for Newfoundland.
We had forty bright seamen for our ship's company
And boldly from the Eastward to the Westward sailed we.

We had not been sailing past two days or three
When a man from our masthead a sail he did see
She bore down upon us our ship for to view
While under her mizzen black colours she flew.

'Good Lord,' cried our Captain, 'what shall we do now?
Here comes a bold pirate to rob us I know.'
''Oh no,' cried our chief mate, 'that ne'er shall be so,
We'll shake out our reef boys and from her we'll go.'

Now when this bold pirate she hove alongside,
With a long speaking trumpet 'Whence you come?' they cried.
Our Captain being aft boys, he answered them so,
'We are come from fair London, we're bound for Cairo.'

'Come haul up your courses and heave your ship to,
For I have a letter I'll send home by you.'
'I will haul up my courses and heave my ship to
But it shall be in harbour, and not alongside you.'

They fired shots after us, but none could prevail,
For the Bold Princess Royal soon showed them her tail,
She chased us to windward but could not make way
So she haul'd up her mainsail and then bore away.

This was the second version of this song that RVW heard in King's Lynn. There is a slight variation on the tune used by Mr Anderson. This set of words was noted by Frank Kidson and included in his paper for the first meeting of the Folk Song Society and included in the Journal. He'd heard them from Mrs Agar of Whitby, a sailor's daughter who had learned the song from her father. He also had it on broadsides in his collection. Given that there was a considerable coastal trade between Lynn and Whitby, it's likely that sailors would have picked up the song from shipmates and from sing-songs ashore. It is a favourite among later generations of singers. Walter Pardon of Knapton, Harry Cox of Catfield, Jumbo Brightwell at the *Butley Oyster* and Sam Larner of Winterton all sang it, as did Bob Roberts of Pin Mill.

United States packet ship "Victoria" of New York.
Library of Congress.

The Loss of the Ramillies

Mr Crisp, King's Lynn Union January 9th 1905

The Loss of the Ramillies

It happened on a certain day
The Ramillies she to her anchor lay
The very same night a gale came on
And away from her anchor the good ship sprung.

The rain it came down in a dreadful shock,
The seas they flew over our fore top.
With close reefed topsails so neatly spread,
We were thinking to weather the old Rame Head.

Our bosun cried, 'My brave fellows all,
Come list awhile for I can't find my call
Now launch your boats your lives for to save
For the seas this night they will sure be your grave.'

The boats were manned and overboard were tossed
Some they got in them but they were all lost
Some went one way and some went another
But the watch down below they all got smothered.

When the news to pretty Plymouth came
That the Ramillies was lost with most of her men
Pretty Plymouth's streets were flowing with tears
For the hearing of these sad, sad affairs.

Now all you pretty maidens, whoever you may be,
That lost your true loves in the bold Ramillies,
There was only two that was left to tell the tale,
How the Ramillies went down in the January gale.

This song tells the story of Admiral Byng's old ship, the *Ramillies*, which was lost in a storm in the Channel on 14 February 1760. This is Roy Palmer's note on the events which led to the song being written:

> This song lasted for a century and a half, on both sides of the Atlantic, apparently without the benefit of print. Conversely and perversely, 'The Fatal Ramillies', a different song on the same topic, while widely printed on broadsides in the nineteenth century, has turned up only once in oral circulation.

The *Ramillies* was a 90-gun ship of the line built originally in 1664 as the Katherine, 82 guns, and rebuilt twice more, finally as the *Ramillies*, in 1749. She sailed from Plymouth to join the blockade of French ports in February 1760, when she encountered a violent south-westerly gale and began to leak. She turned back, but went a bay too far. As the *Gentleman's Magazine* put it:

> the unfortunate Ramillies, Capt. Taylor, with 734 men, being embay'd within the Bolt-Head (which they had mistaken for the Ram-Head, and imagined they were going into Plymouth Sound), and close up on the rocks, they let go their anchors and cut away all their masts, and rode safe until five in the evening (of 15th February), when the gale increased so much 'tis impossible to describe; they parted, and only one midshipman (John Harrold) and twenty five men out of the whole, jumped off the stern on to the rocks and were saved...

The wreck of the *Ramillies* is still in Bigbury Bay, some of her cannon visible in the cove which bears its name, and the villagers of nearby Inner Hope and Thurlestone still talk of the fatal night. Roy Palmer says

> There is one tradition that a local man on board the *Ramillies* tried to warn the officers of their error but was put in irons for insubordination. The Green at Thurlestone used to have a big depression where a mass grave had been dug, but this has now disappeared under the asphalt of a car park. Some 20 years ago (Palmer was writing in 1983) the skeletons of some Ramillies men were found under the dunes. They were collected by the council and taken to the rubbish tip.

Many years later, the song found its way into the repertoire of Jumbo Brightwell of Leiston in Suffolk, and of Walter Pardon in Norfolk, who was recorded singing it at home in December 1974 by Bill Leader, Peter Bellamy and Reg Hall. It is on his CD *A World without Horses*. It was also recorded in Orkney in 1971, sung by 92-year-old Peter Pratt.

In 1905, Vaughan Williams noted the words of the song as Mr Crisp sang it.

The Royal Katherine from a painting of 1664. It was rebuilt in 1702 and became a 90-gun second rate and, in 1756, was the flagship of Admiral John Byng. When he failed to relieve Port Mahon and so lost the island of Minorca to the French, Byng was controversially executed.

Royal Museums Greenwich.

Hills of Caledonia (John Raeburn)

Mr Crisp, King's Lynn Union, January 10th 1905

My— name it is John Rae - burn in Glas-gow I was born— Theplace of all— my

resi dence I'nforced to leave in scorn; Theplace of all— my resi dence I'nforced to go - a-

way To— leave the love-ly hills— and dales of Ca - le-don - i - a.

Hills of Caledonia (John Raeburn)

My name it is John Raeburn, in Glasgow I was born,
The place of all my residence I'm forced to leave in scorn;
The place of all my residence I'm forced to go away
To leave the lovely hills and dales of Caledonia.

My character soon taken was and I was sent to gaol
My friends stood all around me, there was none that could me bail;
And then my old mother her old grey locks did tear
Saying, 'Son, oh son, what have you done to be sent so far awa'?'

When we reached the gangway leading to the ship
The guard stood all around me for fear I'd make a break
The guard stood all around me for fear I'd break awa'
And try to regain the hills and dales of Caledonia.

There is a girl in Glasgow Town, a girl I love so well,
And if ever I return again along with her I'll dwell.
I'll quit all my night-walking and shun bad company
And bid farewell to the hills and dales of Caledonia.

This is said by Robert Ford, writing in 1899, to be a popular street song all over Scotland, sold readily in penny sheet form. Roy Palmer says it is still sung by travelling people, which may be how Mr Crisp heard it. Vaughan Williams noted the words.

Commenting on the song in the *Journal of the Folk Song Society* Vol. II pp.180-181, Frank Kidson says according to Ford's *Vagabond Songs of Scotland* Vol. II 1901, the hero of the ballad was one John Raeburn a baker, who was transported for theft {though innocent} some sixty years ago.

The Cumberland's Crew

Mr Crisp Jan 11th King's Lynn

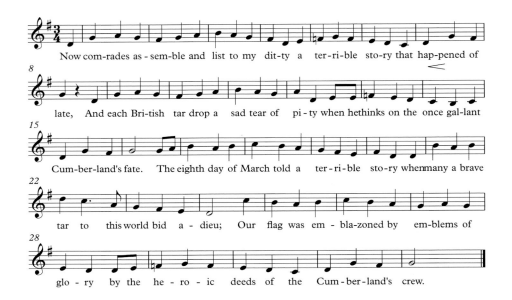

The Cumberland's Crew

Now comrades assemble and list to my ditty, a terrible story that happened of late,
And each British tar drop a sad tear of pity when he thinks on the once gallant Cumberland's fate.
The eighth day of March told a terrible story when a bright tar to this world bid adieu
Our flag was emblazoned by emblems of glory by the heroic deeds of the Cumberland's crew.

On that fateful day about ten in the morning the sky it was clear and high was the sun
When the drums of the Cumberland gave forth a warning which told every seaman to stand by his gun.
An iron-clad frigate down on us came bearing, high in the air she the rebel flag flew,
The pennant of treason she proudly was wearing, determined to conquer the Cumberland's crew.

Then up spoke our brave captain with stern resolution saying, 'Boys of that monster we'll be not afraid.
We have sworn to defend our beloved constitution and to die for our flag, boys, we are not afraid.
We will fight for our country because it is glorious and to the old flag we'll ever prove true,
We will die by our guns, boys, or conquer victorious.' He was answered by cheers from the Cumberland's crew.

Now our noble ship's opened her guns' dreadful thunder, our shot like hail on the rebels we poured
Our people gazed on her with awe-stricken wonder as a shot struck her side and went harmlessly o'er.
But the pride of our navy could never be daunted though the dead and the wounded our decks did bestrew
And the flag of Old England still proudly we vaunted, sustained by the pride of the Cumberland's crew.

Now broadside for broadside we poured down upon her, the blood from our scuppers ran down in dire gore,
Our people gazed on her in awe-stricken wonder as a shot struck her side and went harmlessly o'er.
She struck us amidships, our flanks she did sever while her iron bows struck our noble ship through;
And slowly we sank in the dark rolling river, O still were the cheers of the Cumberland's crew.

Then slowly we sank in Virginia's dark waters; we'll be honoured by the noble, the brave and the true
We'll be honoured by Old England's brave sons and fair daughters with the heroic men of the Cumberland's crew.
We stood by our guns, boys, and never surrendered, and to the old flag, why, we ever proved true;
With our flag proudly flying to our graves we went dying, it was nailed to the mast of the Cumberland's crew.

Clearly this was a new song to Vaughan Williams because he noted all the words. The song is about the Battle of Hampton Roads in March 1862 during the American Civil War. The Confederate frigate, the *Virginia*, was an iron clad ship, fitted with a ram, and driven by steam. She sank two Federal vessels, the frigate *Congress* and the sloop *Cumberland*, both of them wooden ships of the Union navy. The *Cumberland*'s fate was commemorated in a song which became well known in North America, but rarely crossed the Atlantic. Mr Crisp might have learned it from an American shipmate. The details in it remain fairly accurate, except that the sailors defending their constitution against the rebels have somehow become British. A version of the original words was published in a broadside by Firth.[17] Accounts of the battle say the *Virginia* rammed the *Cumberland* on the starboard side and the stricken ship began to sink, though her gun crews kept up a heavy fire as she went down. In the words of one of the *Cumberland*'s enemies, 'No ship was ever fought more gallantly.' The *Virginia* went on to beat four other ships that day and duel with a new Union ironclad *The Monitor*, the following day. The battle demonstrated how vulnerable the wooden ships were when attacked by the ironclad warship, and both the British and French navies stopped building new wooden warships as a result and turned instead to iron-clad ships. Interestingly, the *Cumberland*'s colours were nailed to the mast; in other words, they couldn't strike their colours and surrender, but had decided in advance to fight to the death. Hence the saying, 'nailing your colours to the mast'. The song was published on a broadside as early as 1865.[18]

The sinking of the "Cumberland" by the iron clad "Merrimac" off Newport, 1862. Sketched by F. Newman.
Library of Congress.

The Maids of Australia

Mr Crisp, King's Lynn January 1905

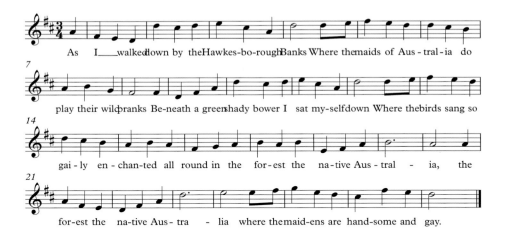

The Maids of Australia

As I walked down by the Hawkesborough banks,
Where the maids of Australia do play their wild pranks,
Beneath a green shady bower I sat myself down
Where the birds sang so gaily enchanted all around
In the forest, the native Australia,
In the forest, the native Australia,
Where the maidens are handsome and gay.

As I sat a-viewing this beautiful scene
When a pretty fair damsel I happened to see
She must be going swimming or so it would seem
By the stream of her native Australia,
By the stream of her native Australia,
Where the maidens are handsome and gay.

She stripped off her clothing, before me she stood,
As naked as Venus that rose from the flood,
She blushed with confusion and smiling said she
For these are the clothes that Australia gave me
The day I was born in Australia,
The day I was born in Australia
Where the maidens are handsome and gay.

Now she dived in the water without fear or dread
Her beautiful limbs she exceedingly spread
Her hair hung in ringlets, the colour was black,
Sir, said she, you will see how I float on my back.
On the stream in me native Australia
On the stream in me native Australia
Where the maidens are handsome and gay.

Now being exhausted she came to the brink
Assistance, kind sir, for I surely will sink
As quick as the lightning I took hold of her hand
My foot slipped and we fell on the sand.

Now we frolicked together in the highest of glee
In the finest Australia you ever did see
The sun it went down and the clouds did resign
Then I left the fair maid of Australia,
Then I left the fair maid of Australia
Just as the sun went down.

Now six months being over and nine being come,
This pretty fair maid she brought forth a son
O where was his father? He could not be found
And she cursed the hour she lay on the ground
In her native, the plains of Australia,
In her native, the plains of Australia,
Where the maidens are handsome and gay.

Peter Kennedy recorded this from Harry Cox in 1953 and it was published in the *Folk Song Journal* five years later. Ewan McColl and Peggy Seeger recorded Sam Larner of Winterton singing it in 1960. He makes no reference to the song collected by Vaughan Williams, but the refrain fits both versions so closely it is quite likely to be the same song.

Kennedy says in *Folk Songs of Great Britain and Ireland*, "The Hawkesbury River reaches the sea north of Sydney at Broken Bay, New South Wales. To date the song seems to have been found in Norfolk but has not come to light in Australia." Whether Vaughan Williams had any words for this is not clear. Perhaps Mr Crisp thought it was too risqué to sing all the words to him.

Spanish Ladies

Mr Crisp King's Lynn Union September 1st 1906

Spanish Ladies

Fare you well and adieu, to you Spanish ladies,
Fare you well and adieu, you ladies of Spain
For we've received orders to sail for Old England
And I hope in a short time to see you again.

Chorus
Then we'll rant and we'll roar like true British sailors,
We'll rant and we'll roar all on the salt seas
Until we arrive at the Channel of old England
And from Ushant to Scilly is forty-five leagues.

We hove our ship to all for to get sounded,
We hove our ship to and soundings took we,
We had forty-five fathoms and light sandy bottom
And we squared our main yard and up Channel stood we.

The first land we made it was called the Deadman
Then Ram Head off Plymouth, Start, Portland and Wight
We passed by Beachy, by Dungeness and Fairlee
Till at length we arrived at the North Foreland light.

Capt. Whall has two further verses, which finish the sailors' voyage:

Then the signal was made for the grand fleet for to anchor,
All in the Downs that night for to meet;
Then it's stand by your stoppers, let go your shank painters,
Haul all your clew garnets, stick out tacks and sheets,

Now let every man toss off a full bumper,
And let every man toss off a full bowl,
And we'll drink and be merry and drown melancholy,
Singing here's a good health to all true hearted souls.

These are the words noted when Mr Crisp sang this song with Mr Leatherday, so it's likely the words would have been the same when he sang them on his own.

Vaughan Williams notes that the two singers called this a Royal Navy song. Capt. Whall, in his *Sea Songs, Ships and Shanties* first published in 1910, includes *Spanish Ladies* as *Adieu and Farewell* and says he collected most of the songs in the mid-1800s when he went to sea. Mr Crisp and Mr Leatherday sing the tune in a minor key and Capt. Whall clearly indicates that he believes the minor key is the original. Roy Palmer says it's a navy song sung by ships returning from the Mediterranean. It was then taken up by merchant seamen and whalermen. He says the earliest text he's seen for the song is from the '*Nellie*'s' logbook of 1769, and uses the version in Captain Maryatt's *Poor Jack* in his *Oxford Book of Sea Songs*. He says even by 1906 it was still much sung in the Navy. Considering Lynn's long history of seafaring, it is no surprise that this song would be sung here.

These are the words noted by RVW when Mr Crisp and Mr Leatherday sang it to him.

Spanish Ladies

Mr Leatherday and Mr Crisp, King's Lynn Union, January 11th 1905

Fare you well and a-dieu to you Spa-nish la-dies Fare you well and a-dieu to you la-dies of Spain For— we've re-ceived or-ders to sail for old Eng-land and I hope in a short time to— see you a-gain.

Later in the week, Vaughan Williams noted another variation of the tune from Mr Crisp, this time without any words. It seems probable that they were the same as the version he sang with Mr Leatherday.

When it was published in the *Folk Song Society Journal* Vol. II, p.161, Frank Kidson says the words are on ballad sheets of the Catnach period. He also says that Captain Marryat first quoted the words in his novel *Poor Jack* and William Chappell in *Popular Music 1856-9* gave the air under the title *Farewell and Adieu*. He says the song can be most aptly described as 'Sailing directions for the English Channel', as almost every notable point from Ushant to North Foreland is mentioned. The Revd Sabine Baring-Gould and Cecil Sharp also collected the song. Sharp notes that Vaughan Williams' version is the only one with the leading note flattened throughout.

The tune is widely known as one of the themes of Sir Henry Wood's *Fantasia on British Sea Songs*, but there's no indication of which collection he used as a source when his fantasia was written to mark the centenary of the Battle of Trafalgar.

Mr Leatherday

The Leatherdays seem to have been very much a South Lynn family; John Leatherday (born 1840) and Robert (born 1842) were living there in 1851 at 44 Friar Street with their widowed mother Mary, who was a charwoman aged 48, and sisters Esther (born 1837) and Mary (born 1848). Of these Esther was styled "servant – out of place". The family had not featured in the 1841 census at all although the children were born in Lynn. It is Robert who was eventually to appear as an inmate of the Union, a widower aged 70 in the 1911 census, and who is thus assumed to be Vaughan Williams' Mr Leatherday.

The census records chart his progress through life. In 1861, as a 19-year-old general porter, he was still at home with his family in South Lynn.[19] Very soon thereafter he must have married as by 1871 he had a nine-year-old daughter, Rhoda. His wife Sarah was a laundress and she and Rhoda were both natives of Lynn, but they now lived in Cambridge, where Robert was described as a brick maker.

By 1881 he was back in South Lynn and alone, although he described himself as "married", not widowed; nevertheless no further reference has been traced to either Sarah or Rhoda Leatherday. Robert was lodging at the *Prince of Wales* public house at what is now the South Gates roundabout.[20]

His whereabouts in 1891 are unknown but in 1901 he was a "labourer in manure works", lodging now with a sawyer's family in William Street, just off Guanock Terrace in South Lynn. The manure works, later known officially and more euphoniously as West Norfolk Fertilisers and popularly as the muck works, had begun production in the 1870s. At one time it was said that if you lived in South Lynn, especially beyond the South Gates, the odds were you worked either for the railway, Cooper Roller Bearings or the manure works. In July 1902 Robert Leatherday was admitted to the workhouse where he was still a resident described as "formerly a labourer (builders)" in 1911.

Mr Leatherday sang 5 songs in 1905:

Creeping Jane
On Board a '98
The Robin's Petition (tune of)
Spanish Ladies (with Mr Crisp)
Spurn Point
In 1906 he added:
Three Butchers

The Prince of Wales pub on London Road, with flock of geese going past. Singer Robert Leatherday was lodging here when the 1881 census was taken.
True's Yard.

Creeping Jane

Mr Leatherday January 1905

I'll sing you a song and a very pret-ty one It's con-cern-ing of Creep ing_ Jane Oh she never does the work like a horse or a mare Nor her val-ly's not the half_ of a pin Fal the dee_____ Fal the dal the di - - do Her val - ly's not the half___ of a pin, fal the dee.

Creeping Jane

I'll sing you a song and a little, little song,
Concerning of Creeping Jane
She never won a race against a horse or a mare
That she vallied not a pin, fol the day etc.

Oh when they came unto the race ground
Oh the gentlemen they viewed her all around
And all that they said against Creeping Jane
She's not able to gallop over ground.

This is the version which Hammond collected:

I'll sing you a song and a very pretty song,
It's concerning of Creeping Jane,
Oh she never does the work like a horse or a mare,
Nor her vally's not the half of a pin, fol the dee,
  Fal the dal the dido
Nor her vally's not the half of a pin, fal the dee.

When Creeping Jane she came to the first mile post
Creeping Jane she keeps lingering behind.
Oh the rider put the whip into little Jenny's waist,
And she passed over the moor like a dart, *fal the dee etc.*

When Creeping Jane she came to the second mile post,
Creeping Jane she looked fresh and gay,
O the rider put his spurs into little Jenny's waist
And he says, 'My little lady, never mind.' *fal the dee etc*

When Creeping Jane she came to the third mile post,
Creeping Jane she looked fresh and gay,
O the rider put a posy into little Jenny's ear
And he said, 'My little lady, never mind.' *fal the dee etc*

Now Creeping Jane she's a-won that race
And she scarcely sweat one drop,
She is able for to gallop o'er the ground
While the others are not able for to trot, *fal the dee etc.*

Now Creeping Jane she's dead and gone,
Another body lies under cold ground.
I shall send to her master to ask for one favour
For to keep her little body from the hounds, *fal the dee etc.*

Vaughan Williams noted two verses from Mr Leatherday. They are similar to the version collected by Hammond from S. Dawe in Beaminster in 1906. A Such broadside version had been printed in the *Folk Song Journal* Vol. I p.233 in 1904. RVW had heard it before from Henry Burstow at Leith Hill in December 1903. Later Cecil Sharp collected it in Oxfordshire in 1923. 'Vally' is value.

Sailors Carousing by
Julius Caesar Ibbetson,
pub.1807.
Yale Center for British Art.

On Board a '98

Mr Leatherday King's Lynn Union January 9th 1905

When I was young and scarce eight-een I drove a roar-ing trade And many a sly trick I have played with many a pret-ty maid, My par-ents found that would not do I soon would spend their store So they resolved that I should go On board a man o' war.

On Board a '98

When I was young and scarce eighteen, I drove a roaring trade,
And many a sly trick I have played with many a pretty maid.
My parents found that would not do, I soon would spend their store
So they resolved that I should go on board a man o' war.

A bold press gang surrounded me, their warrant they did show,
And swore that I should go to sea and face the daring foe,
So they lugg'd me to the boat, Oh how I cursed my fate
'Twas then I found that I must float on board of a ninety-eight.

When first I put my foot on board how I began to stare
Our Admiral he gave the word there is no time to spare,
They weighed their anchor, shook out sail and off they bore me straight,
To watch the foe in storm and gale from on board of a ninety-eight.

Before we reached America they gave me many a drill
They soon learnt me a nimble way to handle an iron pill
In course of time a fight began when bold Jack tars laid straight,
What would I give if I could run from on board a ninety-eight.

But as time fled I bolder grew and hardened was to war
I'd run aloft with my ship's crew and valued not a scar
So well I did my duty do till I got boatswain's mate,
And damme, soon got boatswain too on board of a ninety-eight.

So years rolled by at Trafalgar brave Nelson fought and fell,
As they capsized that worthy tar I caught a rap as well.
To Greenwich College I came back because I saved my pate
They only knocked one wing off Jack on board of a ninety-eight.

So now my cocoa I can take, my pouch with 'bacco stored
With my blue clothes and three cocked hat I am happy as a lord.
I've done my duty, served my king and now I bless my fate
But damme, I'm too old to sing—I'm nearly ninety-eight!

Vaughan Williams liked this tune, which he used in *Norfolk Rhapsody No 1* and elsewhere. He did not note any words but says in the *Folk Song Society Journal* Vol. II p.177 that the words were completed from a ballad sheet printed by F. Paul, Spitalfields. He also notes that the tune has an affinity to the *Gallant Poachers* in the *Folk Song Journal* Vol 1 p.142. Frank Kidson adds that the words are also on a ballad sheet printed by Anne Ryle, Catnach's sister, so it's possible the words were also published by him.

During a talk on the BBC in 1940 Vaughan Williams talked about a 'little suite' of march tunes he had put together for the BBC's Military Band. The third tune he used was this one. 'Then comes a man-of-war song, 'On Board a '98'. This was sung to me in King's Lynn by an old sailor. I spent many happy mornings with him and his friends, listening to their almost inexhaustible stock of splendid tunes.' These were his visits to the King's Lynn Union in 1905.[21]

Spurn Point (Come People All)

Mr Leatherday, Lynn Union, King's Lynn January 9th 1905

Come all good peo-ple and list'n a-while A dread-ful sto-ry to you I'll tell A ves-sel called the In-dust-rie Was lost all on the rag - ing sea.

Spurn Point (Come People All)

Come all you good people and list'n awhile
A dreadful story to you I'll tell
Of a vessel called the Industrie
Was lost all on the raging sea.

About seven o'clock on Sunday night
She struck ground all on Spurn point
The swelling waves ran mountains high
In a dismal state the ship did lie.

But when on shore we came to know
To their assistance we did go
We manned the lifeboat stout and brave
Expecting every man to save.

We hailed the captain who stood at stern:
'We have come to save you and your men.'
'We want no relief,' he then did cry
'We shall get off at high water,' he replied.

'Heave us a rope', we once more did say,
'That alongside your ship we may lay'.
'We want no relief,' he then did cry
'I'd thank you to move off immediately.'

In the space of half an hour or more
The lifeboat crew reached the shore.
We watched her until eleven at night,
Then in distress they hoisted a light.

Into the lifeboat once more we got,
And hastened to the fatal spot,
Before we reached the fatal crew,
The light disappeared from our view.

O then we heard one poor man cry
'For God's sake, help me, or I shall die.
My shipmates are gone, and so must I.'
And down he went immediately.

The Frances Ann lifeboat
setting off to a ship in
trouble off Lowestoft.
Lowestoft Maritime Museum.

The captain was so obstinate
Into our lifeboat he would not get;
Or else all hands we might have saved,
And kept them from a watery grave.

The fear of all shipowners in the days of sail was that the rescuer of any ship in trouble would claim salvage, so all the profit and value of ship and cargo was lost. It was one of the founding principles of the RNLI that they were set up to save life, not property, and generally did not claim salvage, thus leaving the way clear for masters and crew to accept the help of the lifeboat if need be. Spurn Point, at the mouth of the Humber, is a notorious hazard for shipping and the lifeboat house is still permanently manned because the lifeboat is inaccessible at high tide from the mainland. Roy Palmer gives the background to this song thus:

> 'The vessel Industry (Captain Burdon) was stranded upon Spurn Point of the mouth of the Humber on January 4th 1868. Her captain declined the proffered assistance of the lifeboat, and his ship became a total loss.' Perhaps Norfolk seamen would be more aware of another ship called the Industry which was lost there on February 21st 1819. The Hull Advertiser reported, "About seven o'clock on Sunday evening during a very heavy gale E.N.E. The Industry, Richard Evans of Yarmouth, from Leith with potatoes, was driven ashore on the Outer Binks near Spurn Point, and before midnight fell on her broadside and the master and crew were all unfortunately drowned."

Interestingly then, as now, Hull had its own Trinity House, responsible for putting out buoys to mark the channels in the area. They ran the lifeboat station at Spurn Point, which had been paid for by a local landowner in 1810. The RNLI was founded in 1824.

Vaughan Williams noted the tune and first verse of the song from Mr Leatherday in the Union at Lynn. The rest of the text has been added from broadside No 2, issued by W. Forth, Waverley St., Hull, under the title of *The Industry off Spurn Point*.[22]

Lucy Broadwood prints the song to a different tune in *English County Songs*, attributing the words to a sailor called Fotherby from Whitby in 1891.

Ann Gilcrist collected a version of the song from Mr W. Bolton at Southport in 1906. Mr Bolton told her, "It used to be in much favour with 'Turnpike Sailors', a name given, he said, to a class of sham seafaring men who imposed upon the charitable by rigging themselves out in the garb of sailors, thus perambulating the country singing long doleful ballads of shipwreck and other misfortunes and professing to be sailors in distress."

Lucy Broadwood notes when it was published in Vol. II p.178 of the *Folk Song Society Journal* that the tune appears in many collections of Irish music, including *Bunting's Ancient Music of Ireland* 1840 and *S. Holden's Irish Tunes of 1800*. The Scots' version is in *Christie's Traditional Ballad Airs*. 'It is a favourite air amongst country singers, and is met with in England and Scotland very often, not only in connection with the broadside *Charlie Reilly* but many other ballads.'

Vaughan Williams used the tune as one of the themes in the *Norfolk Rhapsody No II*.

The Robin's Petition

Tune Leatherday words West January 11th1905 at King's Lynn Union

The Robin's Petition

When the leaves had forsaken the trees,
And the forests were chilly and bare,
When the brooks were beginning to freeze
And the snow waver'd fast thro' the air,
A Robin had fled from the wood,
To the snug habitation of man:
On the threshold the wanderer stood,
And thus his petition began:

'The snow's coming down very fast
No shelter is found in the trees
When you hear this unpitying blast
I pray you take pity on me.
The hips and the haws are all gone,
I can find neither berry nor sloe,
The ground is as hard as a stone
And I'm almost buried in snow.

My dear little nest once so neat
Is now empty and ragged and torn
On some tree should I now take my seat
I'd be frozen quite fast before morn;
Then throw me a morsel of bread
Take me in by the side of your fire
And when I am warmed fed
I'll whistle without other hire.

Till the sun be again shining bright
And the snow is all gone, let me stay;
Oh see what a terrible night,
I shall die if you drive me away,
And when you come forth in the morn,
And are walking and talking around,
Oh how will your bosom be torn
When you see me lay dead on the ground.

Then pity a poor little thing,
And throw me a part of your store,
I'll fly off in the first of the spring
And never will visit you more.'

This song was published by several ballad sheet printers and seems to have been known as a children's song.

Three Butchers

Mr Leatherday, King's Lynn Union, September 1st 1906

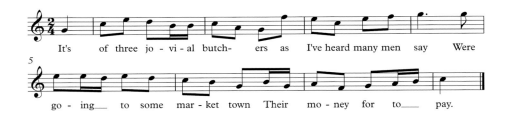

It's of three jo-vi-al butch-ers as I've heard many men say Were go-ing to some mar-ket town Their mo-ney for to pay.

Three Butchers

It was Ips, Gips and Jackson as I have heard men say,
They had five thousand guineas all on a market day.

As they rode over Northumberland as fast as they could ride
Oh Hark! Oh Hark! Says Johnson, I hear a woman cry.

Then Johnson being a valiant man, a man of courage bold
He ranged the woods all over till this woman he did behold.

How came you here, says Johnson, how came you here I pray?
I am come here to relieve you if you will not me betray.

There has been ten swaggering blades have hand and foot me bound,
And stripped me stark naked with my hair pinned to the ground.

Then Johnson being a valiant man, a man of courage bold,
He took his coat from off his back to keep her from the cold.

As they rode over Northumberland as fast as they could ride
She put her fingers in her ear and made a dismal cry.

Then up starts ten swaggering blades with weapons in their hands
And riding up to Johnson they bid him for to stand.

It's I'll not stand says Gibson, so then indeed not I,
No I'll not stand says Gibson, I'd rather live than die.

Then I will stand says Johnson, I'll stand here as I can,
I never yet was daunted nor afraid of any man.

Then Johnson drew his glittering sword with all his might and main,
So well he laid upon them that eight of them were slain.

As he was fighting the other two this woman he did not mind
She took the knife all from his side and ripped him up behind.

Now I must fall says Johnson, I must fall unto the ground
For relieving this wicked woman she gave me my death wound.

'Oh base woman, O base woman, woman what have you done?
Thou hast killed the finest butcher that ever the sun shone on.

This happened on a market day, so people were riding by,
To see this cruel murder they gave a hue and cry.

So now this woman's taken, and bound with irons strong
For killing the finest butcher that ever the sun shone on.

This song caught the imagination of three singers in Lynn: Elizabeth, Mr Crisp and Mr Leatherday. The story of the valiant butcher appears in other collections and on broadsides. The variations seem to be in the number of butchers and some are jolly, others are not.

This is the Catnach version which was widely distributed. Vaughan Williams did not note any words from Elizabeth. It was published in the *Folk Song Society Journal* Vol. I p.174.

Mr Leatherday's 1905 songs include two, *On Board a '98* and *Spurn Point* which went on to be included in the First and Second *Norfolk Rhapsodies* respectively. He helped Mr Crisp out with *Spanish Ladies*. Vaughan Williams called him a sailor and he certainly shows an apparent taste for the sea, although his life certainly appears at ten-year census intervals to be firmly rooted on dry land. On the other hand census returns offer only a "snapshot" at ten-year intervals and he is in fact missing from the 1891 census altogether, giving him twenty years in which to sample the life of a merchant seaman. The Union census return in 1911 only calls him a labourer; returns often refer to former time in the services, although they do not include Mr West's (see next section). Robert's brother John was for some time keeper of the dock gate, a post not unsuited to an ex-sailor, but he appears to have died before 1900.[23]

Mr West

A William West was admitted to the workhouse in 1899 and died there in 1907; aged 81, he was buried at the charge of the Veterans Association. In 1901 the census calls him a former labourer, born at Wereham c1824. The reference to Wereham and also his burial by the Veterans Association indicate he is also the William West, widower, "army pension and coal porter" who in 1891 was lodging at the *Anchor of Hope*, 95 Norfolk Street, a pub run by another ex-serviceman, James Hopkins formerly of the Royal Navy. He may also be the William West who 30 years earlier was working as an agricultural labourer at Wereham. His wife Martha was born there although he himself claimed at the time to have been born at Wilburton in Cambridgeshire. The Wereham connection is nevertheless persuasive and if he enlisted from Wereham it may have "become" for him his place of origin?

Mr West's part in the proceedings was very small; he provided the words for a tune from Mr Leatherday called *The Robin's Petition*, a children's song whose words Vaughan Williams declined to write down, merely saying that West had supplied them. Had they learned it as children themselves, or sung it as young fathers?

Mr Woods

Our sole piece of information regarding Mr Woods is that he was a sailor. He has proved elusive, appearing in the census records neither in 1901 nor, at first sight, in 1911. The Union deaths register gives a Christopher Woods, admitted June 1904, who died aged 80 in September 1906 and a William Wood, admission details not extant, who died in October 1915 also aged 80. William Wood aged 75, formerly of the Royal Navy, was there in 1911.

These two, overlooking whether or not there was an "s" on the name, could possibly be brothers. The 1841 census listed, in Jews Lane (later called Surrey Street) between Chapel Street and the High Street corner of Tuesday Market Place, Christopher Woods, baker aged 42 and his wife Ann (41) plus five children including Christopher aged 14, and six-year-old William; the ages tally with the workhouse record.[24]

The younger Christopher certainly may have become a sailor, as in September 1860 William, son of Christopher Wood, sailor, and Lydia, of Broad Street, was baptised at St Nicholas'. No further trace of Christopher has been found until his apparent admission to the workhouse in 1904 nor, with certainty, of William. There are other William Woods' but none whose age matches the ex-RN William of 1911 and 1915. It might nevertheless be unwise to exclude entirely William Woods, baptised in January 1841, son of John Woods (mariner) and Maria, as five-year discrepancies in age in later life do occur.[25]

By the date of the 1841 census John had become a police officer and the family, including a slightly older child John, were living in the old Gaol House on Saturday Market Place.[26] By 1851 Maria was receiving parish relief as "widow of a deceased police officer" for herself and four children and later references show the family living in Paradise Lane off Norfolk Street.[27] This William too may have gone on to a life at sea. There was also a William Wood who in 1881 was described as "stoker on the Middleton" but he was not born until 1847. There was in fact a Woods family in the North End but research so far has revealed neither a William nor a Christopher in it.

Mr Woods sang only 1 song:

Napoleon's Farewell

Mr Woods' only song reflects the covert admiration for Napoleon at grass roots level which sometimes surfaces in song. Mr Crisp and Mr Carter had also sung songs featuring Napoleon. Vaughan Williams felt obliged to note along with the song "This is doubtful because he was very hoarse".

Napoleon's Farewell

Mr Woods, sailor

Fare-well ye splen-did cit-a-del, met-rop-o-lis called Pa-ris, Where Phoe-bus ev-ery mor-ning shoots forth re-ful-gent beams Where's Flo-ra's bright Au-ro-ra ad-van-cing from the Or-i-ent With ra-di-ant light a-dor-ning the pure shi-ning streams At eve when Cen-taur does re-tire while the o-cean gilds like fire The un-i-verse ad-mires our mer-chan-dise and store, Com mand-ing Flo-ra's fra-grance the fer-tile fields to de-co-rate To il-lum-in-ate the roy-al Cor-si-can a-gain on the French shore.

Napoleon's Farewell

Farewell ye splendid citadel, metropolis called Paris
Where Phoebus every morning shoots forth refulgent beams
Where's Flora's bright Aurora advancing from the Orient
With radiant light adorning the pure shining streams.

At eve when Centaur does retire, while the ocean gilds like fire
And the universe admires our merchandise and store
Commanding Flora's fragrance the fertile fields to decorate
To illuminate the royal Corsican again on the French shore.

My name's Napoleon Bonaparte he conqueror of nations
I've banished German legions and drove kings from their throne
I've trampled dukes and earls and splendid congregations
Though they have now transported me to St Helena's shore.

Like Hannibal I've crossed the Alps, the burning sands and rocky cliffs
O'er Russian hills through frost and snow I still the laurel wore
I'm on a desert island where the rats the devil would affright
Yet I hope to shine in armour bright through Europe once more.

Some say the first of my downfall was parting from my consort
To wed the German's daughter who wounded my heart sore
I stole Malta's golden gates, I did the works of God disgrace
But if he gives me time and place to Him back I will restore.

My golden eagles were pulled down by Wellington's allied army
My troops all in disorder could no longer stand the field
I was sold that afternoon on the eighteenth day of June
My reinforcements proved traitors which caused me to yield.

I am an allied oak with fire and sword I made them smoke
I have conquered Dutch and Danes and surprised the grand Signor
I have defeated Austrians and Russians both Portuguese and Prussians
Like Joshua, Alexander or Caesar of yore.

And to the south of Africa and the Atlantic Ocean,
To view the wild emotions and flowings of the tide
Banished from the royal crown of imperial promotion
From the French of glory to see those billows glide.

Three days I stood the plain, liberty's cause for to maintain,
Thousands I left slain and covered in their gore
I never fled without revenge nor to the allied army cringed
But now my sword is sheathed and Paris is no more.

War, the Exile and the Rock Limpet by J.M. Turner, 1842.

Tate Gallery.

David Gregory, in his book *The Late Victorian Folk Song Revival: the persistence of English melody*[28] says, "This song was collected by Lucy Broadwood and Alec Fuller Maitland from a gamekeeper at Lyne in Sussex in 1893. *Napoleon's Farewell to Paris* illustrated two things that were to become characteristic of the next Edwardian phase of song collecting: the folksong revival: the song had been thought interesting enough to collect and analyse primarily because of its modal melody and the words (noted only in fragmentary form from the singer) had been completed from a broadside ballad sheet." Frank Kidson notes that a ballad sheet by Taylor of London has the words.

Vaughan Williams says the full words were published in the *Folk Song Journal* Vol. I p.14.

The florid style seems at odds with the singer, but maybe it was Mr Woods' party piece when a long song was required!

Mr Chesson

Mr Chesson is the only workhouse singer who appears to have a strong link with the North End. He can be identified with some certainty as John Thomas Chesson, son of William Chesson, labourer, and his wife Susan. In 1841 they were living in the town centre in Baker Lane and John, the youngest of three children, was ten months old. By 1861 he was a seaman, lodging with his widowed father William with a Mary Roberts in Baker Lane. He married Anna Jane Roberts on 16 September 1863 at St Margaret's and the first apparent North End link comes with the baptism of three of his children there on 20 January 1869. The eldest bears the name William Churchman Chesson; this suggests John was related to (John) Churchman Chesson (1843-1906), fisherman.[29] Still described as a sailor, John Chesson and his family were living in Purfleet Street.

By 1891 however he had come to land as a "labouring porter", a term which, like "porter", may include a worker on the docks or quayside. He and Anna were now living in Church Street near St Margaret's with three more children: Catherine (born 1873), Charles (born 1876) and Alice (born 1886). Charles also became a sailor, and as "son of John Thomas Chesson, porter", married Ellen Bunn, a fisherman's daughter, of Lansdowne Street in 1898. In 1901 he and Ellen were living in Burkitt Street and he was keeping a shop there in 1904.[30]

John Chesson's daughter Catherine (Kate) married a Gaywood labourer, Alfred Raines, in May 1897 and by 1901 John was living with them in Brompton Place off Wisbech Road in South Lynn. True to the maxim quoted above with reference to dwellers in that area, Alfred now worked for the railway as a "railway engine washer", a gruelling but important stage in the regular cleaning out of an engine. John was admitted to the workhouse in July 1904 and was clearly there in January 1905, but by June of that year, when he attended the workhouse surgery, his address was once more Wisbech Road. There are many indications in the Union's medical book that poor people living outside were able to use its medical facilities like casual attendance at one of today's drop-in medical centres and were even visited at home. He was an "outpatient" again in April 1906 but he was a resident once more in 1911, described as "formerly a mariner merchant service", and his death was registered there in the January quarter of 1913.

Mr Chesson sang 2 songs:

Erin's Lovely Home
Raven's Feather

Mr Chesson only has two songs, one of which Erin's Lovely Home has been noted above sung by other ex-seamen, suggesting that this song may have stemmed from that part of his life.

Erin's Lovely Home

Mr Chesson, King's Lynn Union Jan 1905

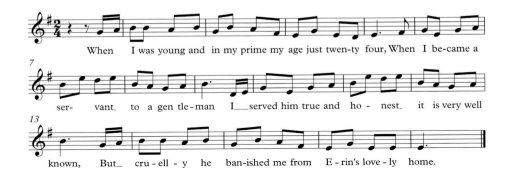

Erin's Lovely Home

When I was young and in my prime my age just twenty-four,
When I became a servant to a gentleman;
I served him true and honest, it is very well known,
But cruelly he banished me from Erin's Lovely Home.

The reason he did banish me I mean to let you hear,
I own I loved his daughter, and she loved me as dear,
She had a heavy fortune, but riches I had none,
And that's the reason I must go from Erin's lovely home.

It was in her father's garden all in the month of June,
When viewing of those flowers all in her youthful bloom,
She said my dearest William, if with me you will roam,
We'll bid adieu to all our friends and Erin's lovely home.

That very night I gave consent along with her to go
 From her father's dwelling place which proved my overthrow,
The night being bright, by the moonlight we both set off alone
Thinking we'd got well away from Erin's lovely home.

When we came to Belfast, by the break of day,
My true love she got ready our passage for to pay
Five thousand pounds she counted down, saying this shall be your own,
And never mourn for those you've left in Erin's lovely home.

But of our great misfortune I mean to let you hear
It was a few hours after, her father did appear,
And marched me back to Omagh gaol in the county of Tyrone,
And there I was transported from Erin's lovely home.

When I heard my sentence it grieved my heart full sore,
And parting from my true love it grieved me ten times more,
I had seven links on my chain and every link a year
Before I can return again to the arms of my dear.

Before the rout came to the gaol to take us all away
My true love came to me and these words to me did say,
Bear up your heart don't be dismayed, I will not you disown
Until I do return again to Erin's lovely home.

This set of words is taken from a 19th century broadside, which Vaughan Williams had in his own collection. Three singers sang versions of *Erin's Lovely Home* to him on his visit. He did not note any of the words, but they had been in the *Folk Song Society's* *Journal* volumes I p.117 and II p.167 and 211, so it's likely Vaughan Williams saw no need to note them again. He had also collected a version of the song from Mr Woolford at Ransbury on 8 August 1904 and from Mr Smith at Salisbury on 1 September 1904.

Raven's Feather

Mr Chesson King's Lynn Union Jan 1905

It's of a dam-sel both fair and hand-some These lines are true, so I've been told Near banks of Shan-non is a lof-ty man-sion Her par-ents claimed great stores of gold.

Raven's Feather

It's of a damsel both fair and handsome
These lines are true as I have been told,
Near the banks of Shannon is a lofty mansion
Her parents claimed great stores of gold.

Her hair was black as a raven's feather
Her form and features describe who can?
But still 'tis folly belongs to nature
She fell in love with a servant man.

Sweet Mary Ann with her love was walking
Her father heard them and nearer drew
And as these true lovers were fondly talking
In anger home then her father flew.

To build a dungeon was his intention
To part true love he contrived a plan
He swore an oath that's too vile to mention
He'd part that fair one from her servant man.

He built a dungeon of bricks and mortar
With a flight of steps for 'twas underground
The food he gave her was bread and water
The only cheer that for her was found.

Three times a day he did cruel beat her
Unto her father she thus began:
'If I've transgressed now, my own dear father,
I lay and die for my servant man.'

Young Edwin found out her habitation
'Twas well secured by an iron door
He vowed in spite of all this nation
To gain her freedom or rest no more.

'Twas at his leisure he toiled with pleasure
To gain releasement for Mary-Ann
He gained his object and found his treasure
Did my young faithful servant man.

Some clothing he bought his love
As man's apparel her to disguise
Crying, 'For your sake I'll face your father
To see me here it will him surprise.'

When her cruel father brought bread and water
To call his daughter he then began
Said Edwin, 'Enter, I've cleared your daughter
And I will suffer, your servant man.'

Her father found 'twas his daughter vanished
Then like a lion he did roar
He, 'From Ireland you shall be banished
Or with my broadsword I'll spill your gore.'

'Agreed,' said Edwin, 'so at your leisure
Since her I freed, now do all you can
Forgive your daughter, I'll die with pleasure,
The one in fault is your servant man.'

When her father found him so tender hearted
Then down he fell on the dungeon floor,
He said, 'True lovers should not be parted
Since love can enter an iron door.'

Then soon they joined to be parted never
To roll in riches this young couple can
This fair young lady midst rural pleasure
Lives blest for ever with her servant man.

When this was transcribed from Vaughan Williams' notebook (possibly by his wife Adeline or by Lucy Broadwood) it carried the note *The Two Affectionate Lovers*. It says 'Tunes to the same words as the ballad—that above quoted, noted by R. Vaughan Williams. The first tune quoted is the one sung by Mr Chesson on 10 January 1905. The other two were from Mr Charles Pottipher at Ingrave in 1903 and from Mr Jarman at Forest Green in 1904. Vaughan Williams notes that many of the tunes to these words are in peculiar time. There is a Catnach broadside called *The Cruel Father and the Affectionate Lovers* where the damsel's hair is "as black as a raven's feather." The song was also collected by F. Gwillim in Weobley in 1905 and published in the *Folk Song Journal*, with a reference that the full words are in the *Folk Song Journal* No 4 p.220. It's titled *The Two Affectionate Lovers*. The journal in which Mr Chesson's tune is printed also has the tune sung by Mr and Mrs Verrall at Monk's Gate on 4 October 1904.

Mr Cooper

Of Mr Cooper very little has come to light. Neither the 1901 nor 1911 census shows a Mr Cooper as an inmate but a George Cooper aged 78 from St Margaret's parish died in the workhouse in March 1906 and, sadly, had to be buried by the Guardians themselves rather than by "friends". The cemetery register shows he was a shoemaker and, almost certainly, the George Cooper who in 1891 lodged with a grocer in Littleport Street. Aged 60, he was born in Snettisham, and described as married, although his wife was not present to be counted on census night.

Mr Cooper sang only 1 song:

The Irish Girl

The Irish Girl

Mr Cooper January 1905

One mor-ning fair I took the air Down by Black-wat-er side Oh then gaz-ing all a-round me 'Twas an I-rish girl I spied An I-rish girl I spied.

The Irish Girl

It was one summer morning down by a riverside
I looked all around me and an Irish girl espied
So red and rosy were her cheeks and cole black was her hair
And costly were the robes that this Irish girl did wear.

The tears ran down her rosey cheeks in sorrow she did cry,
Saying 'My hone true love has gone from me and quite forsaken I
The last time I saw my love he was verry bad
The only thing he ask me was just to tye his head.'

I wish my love was as red as a rose that in the garden grew
And I was the gardiner him I would renew.
Yes every month throughout the year him I would renew
With lilleys I would garnish him sweet William, thyme and rue.

I wish I was a butterfly I would fly to my love's brest
I wish I was a linnet, I would sing my love to rest,
I wish I was a nightingale sing to the morning clear
I would sit and sing to my true love who I do love so dear.

I wish I was in Dublin Town sporting on the grass,
With a glass of wiskey in each hand and on each knee a lass,
We would call or licquor merrerly and pay before we go,
We would role a lass all on the grass let the wind blow high or low.

This song, according to James Reeves in *The Idiom of the People*,[31] was widespread. Vaughan Williams heard it from Henry Burstow of Horsham at Leith Hill in December 1903 and from Mr and Mrs Ratford at Ingrave in April 1904. Lucy Broadwood published it in 1908. It was in the *Folk Song Journal* in 1899. The song seemed to persist in the Norfolk repertoires as well. Walter Pardon said when it was sung by the author at the old Meadow Gardens in North Walsham in the 1970s that it was one of the songs he knew and it was the first time he'd heard anyone else sing it.

The tune noted from Mr Cooper does not entirely fit any of the sets of words from Burstow or the broadsides. As Vaughan Williams was normally faultless in his recording of tunes, no matter how quickly he took them down, we are left with a mystery. However, a version taken down by Peter Kennedy in Belfast under the title *Down by the Blackwaterside* does fit, and he refers back to broadsides and Baring Gould's collecting for its origins. [32] So here are two sets of words. The first version, not written in RVW's hand was in his collection. Maybe Henry Burstow had written it out for him. By the spelling it was clearly from a singer whose spelling was occasionally phonetic rather than correct; Vaughan Williams copied it when he noted the tune from Burstow in 1904.

This is from a broadside published by Such in Borough. (Hawkers supplied, it notes).

Abroad as I was walking down by a riverside
I gazed around me an Irish girl I spied
So red and rosy was her cheeks and coal black was her hair
And costly was the robes of gold my Irish girl did wear.

Her shoes were of the Spanish black all spangled round with dew.
She rung her hands and tore her hair crying, Alas! What shall I do?
I'm going home, I'm going home, said she,
Why will you go a-roving and slight your dear Polly?
The last time that I saw my love he seemed to be in pain
With chilling grief and anguish his heart was broke in twain;
There's many a man that's worse than he so why should I complain?
Oh love it is a killing thing, did you ever feel the pain!

I wish my love was a red rose and in the garden grew
And I to be the gardener to her I would prove true,
There's not a month throughout the year, but my love would renew,
With lilies I would garnish her, sweet William, thyme and rue.

I wish I was a butterfly I'd fly to my love's breast,
I wish I was a linnet, I'd sing my love to rest,
I wish I was a nightingale I'd sing till morning clear,
I'd and sing to you, Polly, I once did love so dear.

I wish I was in Exeter all seated on the grass,
With a bottle of whisky in my hand, and on my knee a lass,
We'd call for liquors merrily, and pay before we go,
I'd hold her in my arms once more let the wind blow high or low.

This is the Irish version given by Peter Kennedy which he recorded in 1952 when he was working for the BBC, but has much earlier roots predating or contemporary with Vaughan Williams' collecting. With a repeat of the last line as a refrain, it fits the King's Lynn tune perfectly and still retains many elements from Henry Burstow's version.

Down by Blackwaterside

One morning fair I took the air
Down by Blackwaterside
O then gazing all around me
'Twas an Irish girl I spied.

So red and rosy were her cheeks
And coal black was her hair
I caught her by her lily white hands
And I asked her to be my dear.

All through the middle of the night
We slept till morning clear
Then the young man arose and put on his clothes
Saying: 'Fare thee well, my dear.'

'That's not the promise you made to me
Down by the Blackwaterside',
'The promise I made is the promise I'll keep
For I never intend to lie.

'Go home to your father's garden
Go home and cry your fill,
And think of your own misfortune
That you brought of your own free will.'

'There's not a girl in this wide world
That would prove more loyal and true.'
'Then the fishes will fly and the seas run dry
Sure, 'tis then that I'll marry you.'

Jemmy's Return, 1784.
National Maritime Museum.

Mr Elmer

Mr Elmer sang most of his songs when Vaughan Williams returned to Lynn in September 1906 and notably seems always to appear in company with Mr Crisp. The two may have been friends: in the 1901 census the two names appear together in what seems to have been a random listing of names. It might mean the enumerator took them down from the men wherever he happened to find them sitting, as one might have expected them to be in alphabetical order from the records. Mr Elmer is described as "George Elmer, widower, general labourer." He was aged 61, born in Lynn, and was still in the workhouse in 1911, although he seems to have left and re-entered several times between April 1908 and August 1910.

There had been an Elmer family in Chapel Street in 1841 but no George has been traced until 1871, when George Elmer aged 29 "excavator" and his wife Mary, who was born in the Rudhams,[33] were living in Surrey Street off the Tuesday Market Place. Other "excavators" were noted above in North Street in 1851 and 1861 and here too there may be a link with the creation of the docks. Beyond that it has not been possible to track him down. In 1881 there seem to have been no Elmers in Lynn although there were several agricultural labourers of that name in the Grimston and West Winch areas just outside the town.

Mr Elmer sang 2 songs in 1905:

It's of an Old Lord

Hares in the Plantation (Unattributed but follows *It's of an Old Lord* in the notebook).

It's of an Old Lord

Mr Elmer January 1905 King's Lynn

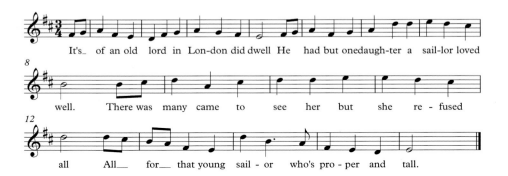

It's of an Old Lord

It's of an old Lord in London did dwell
He had but one daughter whom a sailor loved well
Their (sic) was many come to see her but she refused all
All for that young sailor who was proper and tall.

Her father went to her one day with a frown
Saying, 'Is there a lord or a duke in this town
But he can enjoy your sweet lovely face
For to marry this young man your friends to disgrace.'

Now her father was grieved, but not to the heart,
To think he could force these young lovers to part,
'It would cost me ten hundred bright guineas,' said he,
'I'll send for the press gang and I'll send him to sea.'

They went to get married, got to the church door,
They met with the press gang, about half a score,
They pressed her own true love on to the salt sea
And instead of being married brought sorrowful day.

Now soon you shall hear how it fell to her lot
To be a true lover's messmate though he knew it not,
It was every morning this young couple arose
They got up together and slipped on their clothes.

(some verses evidently missing here.)
Saying, 'I once had a true love in London,' says he,
But her cruel father forced me to sea;
Come tell unto me the day of your birth,
Tell unto me with a good deal of truth.'

For I am your true love and you are my joy
And if I can't have you my life I'll destroy.
'Now we'll send for the parson, the parson with speed,
Now we'll send for the parson and married we'll be.'
'If ever I'm married it will be to you,
Here's adieu to my father and all he can do.'

RVW noted the first verse of this ballad but added the further six verses when it was published in the *Folk Song Journal* Vol. II pp 181-2. He gives variants to fit the words on the third and fourth lines. A version was printed by an Irish broadside publisher under the title *The Lady and the Sailor*, and it's a rich merchant, not an old lord, who has the daughter. But the burden of the story in this and similar songs rests on a father's efforts to stop a well born daughter marrying a common tar.

The Sailor by William Finden, pub.1834.
Yale Center for British Art.

Hares in the Plantation

Unknown singer, King's Lynn January 1905

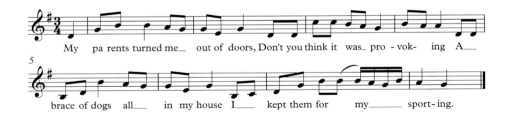

My pa rents turned me___ out of doors, Don't you think it was___ pro - vok- ing A___
brace of dogs all___ in my house I___ kept them for my___ sport- ing.

Hares in the Plantation

My parents turned me out of doors
Don't you think it was provoking
A brace of dogs all in my house
I kept them for my sporting.

When I had two dogs and an airgun too
I kept them for my keeping.
I kept them for my sporting nights
While the gamekeepers laid sleeping

Me and my dogs went out one night
To view the wily creatures
Up jumps the old hare and away she ran
Down into the plantation.

Before I could get half a field or more
Or very little further
Up jumped another old hare and away dogs went
Made hare shriek murder.

Up she jumped and followed out aunt[34]
When the dogs stopped her running.
'Oh pray, poor puss, do lay still
For your uncle is a-coming.'

I picked her up and broke her neck
And into my pocket I put her;
Thinks to myself, 'I had better be going
Before I meets the looker.'

I went into a neighbour's house
And I asked him what he'd give me.
He said he'd give me a crown a brace
If I would bring him fifty.

I went into a public house
And there I gets quite mellow,
I spent a crown, another one throwed down,
Wasn't I a good-hearted fellow?

Vaughan Williams heard this song once before he came to King's Lynn in April 1904 at the *Bell* in Willingale Hoe in Essex; then again afterwards from Noah Fisher at the *Three Horseshoes* in Tibenham in South Norfolk in 1911. It was also collected by Frank Kidson and published in his *Traditional Tunes* of 1891 as *Hares in the Old Plantation* with a refrain added by repeating the last two lines of each verse. He wrote of it as a song 'originally consisting of a number of verses so deficient of rhyme and reason as to be not worth the trouble of transcription, although the air is by no means a bad one.' His version came from Goole. Cecil Sharp heard the song in Somerset in 1903.

The song is clearly related to *While Gamekeepers Lie Sleeping*, an idea which appealed to those who 'walked by night.'

Vaughan Williams heard the song from Noah Fisher in the *Three Horseshoes* at Tibenham on a later collecting expedition in December 1911. He noted only the first two and a half verses of the version he heard in Lynn, so the rest is borrowed from Mr Fisher.

In 1906, Mr Elmer added four more songs:

Lord Bateman
The Fourteenth Day of February (but *not* The Bold Princess Royal, it is noted)
Kilkenny
Bold Robber (Doubtful, according to Vaughan Williams).

Lord Bateman

Mr Elmer at Kings Lynn Union Sept 7th 1906

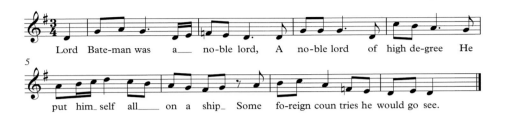

Lord Bate-man was a no-ble lord, A no-ble lord of high de-gree He put him self all on a ship Some fo-reign coun tries he would go see.

Lord Bateman

Lord Bateman was a noble lord,
A noble lord of high degree,
He put himself all on a ship
Some foreign countries he would go see.

He sail-ed east and he sail-ed west
Until he came to fair Turkey
Where he was taken and put in prison
Until his life was quite weary.

And in this prison there grew a tree
It grew so stout and it grew so strong
Where he was chained by the middle
Until his life was almost gone.

The Turk he had an only daughter
The fairest creature ever my eyes did see
She stole the keys of her father's prison
And swore Lord Bateman she would set free.

'Have you got houses, have you got lands?
Or does Northumberland belong to thee?
What would you give to the fair young lady
That out of prison would set you free?'

'I have got houses, I have got land,
And half Northumberland belongs to me;
I'll give it all to the fair young lady
That out of prison would set me free.'

Oh then she took him to her father's palace
And gave to him the best of wine,
And every health she drank unto him,
'I wish, Lord Bateman, that you were mine.'

'Now for seven long years I'll make a vow
For seven long years and keep it strong,
If you will wed no other woman,
That I will wed no other man.'

Oh then she took him to her father's harbour
And gave to him a ship of fame;
'Farewell, farewell, my dear Lord Bateman,
I'm afraid I shall never see you again.'

Now seven long years were gone and past,
And fourteen long days well known to me
She packed up her gay clothing,
And Lord Bateman she would go see.

And then she came to Lord Bateman's castle
So boldly now she rang the bell;
'Who's there?' cried the young porter
'Who's there – now come unto me tell.'

'Oh is this Lord Bateman's castle,
And is his lordship here within?'
'Oh yes, oh yes,' said the proud young porter,
'He's just taking his young bride in.'

'Oh then tell him to send me a slice of bread,
And a bottle of the best wine,
And not forgetting the fair young lady
That did release him when close confined.'

Away, away went that proud young porter,
Away, away and away went he,
Until he came to Lord Bateman's door
Down on his bended knees fell he.

'What news, what news, my young porter
What news have you brought unto me?'
'There is the fairest of all young ladies
That ever my two eyes did see.

She has got rings on every finger
And round one of them she has got three
And such gay gold hanging round her middle,
That would buy Northumberland for thee.

'She tells you to send her a slice of bread
And a bottle of the best wine;
And not forgetting the fair young lady
That did release you when close confined.'

Lord Bateman then in a passion flew
And broke his sword in splinters three
Saying: 'I will give all my father's riches
If that Sophia has crossed the sea.'

Then up spoke this bride's young mother
Who never was heard to speak so free
'You'll not forget my only daughter,
If Sophia has crossed the sea.'

'I own I made a bride of your daughter,
She's neither the better or worse for me;
She came to me with a horse and saddle,
She may go home with a coach and three.'

Lord Bateman prepared another marriage
With both their hearts so full of glee,
'I'll range no more in foreign countries
Now since Sophia has crossed the sea.'

This ballad is very old and very widespread. It had already been heard by Vaughan Williams from Mr Whitby at Tilney All Saints and was in both Lucy Broadwood's *English County Songs* (published in 1893) and in Frank Kidson's *Traditional Tunes* (published in 1891). Kidson says

> many are the airs which have been set to the popular ballad, 'Lord Bateman'.
> …

The common version of the words is undoubtedly much corrupted from a very early metrical poem, and there are numberless copies printed in the English and Scottish ballad books, which were formerly current in a traditional form throughout the land. They are all in general much longer than the one now popular…

The story in all these is of a Christian knight, who sailing into an Eastern land is imprisoned and afterwards released by the daughter of his captor. She afterwards follows him across the seas and arrives at the opportune moment, when the knight, forgetting her who befriended him, is about to wed another lady. It has been asserted, with every appearance of truth, that the hero of the tale was Gilbert a Becket, father of St Thomas a Becket of Canterbury, who in the early times of the Crusades was captured as in the ballad, released and followed to London by the lady. She is said to have known no more than two words of English: Gilbert and London, and to have cried the first through London streets until she found her lover. Fanciful as the legend appears, it is supported by the fact that every ballad known on the subject gives the name of the knight as a greater or lesser corruption of Becket. For instance, 'Young Beckie', 'Lord Beichan', 'Lord Bateman' etc.

Kidson gives the version sung to him by Mrs Holt of Alderhill, Meanwood, which is a different tune from the one Mr Elmer sang. However, the words fit his tune well and there are a mere 21 verses! Given the Lynn singers' love of long songs, this would have been an obvious favourite.

Illustrations from The Loving Ballad of Lord Bateman by George Cruickshank, pub.1839. Google books project.

The 14th Day of February

Sung by Mr Elmer at King's Lynn Union September 1st 1906

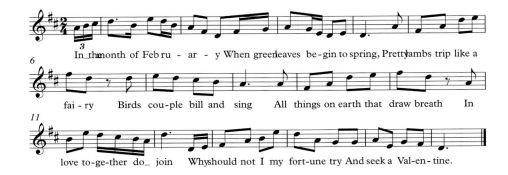

In the month of Febru - ar - y When green leaves be - gin to spring, Pretty lambs trip like a fai - ry Birds cou - ple bill and sing All things on earth that draw breath In love to-ge-ther do_ join Why should not I my fort-une try And seek a Val - en - tine.

The Fourteenth Day of February

Batchelor

In the month of February
When green leaves begin to spring
Pretty lambs trip like a fairy
Birds do couple, bill and sing;
All things on earth
That draweth breath
In love together then do joyn
Why should not I
My fortune try
And seek me out a Valentine.

Thanks, kind Fate, I have my wishes
For I have now met my dear
Whom I greet with honey kisses
Her sweet sight my heart doth cheer
My dearest love
And turtle dove
Good morrow my fair Valentine.

Maid

Surely Sir you are mistaken
For you met some other maid
Young men they are given to scoffing
And as much to her you said.
Then do not stay
Me on the way
With your sweet words that you do coyn
Let me alone
I must be gone
I pray seek some other Valentine.

Batchelor

If true Faith may be believed
On you first I did set sight
Sweet let not my heart be grieved
Who doth love your beauty bright;
Oft I have wisht
I might be blest
With your sweet presence for to joyn,
And ease my mind
Maids should be kind
And loving to their Valentine.

Maid

Sir to me you are a stranger
Maids must look before they leap
In fair speeches oft there's danger
Snakes under sweet flowers creep.
Maids often find
Men's words but Wind
The sun shall set that bright did shine
After a calm
There comes a storm
Go seek some other Valentine.

Batchelor

Fortune fair hath now decreed it
That none but you I should meet
Dearly I do love, believe it,
For you are my only sweet.
My grieved breast
Can take no rest
Which doth my love-sick heart conjoin
Love I require,
Love I desire
Of thee, my beauteous Valentine.

Maid

For your affection Sir I thank you
Before more then my desert
Sure I cannot be so cruel
To procure a lover's smart.
'Tis modesty
For to deny
Yet from my words I may decline
Then banish pain
Make heart again
For I will be thy Valentine.

Batchelor

Now thou speakest like an Angel
And my drooping heart revive
For to give thee all contentment
Day and night then I will strive.
Thy courteous words
Much joy affords
And thy rare beauty so divine
Sweet, let me kiss
My fair mistress
My only joy and Valentine.

Maid

If you intend what you have promised
And do love me as you say
I may yield, but if you flatter,
I can my affection stay.
Now I am free
As you may see
Nor can I say that I am thine
But being bound
No help is found
And then no more sweet Valentine.

Batchelor

When I from my promise alter
Let me then no longer thrive
And let nothing with me prosper
While that I remain alive.
Pains I'll not spare
But will take care
For to maintain thee neat and fair,
And for the best
That can be drest
Then thou shalt eat sweet Valentine.

Maid

Seeing you are so kind hearted
I have freely given consent
And my love to be imparted
Hoping never to repent;
I'll constant prove
To thee my love
For I am thine, and thou are mine,
I'll saving be
As thou shalt see
Sweet husband, friend and Valentine.

Batchelor

A thousand, thousand thanks I render
Back again to thee my love,
Who above the world I render,
My firm faith shall ne'er remove.
Then presently
To church let's hye
Where in hymns and banns let's joyn,
Take hand and heart
Till death do part,
My life, my wife and Valentine.

This proved a difficult song to find, as Vaughan Williams specifies it is not a version of the *Bold Princess Royal*, the first verse of which begins 'On the 14th of February we sailed etc.'

In 1907 a collector called Emily Kemp said she had found a Lancashire rhyme called the *14th of February* but 'I cannot tell, nor can find, any music for it.' However, a black letter broadside, reprinted later, has two songs based around the *14th of February* and *St Valentine's Day*. The opening rhyme says:
'A brace of Valentines I here present
Who now together live in heart's content;
These luckily did meet along the way
In February the fourteenth day.'

The song called *The True Lovers Good Morrow* is a conversation between a batchelor (sic) and a maid and says the tune is *As at Noon Dulcina rested*. Among those for whom the broadside was printed was 'W. Thackeray.' This version is from a broadside by F. Coles, T. Vere and Wright in the Bodleian collection.[35] They are the only words which seem to fit the structure of the tune, but this elusive *14th of February* could be a mystery yet to be solved.

The Bold Robber

Mr Elmer , King's Lynn Union, September 1st 1906

O come all you goodpeople that go out a -tipp-ling I pray give at - tention and list'n to my song, I'll sing you a ditty of a jol - ly bold_ rob - ber Stood sev - en feet high in pro - por - tion quite strong.

The Bold Robber

Oh come all you good people that go out a-tripping,
I pray give attention and list'n to my song,
I'll sing you a ditty of a jolly bold robber
Stood seven foot high, in proportion quite strong.

He robbed a lord and he robbed a lady,
Five hundred bright guineas from each one of them
Till, as he was a-walking he met a young sailor
And bold as a lion he stepped up to him.

'Deliver your money, my jolly young sailor,
You've plenty of bulk in your pocket, I see.'
'Aye, aye,' says the sailor, 'I've plenty of money,
But while I have life, I've got none for thee.

'I've just left my shipping and taken my money,
I'm bound for Old England my friends for to see.
I've ninety bright guineas my friends to make merry,
So I pray, jolly robber, don't you take them from me.'

The saucy bold robber struck the jolly young sailor
Such a blow on the head which brought him to the ground.
'Aye, aye,' said the sailor, 'You have struck me quite heavy,
But I must endeavour to return it again.'

O then they both stripped, like lambkins they skipped,
They went life for life, like soldiers in the field,
And the ninety eighth meeting it was a completement,
And this jolly young sailor the robber near killed.

Says the jolly young sailor to the saucy bold robber
'I hope you won't lay any blame on to me,
If I'd been a robber of ten hundred guineas
I would never have stopped a poor sailor like me.'

Vaughan Williams gives us an interesting modal tune for this but no words. It's similar to the *Saucy Bold Robber* he had heard from Mr Anderson 10 January, 1905. This one was sung to him on 1 September a year later. In his notebook he wrote: "N.B. I am doubtful about this." Mr Anderson's words fit this tune, so maybe it was a song well known among the community at the time. When Joe Anderson's version was published in the *Folk Song Society Journal* Vol. II pp.165-6 Frank Kidson notes "I have never come across this ballad on a broadside or elsewhere". The tune is decidedly old and the song is one of the many narrative lyrics of highwayman exploits which formerly must have been sung around the firesides of most country inns.

Kilkenny

Mr Elmer, King's Lynn Union, September 1st 1906

Oh the boys of Kil-ken-ny are brave ro-ving blades And if ev-er they meet with some fair pret-ty maids, They'll kiss them and coax 'em, and spend mon-ey free, And of all towns in Ire-land Kil-ken-ny for me.

Kilkenny

The boys of Kilkenny are brave roving blades
And if ever they meet with nice little maids
They'll kiss them and coax 'em and spend their money free
And of all the towns in Ireland Kilkenny's for me.

In the town of Kilkenny there runs a clear stream
In the town of Kilkenny there lives a fair dame,
Her cheeks are like roses and her cheeks blush the same
Like a dish of sweet strawberries all smothered in cream.

Her eyes are as black as Kilkenny's black coal,
Which thro' my poor bosom has burned a black hole
Her mind like its rivers is cold clear and pure
But her heart is more hard than marble I'm sure.

Kilkenny's a pretty town and shines where it stands
And the more I think on it the more my heart warms,
For if I was in Kilkenny I'd think myself at home
For it's there I'd get sweethearts but here I have none.

Vaughan Williams did not note words to Mr Elmer's *Kilkenny*, but he had heard the song before from Mrs Berry at Leith Hill Farm in May 1904. The song was also on a broadside called *Boys of Kilkenny*, with a 'Fol de rol etc.' chorus on the end of each verse, presumably a repetition of the last line. According to Roy Palmer, the words of the song have been attributed to Thomas Moore (1779-1852), the friend of Byron and

Shelley, who spent two years in *Kilkenny* in connection with the theatre there. Lucy Broadwood had suggested that the Irish composer Michael Kelly (1762-1826) was responsible for both the tune and the words, which were adapted from traditional sources. He says it was widely sung both in England and Ireland.

This version is on a broadside sold by B. Stewart in Butchergate, Carlisle, and by Wm. Dalton, York.

Notes

1   *Lynn Advertiser,* 7 January 1905.

2   *Lynn Advertiser,* 26 August 1854 reported discussions and a report but no action, while "The buttresses meanwhile continued very slowly to recede from the wall."

3   A drawing by the Revd Edward Edwards actually shows this room constructed in the tower arches, complete with the beds. Higgins D. (2001) *The Antiquities of King's Lynn from the sketchbooks of the Revd Edward Edwards.* King's Lynn: Phoenix Publications, p.21.

4   James, E. (1999) 'The Captain's Apprentice: a study in the development of a folksong' *Folk Music Journal,* 7 (5), pp.579-594.

5   Perrott, V. *Victoria's Lynn: Boom and Prosperity* (1995). Seaford: Vista Books, p.19.

6   For the risks to family life engendered by dependence on the sea and charitable measures to combat them see Richards P. *King's Lynn* (1990) Chichester: Phillimore p.83, examination of the effects of the 1834 Poor Law pp.84 & 86-87.

7   *Lynn Advertiser,* 13 January 1905.

8   Once "The Workhouse" and later "King's Lynn Poor Law Institution", by 1951 it had become "St James Hospital". Information from Kelly's Directories, 1904-1951.

9   Personal reminiscence Elizabeth James.

10   Churchman Chesson married Charlotte Norris, whose brother John Norris married Duggie's sister Sarah.

11   Noticeably the latter occurred in 1861 when he was recorded at some distance from home on board ship.

12   Online ref via Ancestry; the merchant service records are not very complete and cover only two discrete periods, the first ending with 1857. The second group is too late in date to be relevant.

13   To date it has not proved possible to identify which ship of this name he served on. A Norwegian 3-masted barque called the *Ceres* was wrecked on Scroby Sands off Great Yarmouth in October 1910 and the crew rescued by Caister lifeboat. She was built in 1866. There was also a ketch called *Ceres,* built in the West Country in 1811, which traded round the coast, including some East Anglian ports. She was working until 1936, when she sank in Bideford Bay and her crew was rescued by Appledore lifeboat. Information from Beyond Steeple Point website. There was also an American bark called *Ceres* built in 1846. A print of a three masted barque called *Ceres* 'bound for the USA 1881' is also in circulation. Given how busy the Port of King's Lynn was in the 19th century, still home to a Greenland whaling fleet, Mr Crisp could have fetched up on any one of them.

14   King's Lynn workhouse records are in the Norfolk Archive Centre in Norwich.

15   This list of names is not in alphabetical order, suggesting the enumerator might even have compiled it by talking to the men where they happened to be sitting.

16   Palmer, R. (1983) *Folk Songs Collected by Ralph Vaughan Williams.* London: J.M.Dent & Sons Ltd.

17   Bodleian collection, Bod 8498.

18   Minnesota Heritage Songbook website.

19   The address was now at Guanock Field.

20   Still standing but no longer a pub.

21   Cobbe, H. (2008) *The Letters of Ralph Vaughan Williams.* London: OUP, p.298.

22   Palmer, R. (1983) *Folk Songs collected by Ralph Vaughan Williams.* London: J.M.Dent and Sons Ltd.

23   An elasticity between Woods and Wood may appear in there being a household a few doors away headed by a Christopher Wood aged 70, who could be the father of Christopher Woods the baker.

25   e.g. see Mrs Betty Howard (pp.123).

26   Now a museum.

27   Now largely vanished under the bus station and Sainsbury's car park, although a fragment still runs into Norfolk Street under its old name.

28   Gregory, E.D. (2010) *The Late Victorian Folksong Revival.* Lanham, Maryland, USA: The Scarecrow Press Inc., p.494.

29   Churchman Chesson was the son of William and Mary Chesson. His link with Duggie Carter was mentioned above.

30   Kelly's Directory 1904.

31   Reeves, J. (1958 reprinted 1962) *The Idiom of the People.* London: Faber and Faber. pp.130 & 131.

32   Kennedy, P. (1975) *Folksongs of Britain and Ireland.* London: Oak Publications, pp.351 & 373.

33   East and West Rudham are villages 16 miles east of King's Lynn.

34   Aunt and puss are terms for female hares.

35   Ibid. 17, Bod 24229.

The Day Trip to Sheringham

"She had much better go to Sheringham or Cromer, she would hear some songs as is worth hearing on the beach there."

Kate Lee, first secretary of the Folk Song Society, recalling a conversation with fishermen in Wells.

Between the Vaughan Williams' sessions with Mrs Benefer, Elizabeth, Mr Bayley and the workhouse singers, and those with Mr Harper, Mr Smith and Mr Donger, he made a day trip to Sheringham. This day excursion, presumably by train, does not look very fruitful in purely musical terms, as he only secured two songs. On the other hand, we do not know what led to this visit or whether there was any personal reason for making it, to which collecting was perhaps incidental.

Sheringham in 1905 was a 'new town', owing its success to the coming of the railway and the boom in popular seaside tourism, fuelled by the fashionable articles about 'Poppyland'.[1] A century before, 'Sheringham' had been simply the village now called Upper Sheringham, on the edge of, and above, the present seaside resort. Below it a growing number of cottages, increasingly styled 'Lower Sheringham', was largely, though not exclusively, occupied by fishermen. By 1904 Lower Sheringham had greatly outgrown its parent village and Kelly's Directory described there "a considerable fishing station, having about 250 boats employed in the herring, cod, skate, plaice, crab, lobster and whelk fisheries; great quantities of all these different kinds are sent to Norwich and London; about 7 or 8 of the boats are large and fitted for deep sea fishing." There is no harbour at Sheringham; the boats operate from the beach and slipway, but it was a big operation and Vaughan Williams might have concluded that he too might net a good catch. It is also possible that he had in mind

a remark made to Mrs Kate Lee when she enquired for songs among the fishermen at Wells next the Sea in 1897: "One of the other men said, Oh, no, she had much better go to Sheringham or Cromer, she would hear some songs as is worth hearing, on the beach, there".[2]

The east and west railway links, which arrived in 1887, were a vital part of this commercial success, but they had also given Lower Sheringham a vital new industry, for by 1892 it was already "much frequented as a seaside resort". By 1904 Kelly's had added, "and on account of the increasing number of visitors a large number of private lodging houses have been erected, a fine hotel has opened between the railway station and the golf links and another on the sea front." Its new church of 1897 was still a chapel of ease to the ancient parish church up in the old village, but it had nevertheless captured the incumbent, who lived in the new vicarage.

In 1901 the resort had been established by Local Government Order as "Sheringham", a new civil parish and Urban District "out of parts of the parishes of Beeston Regis and Sheringham, the remainder of the ancient civil parish of Sheringham being constituted the civil parish of Upper Sheringham".

Annie Thirtle, writing in *Memories of Old Sheringham* recalls what the town was like in the early 20th century:

Sheringham station and goods yard in its heyday, when trains ran through from the East Midlands.
Peter Brooks collection.

opposite: Sheringham beach.
Anne Roberts.

Sheringham clock tower was built as a reservoir; it had a horse trough on one wall and a tap on another—one of just two public sources of water in the town for anyone who did not have their own well.

Peter Brooks collection.

There were no Avenues or Priory Road. They were all fields. The main Cromer Road was called Top Road, which we used to cross, to Common Lane, which was nothing more than a cart rut... The Co-op Street was called the Piggery, which led to the High Street, where there were mostly small cottages, except for a few little shops such as butchers, bakers, etc., and greengrocery barrows lining the street... Most of the cottages were owned by the fishermen and were usually built from the stones from the beach. The houses all had names instead of numbers. The fishermen also owned beach chairs, which they let in the summer season...[3]

All the boarding houses looked spick and span. The occupants used to employ all the local young girls for the summer season, and didn't they work hard! All the front of the house had to be cleaned up before breakfast, steps scrubbed and brass knockers cleaned. They looked a picture. The fishermen's wives also took in visitors. Nearly all the cottages had 'Apartments' cards hung in their windows. The cottages were painted and decorated every year.

Vaughan Williams' intended course of action when he got off the train is unknown, but it may well have been simply—go in and ask. His second stop, the *Crown Inn*, might therefore have been selected as a good place to start. He began, however, no further from the station than the level crossing immediately outside.

Mr. B Jackson

It would be interesting to know exactly how Vaughan Williams came across Robert, or Bob, Jackson "at the level crossing", where he was the gatekeeper.[4] The crossing over busy Station Road lies between the old station, at which Vaughan Williams would have arrived and which is now the terminus of the North Norfolk Railway's heritage line to Holt, and the present post-Beeching railway station, built on the Cromer side of the road when the line west of Sheringham was closed in the 1960s. At the time the level crossing was closed but was restored in recent years for occasional access for visiting steam engines from the main passenger system over to the North Norfolk Railway.

Robert Jackson, born at Edgefield,[5] was the son of a shepherd. Information about him from the census returns has been admirably fleshed out by Adrian Vaughan's article on the early days of Sheringham Station in *Joint Line*, the in-house magazine

The fish buyer (in the bowler hat) makes his purchases. The photo is dated about 1895.
Bennett Middleton.

of the North Norfolk Railway This relates that "He was born in 1859 and at the age of eleven, whilst working for his living on a farm, his right arm had been pulled out of its socket by a hay-cutting machine. He then became a cattle drover and worked at that for ten years."

By the date of the accident his father, Samuel Jackson, had taken on *The White Horse* in Ramsgate, Edgefield, where young Robert lived with his parents and four sisters; interestingly they had a lodger who was also a drover. In 1881 he was lodging, along with a railway navvy, with the Blogg[6] family at nearby Hunworth as "Night-watch on railway" above which the enumerator squeezed in "now in course of construction". He had joined the Lynn and Fakenham Railway (forerunner to the Eastern and Midland Railway, later the Midland and Great Northern) in 1880 as a night watchman at Melton Constable.[7]

The Bloggs lived on The Green, a few doors away from a widowed agricultural labourer called Bayfield and over the next few years Robert married Bayfield's daughter Sarah. In time he moved to South Lynn as nightwatchman, then to Holt, from which the line was being continued to Cromer. In 1887 he became gate keeper on the railway at Sheringham, where in 1893 he was earning 15 shillings a week. By 1901 he, Sarah and four of their children were living at California House, Brick Kiln Lane, off the Cromer Road. In the 1911 census however this long-serving railway employee, still only in his 50s, was now listed as a "vermin destroyer". Dave King of the North Norfolk Railway provided the following explanation for what appeared at first sight to be a curious change of employment: "The meeting with Ralph Vaughan Williams was just before the next section of railway opened—the Norfolk & Suffolk Joint—giving access to Sheringham for the Great Eastern Railway and making the place much busier. This meant that a new signal box was constructed (Sheringham East) to control the eastern side of the station and the level crossing. As Robert was only a crossing keeper he probably couldn't qualify as a signalman with only one arm, so I presume that the commissioning of the East box in 1906/7 meant another change of job. I can see no reason why Robert would not continue working for the M&GN as 'vermin catcher' until retirement, but cannot confirm this."[8]

Mr Jackson sang:

Come Nancy Will You Marry Me?

Come Nancy Will You Marry Me

Bob Jackson at Sheringham level crossing January 12th 1905

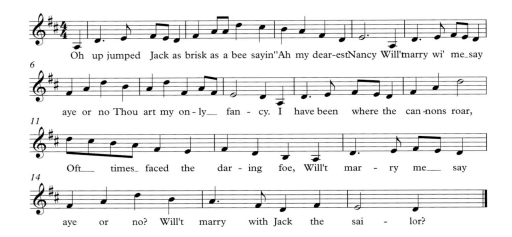

Come Nancy Will You Marry Me?

It was down in yon green valley in the pleasant month of June
The birds were sweetly singing, all nature was in tune,
It was there I first saw Nancy, she's the girl I did adore,
For she was my only fancy and I could love no more.

I said, 'My dearest Nancy, would you be kind and marry me?
I have not stores of riches, but I have stores of love for thee,
There's richer men than I am, but none could love you more,
And if I had gold like mountains it would be yours also.'

'For to have you in my prime, then it would be a pretty thing.
For I have the conceit, love, that I can dance and sing,
I am for some rich gentleman, I have you to be gone,
For your riches will not last me and your love will soon cool down.'

'Oh must I go in sorrow, and must I take my leave,
Must I lament for Nancy who for me does not grieve?
For I am broken hearted it's plainly to be seen
Oh must I go in sorrow and wear the willow green?'

It was but a few months after this fair one changed her mind
She wrote to me a letter thinking I would prove kind.
That what she had said to me she was sorry for and she hoped I
would forgive
And would grant to her one favour her heart and hand receive.

I wrote to her an answer, and somewhat scornfully
I said, 'My dearest Nancy, it's for you I do not grieve,
For there is another more suiting that has taken up your place
I like you to know I can dance and sing as I never had seen your face.'

Come all you wild young females a warning by me to see,
Never slight your own true love while he is kind and free,
For riches will not last you, and beauty will decay,
And when you slight your own true love, his love will fade away.

Vaughan Williams did not note the words to this song and his notebook has it as 'Unknown name', although he indexes it as *Come Nancy Will You Marry Me*. There is no obvious set of words in other collections or broadsides. These verses are from Creighton and Senior collected from John Roast of Chessetcook in America. There seems to be very little information about the song, and this set of words from across the Atlantic seems to be the only source.

Another possibility is that it is a version of the *Tarry Sailor*, which Vaughan Williams collected from Sally Brown at Ranworth in the Norfolk Broads when he returned to Norfolk in 1910.

So late it was one Saturday night
On the quay side I was a walking;
There I beheld a pretty maid,
To her father she was a talking.
She said, 'My true love's come on shore
It's the only lad I do adore.'
Your folly now you must give o'er
Will you wed with a tarry sailor?

'Oh father dear, do not us part
Or strive to separate us;
For if you do it will break my heart
Great grief it will create us.
His love to me is most sincere
And mine to him shall firm endure;
Betide me life or death, I'm sure
I'll wed no other sailor.'

Up comes Jack brisk as a bee
Saying, 'My dearest Nancy,
Now I am safe returned to thee
My heart's delight and fancy.
I've been where stormy winds do blow
And oft have faced my deadly foe
Say, will you have me, aye or no,
And wed poor Jack the sailor?'

'Two hundred pounds left by her aunt
Three hundred more I'd give her;
But if she marry without my consent
A farthing I won't leave her.
Besides to marry she's too young
And sailors have a flattering tongue,
So from my presence quick begone
If you wed that tarry sailor.'

Says Jack, 'I don't regard that sum
My dear, I've gold in plenty
Believe me sir, I do not come

To court with pockets empty.'
Five hundred guineas in bright gold
Upon the table there he told
And swept them in her apron fold:
'Take that, and Jack your sailor.'

Her father seeing his heart
That he behaved so clever,
Said, 'Tis a pity you to part
And I'll not do it ever.
As you so freely give your store
And you each other do adore
Now take her Jack, here's as much more,
For you are a clever sailor.'

Now messmates we've got safe to port
For I am sweetly married
I hope my lads we'll have some sport
And crown the day with claret.
My frigate she is rigged tight
With silks and rings so gay and bright;
I swear my lads to board tonight
And prove myself a sailor.'

This version is from Roy Palmer's *Folk Songs Collected by Ralph Vaughan Williams*, in which he has supplemented the fragmentary words sung by Sally Brown with words from a Kendrew of York broadside. The tunes have some similarities, but neither is a perfect fit for the note taken from Mr Jackson. However, it seems more likely that he would pick up a song with currency among wherrymen on the inland waterways than one from across the Atlantic. Other singers seem to have remembered this song starting with verse 3, which includes the proposal, rather than the two verses of

Three generations of the Emery family. Left to right—Robert, Reg, Harold, Sidney, Jimmy Lewis and Chris.

Emery collection.

preamble. Perhaps they preferred to cut to the chase of this story.

There is a possibility that Mr Jackson had simply picked up on a different ballad and the 'Come Marry Me' phrase was the one which stuck in his mind. The titles noted by Vaughan Williams in Norfolk sometimes differ from those chosen by the broadside writers or other singers.

Mr. Emery

After hearing Bob Jackson sing, Vaughan Williams proceeded to the *Crown Inn*, where he met Robert Emery, presumably by chance, although as boatbuilders favoured by fishermen round the north coast, the Emerys may have been known by someone in the Lynn fishing community. This inn was rebuilt in 1935, so the *Crown* still on the front at Sheringham is not the building Vaughan Williams saw, which itself was an early 19th century rebuild after the original fell into the sea in 1800.[9] Nevertheless it still occupies the original spot, only a few yards across Lifeboat Plain from a building still recognisable as the workshop[10] where the Emery boat-building business was based. That relationship helps confirm that "Emery" is the more likely reading of the name in the composer's notebook which has often been read as "Enery".[11]

There are several descendants of Benjamin Emery, a carrier on the road to Norwich, and his wife Sarah, born respectively at East Beckham and Beeston Regis, both very close to Sheringham. Their sons, Lewis, who died at Erpingham in 1902 and his brother George[12] were born c1818 and c1820. By 1851 Lewis was a master

carpenter, employing one man and living with his first wife Sarah at The Street, perhaps the later High Street, in Sheringham lower part.

Lewis was known as "Buffalo" Emery, because he was very strong. His great great grandson Mike Emery says he was reputed to have carried a deep-sea ship's carpenter's heavy metal vice up the beach on his back. "I doubt it because they weighed half a ton," he said. "I think it was one of those tales." Buffalo's skill as a boatbuilder was no tale, however. He established the business in 1850, which ran to four generations before it finally closed in 1981. The family was proud of being chosen to build Sheringham's sailing and pulling lifeboat, the *Henry Ramey Upcher*.[13]

In a 1953 BBC programme, *Down to the Sea*,[14] Reg Emery, said:

My family has been building boats for the local fishermen for more than a hundred years and we're still doing so today. About 1870 my grandfather Lewis Emery, had his four sons, James, Robert, Ben and John working with him… Now the shape and construction of these boats hasn't altered at all in living memory, and there is no reason why they should for they are perfectly suited for this part of the coast. They are double ended, that is pointed at both stem and stern, and are quite open, having no deck of any sort. I have recently built them up to 30 feet for the whelk fishing at Wells and Brancaster, but the Cromer and Sheringham men want them about 19 feet. They have a width of about seven feet and a depth of just three feet, so they are quite beamy boats, and need to be for safety when handling pots in anything of a sea.

At Sheringham we are very proud of the fact that every boat is handmade, the only machinery we use being an electric drill. The keel, deadwood, stem and stern posts come out of best English oak, are cut with an ordinary handsaw and shaped with an adze. There are eleven planks on either side made from oak and English larch, half an inch thick. Inside there are 36 timbers, or ribs, also of oak, which are steamed to shape, and fitted after the hull has been planked up. This is done clinker fashion. We don't use any moulds at all. We do everything by eye and careful measurement.[15]

The last boat was built in 1957, the year Reg Emery died, after which the firm worked on repairs only.[16]

Lewis' brother George was a fisherman, still at home in 1851 with his parents and younger siblings at East Beckham. By 1861 he too was in Lower Sheringham: he was married and keeping the *Windham Arms*. By 1871 he had moved on to *The Lobster* on the corner of Bridge Street and High Street[17] but the 1881 census recorded him as just a fisherman once more, living in Mill Road with his wife Maria.

By 1891 he appears to have given up fishing and become a carpenter, perhaps in association with Lewis Emery's boat-building business, which had become a family concern. Lewis' first wife had died by 1861 and he had married Ann West, herself from a Sheringham fishing family. By 1881 his sons James and 16-year-old Robert were styled carpenter and assistant carpenter respectively and presumably working with their father.

By 1901 Lewis himself was "formerly carpenter and boat builder" and in 1902 he died. By then George was a widower, living at Hill View, Cromer Road, and working, at the age of 80, as a gardener. The 1900 Kelly's notes "George Emery, Apartments, Hill View, Cromer Road." In view of his age and background, however, it is possible that his son George, born in 1848 and a saddler, living in Great Yarmouth, might also have been involved in the owning and letting of these apartments. It is tempting even to see a mutually convenient arrangement which also provided serviced accommodation for his octogenarian and widowed father. At the date of the census the other residents were apparently single working men rather than holiday visitors.

Lewis' business was now still flourishing in the hands of his son Robert. James had been called a boat builder in 1891, and

Sheringham lifeboat Henry Ramey Upcher launching under sail. Poppyland photos.

carpenter in 1901 and 1911. He was not working for himself, so although the elder brother, he clearly had not inherited the business, but Mike says he 'lent a hand' when needed. In 1911 his home was Rivulet House in Mill Lane, which had been Lewis' and Ann's home also. Ann, who had been twenty years younger than Lewis, still owned the house; she had been offering "Apartments" there as early as 1908.

It was James' younger brother Robert, a carpenter in 1891, who was styled boat-builder in 1901 and 1911 and succeeded their father as head of the firm. In the latter year his own son Robert was also so described, and their address was Life Boat Plain. In 1915 one of the two built the *Q J & J* for John James Davies, the stepfather of the famous Cromer lifeboatman Henry Blogg.[18] The firm is very much a part of Sheringham history and a mural showing the Emery boatbuilders appears on the promenade seawall.

Of the Emery men it was Robert senior whom Vaughan Williams met in the *Crown* in January 1905. His great grandson Mike Emery says Robert was known as quite a character, and a teller of yarns:

Well, I know that he liked to have a drink, that's for sure, and I think it was almost the ruination of the business in a way. They got through it, but he spent quite a bit of money in the pub. And once in the pub, he liked to burst into song, and jump on the table and sing the song and he liked to be the centre of attention.

The *Crown* is just across Lifeboat Plain from the Emerys' workshop[19], and Robert's favourite song was *Kelly from the Isle of Man*[20], which did not make an appearance until 1908. But in 1905 he did sing one song which the composer noted.

Mr Emery sang:

Near Scarborough Town

Robert 'Cally' Emery.
Emery collection.

Near Scarborough Town

Mr Emery at the Crown Inn Sheringham Jan 12th 1905

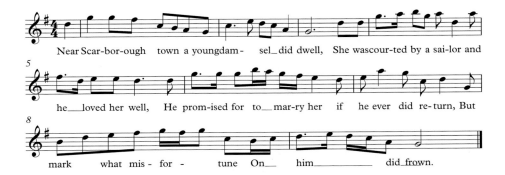

Near Scar-bor-ough town a young dam - sel_ did dwell, She was cour-ted by a sai-lor and

he_ loved her well, He prom-ised for to_ mar-ry her if he ever did re-turn, But

mark what mis - for - tune On_ him_ did_ frown.

Near Scarborough Town

In Scarborough Town a young damsel did dwell
She was courted by a sailor and he loved her well.
And he promised for to marry her if he ever did return
But mark what misfortune all on him did frown.

As they were a-sailing to their great surprise
A storm from the east began for to rise
Twenty-five of them they took to their boat
And short of provisions, they all went afloat.

It fell to her love's lot for him to be one
And he lost his dear life in the watery pond
The wind it blew high and the billows did roar,
Which tossed this young sailor all on the sea shore.

And when this sad news his true lover did hear
She was wringing her hands and tearing her hair
Crying, 'Oh you cruel waves toss my true love on shore
That I might behold his sweet features once more.'

As she was a walking along the sea strand
She saw a drowned sailor lie dead on the ground
And when she came near to him it put her to a stand
For she knew 'twas her true love by a mark on his hand.

She kissed him, she hugged him, she called him her dear
Ten thousand times over she kissed him there
Saying, 'I'm very well contented, love, to lie by your side.'
And a few moments after, this young damsel died.

In Robin Hood's churchyard this young couple were laid
And for a remembrance a stone at their head
Saying, 'All you constant lovers that here do pass by
See this unfortunate couple how happy they lie.'

Mains'l Haul, now known as Martin's Cross. Vaughan Williams, his wife Adeline and her brother Hervey lived there in 1921, one of six addresses they had in Sheringham over the course of two years 1919-1921.

Colin James.

No words were noted with this song. George Gardiner collected it from William Bone in Hampshire in 1907 but he didn't supply all the words. Frank Kidson and Lucy Broadwood noted in the *Folk Song Journal* no 13 that the song tells a true story of a young girl who lived in Stowbrow near Whitby. Mr Bone, like Mr Emery in Norfolk, had the story taking place near Scarborough.

Mr Emery's song is interesting for its strong Yorkshire base, with frequent references in its scenario to Robin Hood's Bay and nearby Stoupe (Stow) Brow. Although walkers on the coastal Cleveland Way might query its proximity "near to Scarborough Bay", Bay Town's position, as seen from a boat well out to sea, would probably be gauged from the most obviously visible landmarks either side of it: Whitby Abbey to the north and Scarborough Castle on its headland much further to the south.

The song was also collected by George Butterworth, but he gives no indication of the singer or where it was collected. It is listed next to his collecting in Winterton and Ormesby in March 1913.

Before Vaughan Williams returned from the First World War, Adeline Vaughan Williams took rooms in Sheringham, hoping the climate of the East Coast might be good for her invalid brother, Hervey, who was diagnosed with tuberculosis and fragile mental health. She had looked after him since her mother had died in a road accident during the war. 'So it was in rooms at the

seaside that Ralph settled down to revising the *London Symphony* and *Hugh the Drover* and there that he started to shape the quiet contours of the *Pastoral Symphony*,' according to Ursula Vaughan Williams in her biography of RVW.[21]

But interestingly, he does not appear to have collected any more songs there, even though in his travels he was usually on the lookout for a song, and the Emery family were still living and working as boatbuilders in the town. Maybe the impact of his war service and the loss of his fellow collector and friend George Butterworth, who died at the Somme, had disheartened him. A spell with Adeline at Sheringham before he went back to the Royal College of Music might well have been a welcome respite, although his London friends and associates were pressing him to return.

His letters show they moved around in the town. He wrote from Northern Lights, Sheringham in August and November 1919,[22] so this might well be where Adeline and Hervey had taken rooms in 1917.[23] On Christmas Day 1919 he was at The Sun-Dial (note new address, he adds) in Curtis Lane;[24] in March 1920 he is there but by April 1921 he writes to his cousin Randolph from Mainsail Haul[25] in St Nicholas' Place with yet another move in prospect:

> Adeline went out this morning & interviewed the nice landlady she knows of—she has not got her *best* rooms vacant—they are all quite nice—but this sitting room and bed room face *north* (N.B. seawards here) & there is also a bed room on the top floor which faces south. Adeline is writing all this to Iris.
>
> The address is
> Mrs Jenkinson
> The Little House,
> South Street,
> Sheringham.
> … We have just moved into a new furnished house with the above appalling name.'[26]

In August 1921 he writes from yet another address, Taormina,[27] which he says is in Augusta Street, but was later listed as in St

Nicholas' Place, near Martin's Cross. Later that year he also writes from Clover Lawn in South Street.[28] The three addresses are close to each other and are substantial Edwardian houses. We are indebted to researcher Lesley Lougher and Cynthia, who now live in South Street, for identifying these houses and so giving us a flavour of the style in which the Vaughan Williamses lived in Sheringham. Mike Emery remembered the houses were on his paper round as a 13-year-old, but over the years the names of the houses have changed or been replaced by numbers.

In her biography of Ralph, Ursula Vaughan Williams says there is little information about their time in Sheringham. 'One tiny glimpse of the life at Sheringham remains, for Veronica, daughter of Iris and Ralph Wedgwood (the Randolph of Ralph's Cambridge days), was sent to convalesce there after some childish illness. She went to tea with Ralph and Adeline several times, and she remembers how, the night before she was to go home to her parents, Ralph, realising he had not said goodbye, came round to see her. He persuaded her nurse to let her get up, for it was long past an eight-year-old's bed-time in those stricter days, and paid a formal and affectionate farewell call which she much enjoyed.'[29]

When Ralph and Adeline returned to London later, he took up a post at the Royal College of Music. Among his early pupils was Patrick Hadley, who later came to live at Heacham near King's Lynn. It was through him that Vaughan Williams came to the second King's Lynn festival in 1952 and gave his lecture on collecting folk songs in East Anglia.

Looking west from Lifeboat Plain, late 19th century. The large number of boats on the beach indicates how many families depended on fishing.
Peter Brooks collection.

Notes

1 Information of the development of Sheringham from Kelly's Norfolk Directories of appropriate dates.

2 Mrs Kate Lee: "Some Experiences of a Folk-Song Collector" jfss/1899/1/9.

3 Sheringham History Group (2003) *Memories of Old Sheringham*. Sheringham, pp.1-3.

4 Vaughan Williams calls him Mr B Jackson and the MGN records refer to him as Bob. The census naturally calls him Robert.

5 A village near Sheringham.

6 Apparently no relation to the famous lifeboatman Henry Blogg of Cromer.

7 Hunworth was stated by Kelly's in 1883 to be "4 miles NE of Holt Station".

8 Email from Dave King to Alan Helsdon, 16 March 2014.

9 Sheringham Museum Trust. (1996) *Sheringham and District*. Stroud: Sutton.

10 Now a holiday cottage.

11 No-one by the name of Enery has been recorded in Norfolk.

12 Died at Erpingham in 1908.

13 The *Henry Ramey Upcher* is now in Sheringham's museum, The Mo.

14 Produced by Roy Clarke.

15 Childs A. and Simpson A. (2004) '*Time and Tide*'. Norwich: Mousehold Press, pp.18-19.

16 Weatherhead F. (1981) *North Norfolk Fishermen*. Stroud: History Press, p.36.

17 parts of this still exist: "*Some of the hay lofts and six original stables, complete with stalls and tack-hooks, survive. They were still in use by Gerald Pegg as a riding school and livery stable in the 1930s.*" Sheringham Museum Trust. (1996) *Sheringham and District*. Stroud: Sutton.

18 *Eastern Daily Press*, 8 February 2014. Mike Emery said the family was related to the Bloggs through his mother's family.

19 The old workshop is still there, called The Boat House. The Sheringham Society has put a blue plaque on it marking the long association with the Emerys.

20 The song was composed in 1908 for music hall singer Florrie Forde, three years later than Vaughan Williams' visit to Sheringham.

21 Vaughan Williams U. (1964) *RVW A Biography of Ralph Vaughan Williams*. London: OUP, p.134.

22 Letters VWL 452, 358, 453,454, and 456. We have been unable to identify where this house was.

23 According to Keith Alldritt's 2015 biography of Vaughan Williams, he returned home from the war to find their London house shut as Adeline had moved to Sheringham.

24 VWL 457, 486,460, 462, 461. The house, designed by arts and crafts architect John Sydney Brocklesby is still there. It is just behind where Mike Emery now lives in Hill View.

25 Now called Martin's Cross. It's thought this is where he revised his Sea Symphony. VWL 473.

26 Cobbe H. (ed) (2008) *Letters of Ralph Vaughan Williams*. London: OUP, pp.124-128. The Little House is No 16 South Street. In 1918 it is listed with Armine and Arthur Jenkinson living there.

27 The house was owned in 1931 by George Grant Lockhart Ross of Hanover Square in London, who also owned Cranmer Hall at Sculthorpe, near Fakenham.

28 VWL 4091 and Adeline's letter VWL 475. The house is still there on the corner of South Street and Montague Street.

29 Ibid 21, p.135.

Opposite: Fishermen at Sheringham,
early 20th century,
Poppyland photos.

The Legacy of his Visit

"These songs will stand the supreme test of time and their eternal beauty will not fade....
These songs are the whole edifice on which a great art can be built."
RVW lecture on folk songs at King's Lynn Festival 1952

However enthusiastic he was about collecting in those early years, Vaughan Williams remained first and foremost a composer. Maybe that is why the biographical details of singers and words to these tunes are thin on the ground in his notebooks. His central purpose was to search out the English voice, the melody and beautiful modal character of the songs and the "old ballads". No wonder he said the King's Lynn tunes were "a rich harvest" when so many were in modes.[1] He was already keen on the modal sound. In his talk in 1957 on Parry and Stanford he recalled Stanford setting his pupils an exercise in the 1890s writing masses and motets in strict modal counterpoint.

> I was let off this discipline because Stanford found that I was too far gone in the modes already. Also, he found in my work too much seriousness and even stodginess; so he decided that I must write a waltz. True to my creed I showed him a modal waltz![2]

He is sometimes accused of taking too little note of the words of the songs and taking too little interest in the singers. It is perfectly possible that the singers, many of them elderly, could not recall all the words of songs, but often he notes a snatch of the words which can direct us to other collections or to broadside versions. When the song was completely new to him, he noted all the words the singer could offer, as he did with *The Captain's Apprentice*.

Vaughan Williams was busy composing at the time of his visit. He had also been asked by Percy Dearmer to be the musical editor of the *English Hymnal*. In the same year as he sat in the workhouse in King's Lynn hearing old songs, he was looking for good melodies to include in the hymnal. In 1904 he was also involved in the start of the Leith Hill Music Festival being organised by his sister Meggie, Lady Evangeline Farrer and Lucy Broadwood. He was the musical director and the festival involved amateur choirs from all over the area. Vaughan Williams would write arrangements for them and conduct, all part of his conviction that musicians should share their music with their fellows.[3]

Can the songs be heard in his music?

There's no doubt that the West Norfolk visit gave Vaughan Williams some of the tunes to which he returned time and again. *The Captain's Apprentice*, collected from James 'Duggie' Carter, is described by Michael Kennedy, Vaughan Williams' musical biographer, as one of the most beautiful English folk songs.[4] *Along with Bushes and Briars*, from Essex, and *Dives and Lazarus*, they remained influential for the rest of Ralph Vaughan Williams' life.

The impact of the songs he heard in that week was immediate. He decided to write a *Norfolk Symphony*, to rhapsodise them. Within two weeks of returning from Norfolk, he and Adeline were with Lucy Broadwood, who recorded in her diary on 25 Jan 1905:

> Barbara and I had tea with the Vaughan Williams and he played Norfolk fishermen's tunes and Sussex tunes to us—he is writing a rhapsody on folk tunes of his collecting.

opposite: Fishing trawler today on King's Lynn South Quay.
Anne Roberts.

In his book *National Music*[5] he writes of those early years of collecting, "We knew somehow that when we first heard *Dives and Lazarus* or *Bushes and Briars* that this was just what we were looking for. Well, we were dazzled, we wanted to preach a new gospel, we wanted to rhapsodise on these tunes just as Liszt and Grieg had done. We did not suppose that by so doing we were inventing a national music ready-made—we simply were fascinated by the tunes and wanted other people to be fascinated too…"

The Norfolk Rhapsodies

Michael Kennedy writes that this is the period when the mature Vaughan Williams emerged.[6]

> He wrote the three Norfolk Rhapsodies… The Rhapsodies, light weight works, were favourably received by the majority of critics and also by the public, for the newspapers were nearly always able to report that the composer was 'loudly cheered'. *The Times*, after the first performance of the first rhapsody at the promenade concerts of 1906, described it as a 'very taking and charming orchestral piece'. By treating folk tunes, the critic thought, the composer had 'shirked a great part, perhaps the greatest part, of the composer's responsibility. It is at any rate the part in which very many modern composers fail, the originating of new and beautiful themes.' But the piece as a whole is quite his own… the result sounds like a piece of music and not a patchwork. It is unnecessary to remark on the dainty colours of the score, an art which is nowadays almost common property, but the first section, in which various instruments, like people sitting round and suggesting what song shall be sung, in turn suggests fragments of tunes used, is particularly happy.'[7]

The *Norfolk Rhapsodies No. 2* and *3* were first performed at the Cardiff Festival in 1907. The *Times* correspondent says the seven folk tunes "of the utmost distinction and vigour" were used. He found that *Ward the Pirate* was the most splendid: "All are scored with remarkable skill, and the thematic development is ingenious and often most humorous. The last piece of the set is a most inspiring march and both, played under the composer's direction, fairly brought down the house."[8]

The second and third rhapsodies were withdrawn by Vaughan Williams within a few years and were not performed after 1914. They were not published. RVW revised the first and although Kennedy says that the songs RVW collected in Norfolk were better restored to future generations through his arrangements of them some years later, in fact the *Norfolk Rhapsody No. 1* has remained in the repertoire of many orchestras ever since. The score of *No. 2* was still extant and was eventually edited by Stephen Hogger and published by Oxford University Press under the auspices of the Vaughan Williams Memorial Trust in 2018. Two missing pages were reconstructed by Stephen Hogger and the work was recorded by the London Symphony Orchestra conducted by the late Richard Hickox in 2002. It was the first time it had been heard since before the Great War. But the third rhapsody is sadly quite lost. We only have the programme notes from that Cardiff festival to tell us about it. However, in 2018 David Matthews used those notes as the framework of a piece entitled *Norfolk March*.

As these three rhapsodies were Vaughan Williams' immediate reaction to his week in King's Lynn, it is worth looking at them in detail. The songs quoted in the rhapsodies are in No.1, *The Captain's Apprentice* (collected from Duggie Carter); the *Basket of Eggs* (Anderson); *A Bold Young Sailor He Courted Me* (Anderson), *Ward the Pirate* (Carter) and *On Board a '98* (Leatherday).

This is the analytical programme note written by W.A. Morgan at the time of the first performance after quoting the songs which were used:

> The composition opens with an introductory Adagio founded on the rhythm of the tune *The Basket of Eggs*. At the sixteenth bar the solo viola introduces the melody *The Captain's Apprentice* (freely, as if improvising), lightly accompanied. Presently the original rhythm appears

in the horns, which later take up the tune of *The Captain's Apprentice*. The tempo soon quickens, and the flutes in thirds have the theme of the *Basket of Eggs*. The next song to be introduced is *A Bold Young Sailor He Courted Me*, which is given to the *cor anglais*, accompanied by the harp. After it has been handed on to other wind instruments it finally makes its entrance on the strings. In this way we arrive at a climax, which ends in a glorified version of the second tune. Fragments of this are now treated in various ways until the time changes to allegro. We are now concerned with the first tune. When it appears in the oboe, it is accompanied by embroideries in the strings and the woodwind, which are an anticipation of the fifth tune.

Presently, while these persist, the trumpets and trombones announce a version of part of the fourth tune, *Ward the Pirate*, in augmentation; and this is succeeded by the fifth and last melody, *On board a '98* first heard on the strings. Eventually the whole orchestra joins in its treatment, and an augmented version of the third tune enters in the strings, horns and trumpets, while the woodwind and glockenspiel give out the fifth. Its course is interrupted from time to time by suggestions of the fourth tune, which first appears on the trombones. Ultimately this is heard on the brass *brillante e marcato*, accompanied by fragments of the fifth tune. This marks the beginning of the coda, which is mainly evolved from the second bar of the opening melody, and ends brilliantly.

But that is not the *Norfolk Rhapsody No. 1* we hear today. Vaughan Williams revised it and honed it, so by 1914, when it was performed at Bournemouth, it had changed. Vaughan Williams had been to study orchestration with Ravel in Paris and learned a lighter touch with the orchestra. So when the Rhapsody No 1 re-appeared, according to Michael Kennedy, "the flutes have the

rhythm of the *Basket of Eggs*, but it is of *The Captain's Apprentice* that the clarinet hints. *Ward the Pirate* has disappeared, and the whole of the coda has been rewritten. There is no glockenspiel, and the 'brilliant ending' is now a slow fade out by way of a return to the opening landscape. The noble and tragic beauty of *The Captain's Apprentice* permeates the entire work."

Writing in 1950, Hubert Foss looked back at this rhapsody in his study of Vaughan Williams: "Though in a sense the *First Norfolk Rhapsody* might be called landscape painting, it is a deeply considered work. If the grand orchestral clothes sit a little 'beginnerly' on the simple tunes, those tunes are allowed to walk their own way freely. The sum total is a moving piece of music which inspires and retains affection as well as admiration."[9] The final version of the *Norfolk Rhapsody No. 1* was published in 1925 by Oxford University Press.

The *Norfolk Rhapsody No. 2* in D Minor also appeared in 1906 and was first performed at the Cardiff Festival, Park Hall, Cardiff on 27 September, along with the Rhapsody No. 3 in G Minor and Major. For *No. 2* Vaughan Williams used *Young Henry the Poacher* sung to him by Mr Anderson; *Spurn Point*, collected from Mr Leatherday at King's Lynn Union on 9 January 1905 and *The Saucy Bold Robber*, which was collected from Mr Anderson and Mr Elmer at the Union.

Vaughan Williams conducted the first performance. Once again, the programme notes were written by W.A. Morgan:

It opens with three bars of introduction larghetto, when the tune of *Young Henry the Poacher* is heard by the wood wind played *andante sostenuto*; the last two phrases being repeated by the strings as a refrain. The tune is then heard in varied form by the violoncellos and violas in a figure… (quotes the figure)… suggested by the tune itself. The tune does not at present reach its cadence, but is developed in animated tempo until the climax, when the premonition of the second subject is heard, first by the strings, then by the horns and finally by the oboe. The second tune *All on Spurn Point* now appears in its complete form, being played by the solo horn, after which it is repeated by a combination of instruments, and an extended cadence leads to the third tune, the *Saucy Bold Robber*. This latter tune forms the basis of a short scherzo, which is first given in sparkling style by the piccolo and oboe, and afterwards by the full complement of woodwind, with an accompanying figure on the strings derived from the last bar of the tune. After a suggestion of canon, the *scherzo* gradually dies away, and gives place to a version of *Young Henry the Poacher*, accompanied *tremolando* on the violas, but is interrupted from time to time by the figure given in the example above. The movement ends *pianissimo* with a reference to *Spurn Point*.

The programme notes that the work was written in 1906. The notes are quoted in full because both works can still be heard. The first rhapsody is a firm favourite with orchestras and audiences.

Alas, we only know about the third rhapsody from Mr Morgan's programme notes. The music has vanished. Vaughan Williams used *The Lincolnshire Farmer* collected from Mr Whitby at Tilney All Saints on 8 January 1905; *John Raeburn* collected from Mr Crisp and Mr Donger in King's Lynn on 13 and 14 January; *Ward the Pirate*, collected from Mr Carter in the North End on 9 January and *The Red Barn* collected from Mr Whitby on 8 January.

Vaughan Williams' original intention of making them into a *Norfolk Symphony* was never realised. His musical life was moving on and, in particular, the work on the *English Hymnal* was taking up much of his time.

The English Hymnal

In 1904 the Revd Percy Dearmer appeared at the Vaughan Williams' home in Barton Street and asked him to edit the *English Hymnal*. Vaughan Williams said he had no experience of hymn books, but Dearmer said he'd been recommended by Cecil Sharp and Canon Scott Holland, and

also hinted that if he refused, the next to be offered the job would be H. Walford Davies, a musician with whose ideas, according to James Day, Vaughan Williams emphatically disagreed.[10] Dearmer said it would take a couple of months and about £5 in expenses. In the event it took two years and cost Vaughan Williams £250 (a considerable sum in 1904) of his own money. But it gave him the chance to use some of the tunes he had been collecting, among them Mr Anderson's *Young Henry the Poacher*, which became the tune for *O God of Earth and Altar*. Vaughan Williams gave the tune the title *King's Lynn*. He wrote some tunes himself, and already there's a sense of these Norfolk tunes getting into his musical bloodstream. On the *English Hymnal*'s 50th anniversary he was quite clear why he had used folk tunes for some of the hymns. 'Why should we not enter into our inheritance in the church as well as the concert hall?'[11]

Arrangements of Folk Songs

In 1908 he published *Folk Songs from the Eastern Counties*, which was edited by Cecil Sharp. From Norfolk all the songs included are from King's Lynn:

On Board a '98 (Leatherday)
The Captain's Apprentice (Carter)
Ward the Pirate (Carter)
The Saucy Bold Robber (Anderson)
The Bold Princess Royal (Smith or Anderson)
The Lincolnshire Farmer (Whitby)
The Sheffield Apprentice (Anderson or Mrs Howard)

He returned to *Ward the Pirate* again in 1912 and arranged it for mixed chorus and a small orchestra, but the work was unpublished. Mr Harper's *Just as the Tide was a Flowing* was arranged for unaccompanied chorus the following year as one of *Five English Folk Songs*. He came back to the song as a unison arrangement with piano accompaniment which was published in 1919 as part of the *Motherland Song Book Vol IV*. *Spanish Ladies*, sung to him by four singers, appears in the same volume. The first volume of the *Motherland Song Book* included the hymn *Oh God of Earth and Altar*, set to the tune of *Young Henry the Poacher*. The hymn appears again in the *League of Nations Song Book*, published in 1921 and edited by Percy Dearmer, who'd originally persuaded Vaughan Williams to be the musical editor of the *English Hymnal*. Clearly the hymn and its tune had made an impression.

In 1926 he wrote *Six Studies in English Folk Song*. Michael Kennedy wrote, "These studies are not exact transcriptions of identifiable folk songs; nevertheless, the origins of the studies are identifiable."[12] He discerns *Spurn Point*, sung by Mr Leatherday at King's Lynn Union, and *Van Diemen's Land*, sung by Mr Donger in the North End, as two of the songs he used. The third was 'Lovely on the Water', collected in South Walsham during a later expedition to the Norfolk Broads.

Even though Vaughan Williams was concentrating more on operatic and orchestral works through the 1920s and 30s, the King's Lynn songs were still part of his work. The Norfolk version of the *Bold Princess Royal* and *Ward the Pirate* are included in a volume of *Folk Songs Volume II*, a selection of 33 less-known folk songs arranged by Cecil Sharp, Vaughan Williams and others, published in 1935.

Mr Harper's *Oxford City*, a tune closely related to Vaughan Williams' favourite *The Captain's Apprentice*, made it into the *Penguin Book of English Folk Songs* written with A.L. Lloyd in 1958 but published in 1959, the year after Vaughan Williams' death. For the modern singer, perhaps, its words were less savage than those of Mr Carter's song. *Ratcliffe Highway*, sung to Vaughan Williams in 1905 by Mrs Betty Howard in the North End, is also in the book.

Symphonies

As we have seen, Ralph Vaughan Williams' first intention after his return from King's Lynn was to write a *Norfolk Symphony*. By the time he wrote the *Sea Symphony*, which was first performed in 1910, he had absorbed the idiom of his two years' collecting into his musical language. Critics and commentators at the time and since said that his composition was heavily influenced by folk song and continued to be so. The melodies, the phrases and turns of folk songs were now appearing as the ingredients of the musical feast which Vaughan Williams produced, but songs were not quoted in their entirety. However, as you listen you can hear their familiar figures woven into his music.

In 1935, A.L. Bacharach wrote that Vaughan Williams and Holst came under the influence of the folk song revival, but neither remained enslaved by it. Vaughan Williams, in particular, has so absorbed the spirit of English folk music into his system that it seems to have become an integral part of his own intellectual process. He no longer presents us with rhapsodies, literal stitchings-together of collected tunes.[13]

In 1932 he gave a series of lectures on National Music, which were published two years later by Oxford University Press. He talks in detail about folksongs and then looks at their importance to the modern composer.

Has it anything to say to us as creative artists? Well, I would suggest that to say the least of it, it acts as a touchstone. Artistic self-deception is the easiest thing in the world and we must be continually testing ourselves as to our sincerity, to make sure all our emotions are not vicarious. Will not the folksong supply this test? In the folk song we find music which is unpremeditated and therefore of necessity sincere, music which has stood the test of time, music which must be representative of our race as no other music can.[14]

During the Second World War Vaughan Williams continued to believe that musicians should be useful to their fellows. He composed some pieces to be broadcast on the BBC Third Programme, including a 'little march suite.' Speaking about it during the programme, he said, "Last time I had the pleasure of speaking to you we heard some splendid marching tunes, all of them good for singing – tunes which really belong to us because they have been sung for generations of our forefathers. I promised you then that, if I was allowed, I could show you a lot more, and here they are – nothing precious about them – tunes with real blood in their veins and real muscles in their limbs…

We will finish up with three march tunes which I have put together in a little suite…. Then comes a man-of-war song, *On Board a '98*. This was sung to me in King's Lynn by an old sailor. I spent many happy mornings with him and his friends listening to their almost inexhaustible stock of splendid tunes."[15]

When that was written, Vaughan Williams still had some extraordinary compositions ahead of him. Their variety and originality took him far beyond the folk song collecting he did before the Great War, but he remained involved with the English Folk Dance and Song Society; he presented the handsome silver badge which is worn by the Squire of the Morris Ring of England. And he remembered the people of King's Lynn who sang to him half a century before when he came to the King's Lynn Festival in 1952, praising Gillian Martin, then still at King's Lynn High School for Girls, who sang illustrations for him, for the simplicity with which she sang.

The *Lynn News and Advertiser* covered his visit and the concert, which was attended by the Queen Mother and Princess Margaret.

Wednesday, when Lynn Festival received its second royal visit in three days, is a day that will be remembered by hundreds of residents and visitors and particularly by Gaywood Park Schoolchildren…

For an hour and a half the royal party sat in the assembly room of the town hall listening to Dr Vaughan Williams' lecture on East Anglian folk songs. Then they walked to St George's Guildhall where the children of Gaywood Park Secondary School were presented to them following a performance of the festival pageant, 'The Guild of St George.' … For two Lynn schoolgirls in particular the occasion was a great one. One was the Mayor's daughter… The other 15-year-old Gillian Martin, a pupil at

Lynn High School. Gillian, daughter of Mr and Mrs D.B. Martin, of 410 Wootton Road, Lynn, had the honour of being presented to the Queen Mother and Princess Margaret after she had sung before them in the Assembly Room at the Town Hall— and Dr. Ralph Vaughan Williams, the eminent composer, congratulated her on her performance.

The occasion was a lecture recital by Dr. Vaughan Williams, one of the events of the Lynn Festival. Gillian, a soprano, and 22-year-old Cambridge undergraduate, Mr. John Flower, were chosen to sing folk songs to illustrate it. They did not know until a few days before they were due to sing, that the Queen Mother would be among the audience to hear them. But Gillian, charming in a blue dress with her long brown hair gathered back into a crisp blue bow, remained 'as cool as a cucumber', to quote Mr Flower. And when it was her turn to sing she stepped gracefully on to the flower-decked platform and sang her song beautifully.

Afterwards she admitted feeling nervous before she began to sing. But when she began her confidence returned and she sang with an assurance that would have done credit to a performer of wide experience. And for Gillian this was her first big performance. She had sung in public once previously when Dr. Patrick Hadley, Professor of Music at Cambridge University, who heard her when he listened to High School girls singing carols last Christmastime. He chose her to sing the solos then. Mr and Mrs Martin, sitting with an audience which filled the Assembly Room, and overflowed into the Stone Hall, were able to share in their daughter's triumph. Mr. Flower's mother and father, who live in London, were not able to travel to Lynn to hear him. Mr Flower is an exhibitioner up at Caius College.

Dr. Hadley, who accompanied Gillian and Mr Flower, made the presentations in the Mayor's parlour. Dr. Vaughan Williams was also received by the Queen Mother and her daughter. There is a permanent reminder of the happy occasion in the Town Hall. A very special page in the visitors' book bears the signatures Elizabeth R, Margaret, Ralph Vaughan Williams, Patrick Hadley, Gillian Martin and John Flower.[16]

Ursula Vaughan Williams remembered going to the talk and then to St Nicholas' Chapel in Lynn for a concert conducted by Sir John Barbirolli:

At Paddy Hadley's invitation Ralph was to lecture on East Anglian folk songs at the first King's Lynn festival. We drove up through Essex stopping at Saffron Walden, where Ralph used to practise the organ when his unit was stationed there and by Ely, where we walked round the cathedral while Ralph described how he used to come over from Cambridge on Sundays to hear the choir. We arrived at Paddy's house at Heacham in time for a bathe before having dinner in the garden with Angus Morrison, our fellow guest. We drank Moselle while hundreds of shooting stars fell out of the sky and the air was gentle and summery and smelt of lavender fields, now almost ready to be cut. There were more bathes, rehearsals, the Lanchester Puppets and concerts. Ralph's lecture was an afternoon affair: to illustrate it he had two young singers, one of Paddy's students from Caius and a schoolgirl from Lynn (John Flower and Gillian Martin) who sang with absolute simplicity, just as Ralph liked folk songs to be sung.

The Queen Mother and Princess Margaret were in the audience and Ralph was presented to them afterwards. He knew his subject well and had plenty to say about it; when his duty was done and he could be audience again and enjoy his fifth symphony which John Barbirolli conducted in St Nicholas' Chapel where the angels in the roof were a constant pleasure to the sight.[17]

This was how the *Lynn News* reported the talk given by Vaughan Williams that day:

Dr. Ralph Vaughan Williams, the celebrated British composer, had just begun to give his illustrated lecture at Lynn Town Hall on Wednesday afternoon when a man's voice interrupted him. The lecturer paused for a moment to listen to the burst of song. Then he teased the audience, which included Queen Elizabeth the Queen Mother, Princess Margaret and the Earl of Dalkeith, asking them if a song so exotic could be English. Surely, he said, an English folksong should be crude and clownish, smelling of John Bull and roast beef. Then he admitted he had first heard the song sung nearly 50 years ago by a Lynn fisherman.

It was in 1903, he continued, that he first sought the Eastern Counties for folk songs. Two years later he visited Lynn. First he went to the outlying villages, Terrington and Tilney, but found very little there. He returned to Lynn where he met a clergyman who was intimate with the North End fishermen. They both went to hear them sing and, said Dr Vaughan Williams, "I reaped a rich reward there." Speaking of the folksong he said that it appeared to be something personal rather than local. It ran in families and individuals, and often it was jealously guarded. It did not belong to one class or section of society.

During the talk, Vaughan Williams lamented the way folksongs had become unfashionable. He wanted to reclaim them before it was too late.

These songs are not old and quaint relics of the past age," remarked Dr Vaughan Williams. "The collectors would not have taken all that trouble for museum pieces. This art is as alive today as it ever was. These songs will stand the supreme test of time and their eternal beauty will not fade. It is true that our better nature is being debauched by Hollywood and other evil influences. For the moment we have sold our souls to Tin Pan Alley. But we are able to redeem them. The question is, will the folk song survive their new incarnation. I believe they have the vitality and strength which will enable them to live in their new surroundings. These songs are the whole edifice on which a great art can be built.

Fifteen-year-old Lynn High School pupil Gillian Martin and Cambridge undergraduate John Flower sang songs to illustrate Dr Vaughan Williams' lecture.

Vaughan Williams maintained his connection with the King's Lynn Festival. His former pupil Patrick Hadley, who lived at Heacham and was one of the directors. In the ensuing five festivals, held towards the end of July each year, all but one included his work. The 1953 festival saw the first performance of his prelude on an old carol tune, given by the BBC Chorus and the Boyd Neel Orchestra conducted by Georges Enesco. In 1955, the Halle Orchestra under Sir John Barbirolli played *Variations on Dives and Lazarus* in St Nicholas' Chapel. It went down well with the critic for the *Lynn News and Advertiser*:

> For many years Vaughan Williams has been absorbed with the revival English Folk Music, which he has resurrected in such a way that its beauty and freshness is apparent at the very first hearing. So it was with his *Five Variations on Dives and Lazarus* in which his use of the harp and woodwind sections is masterly. Bringing the national scene alive, this work was a fine inclusion in the programme.

The Queen Mother and Princess Margaret were there to hear it.

Vaughan Williams was due to conduct the BBC Midland Orchestra and Chorus in the 1956 festival, The programme included his own *Serenade to Music* and the premiere of Patrick Hadley's *Fen and Flood*. The *Lynn News and Advertiser* said this included the 'particularly interesting old sea song, *The Lynn Apprentice*'—so Duggie Carter's song was again inspiring a composer. One of the main singers was Fred Calvert, the local police superintendent well known for his fine singing voice. Hadley's piece, according to the paper, was really a musical description of how the Fens changed up to the time of the flood (the disastrous 1953 floods were still very fresh in the minds of West Norfolk people) "expressing the hope they will be prevented in future with the words 'the waters shall not win." There was a discussion of the work on the BBC Midland and Home Service that Friday evening.

However, the paper then noted that Vaughan Williams was not able to come to King's Lynn because of a thrombosis and Stanford Robinson would stand in for the whole concert. Ursula Vaughan Williams wrote to the festival to say, "he is well in himself but must stay in bed for the time being."

Hadley was just one of the composers who was influenced by Vaughan Williams and his love of English folk music. He was paving the way for a new generation of English music, some of it far removed from the lyrical *Norfolk Rhapsodies*. Vaughan Williams had the capacity to use the music of many centuries as a touchstone, bringing together ideas from the Tudors onwards into a distinctively English style. By 1905 he had begun that musical journey by listening to ordinary people singing him their old songs, not least the sailors and fisherfolk of King's Lynn and Mr Whitby and Mr Poll in the Tilneys nearby.

The late Roy Palmer, in his book *Folk Songs Collected by Vaughan Williams*,[18] pays a fitting tribute:

> Vaughan Williams is a composer of the first rank who owes a great deal to folk song, but folk song owes a great deal to him…. The predominant feeling should be immense gratitude that he should have made his collection at all, and beyond that to

have spent so much time in annotating,
arranging and promoting folk song.
We are deeply indebted to him.

Notes

1   Modes were an older system of scales mostly superseded by the conventional major and minor scales. They are based on the patterns of 'white' notes on the piano e.g. the scale starting on D is the Dorian, and characterised by a flattened 7th note etc.

2   Vaughan Williams R. (1959) *Heirs and Rebels*. London: OUP, p.101.

3   In his book '*National Music*', RVW wrote: "The composer must not shut himself up and think about art, he must live with his fellows and make his art an expression of the whole life of the community."

4   Kennedy, M. (1964) *The Works of RVW*. London: OUP, p.84.

5   Vaughan Williams R. (1934) *National Music. 1st edn*. London: OUP, p.82.

6   Ibid. 4, p.87.

7   Ibid.

8   Ibid. first ed p.88.

9   Foss, H. (1950) *Ralph Vaughan Williams: a Study*. London: George G.Harrap & Co Ltd, p.112.

10   Holmes P. (1961) *Ralph Vaughan Williams*. London: J.M.Dent and Sons, reprinted (1998) OUP, p.30.

11   Ibid. p.31.

12   Kennedy M., (1964) *The works of RVW*. London:OUP, first ed.

13   Bacharach, A.L. (1935) *The Musical Companion*. London: Gollancz, p.460.

14   Vaughan Williams, R. (1934) *National Music*. London: OUP, p.73.

15   Cobbe, H. (2008) *Letters of Ralph Vaughan Williams 1895-1958*. London: OUP, pp.298/9.

16   *Lynn News*, 26 July 1952.

17   Vaughan Williams U. (1964) *RVW A Biography of Ralph Vaughan Williams*. London: OUP, pp.323-4.

18   Palmer, R. (1983) *Folk Songs Collected by Vaughan Williams*. London: J.M.Dent and Sons Ltd, p.xxii.

The North End of Lynn Today

"In a very few years, we in Lynn have managed to sweep away a complete community which developed over at least 600 years."

Pat Midgeley founder of True's Yard Museum

When Vaughan Williams visited the North End it was a maze of small houses, narrow streets and yards. But there is hardly any of it left, swept away by slum clearances and road building. Families were moved out on to council estates, most of the pubs were demolished and the North End was split by a busy road.

The changes began with the 1930 Slum Clearance Act which allowed clearance of houses which were "by reason of disrepair or sanitary defects unfit for human habitation"; a further factor might be "the narrowness or bad arrangement of the streets", seen as "dangerous or injurious to the health of the inhabitants".

The local authority began a phased campaign to clear all the yard dwellings from the town. In the North End this left, for the time being, largely just the houses fronting the streets.[1] North Place seems to have been left intact, as Clarence Bailey was still living there in the 1960s. Many of the residents were re-housed in what are now the older parts of the North Lynn housing estate, north and east of Loke Road as extended in the 1920s. In due course new estates south and east of the town expanded this accommodation, as the campaign in the town continued throughout the 1930s.

The next major development in the North End, which was to devastate Pilot Street and North Street themselves, came in the 1960s. In the late 1950s an economic regeneration plan set out to rescue Lynn from what was seen as impending business stagnation. An offer from Dow Chemicals to set up their factory on the riverside land

north of the town's dock was seen as a real coup for the regeneration working party: investment by such a major company might boost the confidence of other firms to relocate to Lynn.

A condition of the offer was a good access road guaranteed from the town. As a result, John Kennedy Road, an extension to the town's Victorian artery Railway Road, was created in 1960, cutting ruthlessly across Austin Street and Pilot Street, and passing the end of North Street. Beyond the Docks Railway crossing and Loke Road it joined Estuary Road and swung right between the Bentinck Dock and Savage's works; it was later extended as the town's northern bypass.[2]

The abbreviated southern end of Pilot Street survives as a cul-de-sac, terminating at the ancient timber-framed former *Grampus* public house, now Grampus House. A line of houses on the site of the

Pilot Street today looking towards the blocked end of the street. Beyond the old Grampus (now Grampus House) virtually everything up to the docks railway line next to the Tilden Smith was demolished. The first new house beyond Grampus House is on the site of the Fisherman's Arms: most of the rest are over St Nicholas' School and the street itself.
Colin James.

opposite: True's Yard today.
Anne Roberts.

Cottage demolition in Pilot Street: The exposed wall suggests that the cottage of which it was part was very old, as its derelict neighbour also appears to be. Ironically St Nicholas' Chapel behind it is being repaired and this dates the picture to 1965-6. The cottage is probably right on the corner where Pilot Street becomes Chapel Lane. This side of the street was not built on thereafter—see picture below.
True's Yard.

Pilot Street as surviving now: The lefthand house of the ancient jettied pair was the Grampus pub. At the far end of the street is a former butcher's shop. The cottage in the previous picture would have been just opposite it.
Colin James.

old St Nicholas' school extends right across the blocked end.[3] In the late 1960s the street looked very bleak and forlorn. In 1969 the *Eastern Daily Press* described "just 12 properties and close on half of those boarded-up or derelict. The occupied ones are neat and cosy-looking, and in a gap in the row one can see a well-trimmed garden with a magnificent honeysuckle in full flower. They face onto uneven footpaths and a badly worn granite-sett street patched here and there with asphalt, on to a patch of weed-ridden land used as a car park and then on to St Nicholas' Chapel and, near to that, a shoe factory."[4]

This last was in fact the old school, later replaced by the houses which now close the north end of the street. On the "patch of weed-ridden land" had stood the former homes of John Bayley's brother Jacob and Betty Howard's son Robert. The surviving houses on the opposite side line a street still paved with setts but in good order. The northern half of Pilot Street, from the *Grampus* to the railway crossing and *Tilden Smith*,[5] disappeared completely. At the same time virtually the whole of North Street was demolished and the road widened for easier access from the new road to the docks. The homes of Duggie Carter and William Harper in Watson's Yard and of Joe Anderson in Churchman's Yard now lie under the road itself.

An enquiry held in April 1958 had conveniently declared 50 houses in the North End "not fit for human habitation", perhaps quoting the standards laid down in the 1957 Housing Act, which the Town Clerk described as "'the first bite of a rather large bun" of slum clearance in the North End".[6] The national press commented that the local authority was "taking advantage of the clearance to drive a road . . . through the North End to a new industrial estate in the dock area." The demolition included "seven [houses] originally scheduled by the Ministry of Works for preservation because of their architectural interest" and the report continued, "It is difficult to feel much regret over North Street, but Pilot Street makes more of an appeal to one's sympathy."[7]

The new roadway, named for John Kennedy who became President of the USA during its construction, went through despite protests and the formation of a North End Society to fight the plans. It is interesting to see that one of two people who declared to the *Manchester Guardian* reporter that they "were determined to stay in their houses until they fall about their ears" was "Mr Bailey, retired fisherman of North Place". He was none other than John Bayley's grandson Clarence. Perhaps not however a continuous occupation although he and his aunt Susanna were there in 1911. Bob Booth has Susanna Bailey in North Place in King's Lynn in the 1930s.[8]

In the 1980s two cottages and the remains of True's Yard were spotted by the late Pat Midgley, who saw them from the balcony of a neighbouring building and realised it was the only yard to have escaped the bulldozers. It became part of what is now the True's Yard Fisherfolk Museum complex on the corner of North Street and St Ann's Street, including its two fishermen's cottages.

Just north of the *Grampus* in Pilot Street, the *Fisherman's Arms* was demolished but provided with a new building on the far side of the new road,[9] as was the *Victoria* on the corner of Loke Road. All the other pubs of Pilot Street and North Street disappeared, except for the *Tilden Smith*. Re-named the *Retreat* as a condition of release from the brewery in the 1970s, it closed during 2013.

This redevelopment almost certainly had a knock-on effect on the singing tradition even in the few remaining pubs, by the demolition of so many nearby houses. A healthy tradition, if in the hands of elderly singers, had been reflected in the BBC recording at the *Tilden Smith* in 1955, but it was clear from comments made in 1967 to Mike Herring during his research, that it would not outlast the few 1955 singers still living. He remarked to Bussle Smith's daughter that her father, then 83, was "the only singer I've found still with old songs. Turkey Stevens has odd bits of old ones that he can remember old fellows singing . . ." She replied sadly "Now there's not many old ones left; they don't go up there to keep

John Kennedy Road: On the extreme left are the back of the ancient Grampus House in Pilot Street and the modern house on the site of the Fisherman's Arms; the site of the Methodist chapel is under the road. The car wash, initially built as a car dealership, marks where Henry and Lol Benefer's shop used to be and actually echoes its curved front on the corner of North Street, where the new road picks up the old Pilot Street line. Colin James.

The Tilden Smith: Later re-named The Retreat but now no longer a pub. On its lefthand edge the old "Pilot Street" nameplate still survives. A heritage plaque on the side wall records its former connection with folksong. The Docks Railway beside it is no longer used. Colin James.

North Street today: The filter lane between the island with the lights and the car wash frontage indicates the original width of the street; the island lines up with True's Yard Fisherfolk Museum at the far end. On the opposite side, the former street frontages and Churchman's and Watson's Yards, where Duggie and Joe lived, are under the road and the car park.

Colin James.

remembering it." It was also apparent that none of the songs collected by Vaughan Williams had survived in the local community: none of them is in the 1955 BBC recording, or 1965 and 1966 recordings by Mike Herring. The repertoires were completely different and notes at True's Yard suggest the same.

True's Yard Fisherfolk Museum opened in 1991, thanks to the drive and energy of the late Pat Midgley, who was awarded the MBE for her work there. It has expanded since into the former *Naval Reserve* pub on St Ann Street and the neighbouring tattoo parlour, which turned out to be the last surviving smokehouse in King's Lynn. The museum continues to give as full a picture as possible of the vanished North End and its way of life,

Savage's fairground engineering works closed in 1973 and the site has twice been redeveloped for commercial use. The streets of terraced houses off Loke Road survive and have inherited the name of North End, between which and "North Lynn" a very firm distinction at a point along Loke Road is maintained. Fishing boats in the Fisher Fleet beyond the Alexandra Dock now fish mainly for shellfish and shrimps in the Wash, many of them crewed by the descendants of the old Northenders.

Gradually, first hand memories of the old North End are dying out. Writing in 1987, Pat Midgley said that "in a very few years, we in Lynn have managed to sweep away a complete community which developed over at least 600 years.

The Northenders remain bitter to this day. The £30 which property owners received for their houses seemed a derisory figure even then. They were rehoused in council houses throughout Lynn. It is this that they can never forgive, the loss of their close-knit community and life. Today, very little remains of the old North End."[10]

But their stories, an important photographic archive of their lives, and their songs have survived; the tunes, as Ralph Vaughan Williams said in a BBC broadcast, "that have been sung for generations of our forefathers…with real blood in their veins and real muscles in their limbs.'[11] Perhaps, as much as anyone, he has handed down the spirit of the old North End in their "seemingly inexhaustible stock of splendid tunes."[12]

Notes

1   The clearance over the next few years was probably less complete than had been envisaged, owing to the outbreak of World War 2 and the works necessary after it. The overall plan is quoted by Bob Booth (2013) in his introduction to *King's Lynn: An Illustrated Street Directory 1933*. King's Lynn:Tricky Sam Publishing, p.11.

2   Parker A. and Howling B. (2004) *King's Lynn: A History & Celebration*. Salisbury: The Francis Frith Collection for Ottakar's. p.101. Winifred Tuck's notes on the development of the Loke Road area also show that such a road was considered by the Streets, Buildings and Markets Committee as early as 23 February 1938 but rejected as too expensive a project. (King's Lynn Library local collection.)

3   At the other end of the row they reach St Ann's Street across the site of Fred Humphrey's works.

4   *Eastern Daily Press*, 11 June 1969.

5   The name Pilot Street still survives on the side of the former *Tilden Smith*.

6   *Eastern Daily Press*, 15 February 1958.

7   *Manchester Guardian*, 7 May 1958 Cutting in Pilot Street file, King's Lynn Library.

8   Booth R. (2006) *King's Lynn in the 1930s*. King's Lynn: Tricky Sam Publishing, p.21.

9   Now a Chinese restaurant.

10   Midgley P.W. (1987) *The Northenders, a disappeared community*. King's Lynn: True's Yard Museum publication, p.39.

11   Cobbe H. (2008) *Letters of Ralph Vaughan Williams*. London: OUP, p.208.

12   Ibid. p.209

Appendix 1: Previous Research

Tribute should be paid to two researchers whose work in the 1960s laid the foundations for further investigation. In 1967 Mike Herring recorded conversations with several North End residents in the hope of finding surviving first or second generation descendants of the singers.[1] His tape provides fascinating glimpses of North End singers in the half century after Vaughan Williams' visit and also valuable clues whose significance was appreciated increasingly during the research for the present book.

Secondly, in 1971 Edgar Samuels completed a thesis for the University of Uppsala, entitled *Vaughan Williams and King's Lynn 1905*.[2] His particular focus was the exploration of five songs sung by Mr Carter but he highlighted what was going on in the town in January 1905, including the stormy weather which kept the boats at home. He suggested a connection between Vaughan Williams' appeal in the *Morning Post* for songs and the visit to Tilney which initially brought him to West Norfolk in January 1905. He also raised for the first time the possibility that a photograph showing a cleric with two fishermen, found among Vaughan Williams' papers, might show the anonymous clergyman who, the collector said, introduced him to the King's Lynn fishing community. He thought the obvious candidate would have been the curate in charge of St Nicholas' Chapel and identified him as the Revd Alfred Huddle. In the light of that he suggested that the other two men in the picture were Mr Carter and Mr Anderson, who were the first two fishermen visited and therefore perhaps the two best known to Mr Huddle.

The works of both Mike Herring and Edgar Samuels provided a catalyst for local investigation. Copies of both tape and thesis, held in the Lynn Museum collections, inspired an exhibition on Norfolk folk music, called *Singing and Dancing was All My Delight*, which was staged for King's Lynn Festival in 1976, at 27 King Street, then the local museum of social history. During its compilation members of Mr Carter's family approached the museum, offering for the exhibition their own copy of his head and shoulders portrait from the above photograph, which was later presented to the museum. They also offered an opportunity to tape the reminiscences of Mr Carter's daughters and granddaughter, now held at Lynn Museum and transcribed by the author who had curated the exhibition. They confirmed the names of the three men in the photograph, proving Samuels' identification of the three men in the photograph correct.[3]

Another valuable piece of work was done by David Jackson, who collated all the published versions of Vaughan Williams' West Norfolk collection and lodged a copy with True's Yard Fisherfolk Museum.

In 2005 two programmes of songs collected in Lynn in January 1905, were performed to mark the centenary of the composer's visit.[4] *The Tudor Rose* in St Nicholas' Street was so well attended that people were standing on the stairs; the second filled a larger venue. Later in the year another well attended presentation at what is now known as Marriott's Warehouse marked the bicentenary of Trafalgar. This book and the recent research into the individual singers as a group had their origins in these events, which flagged up how many of the 1905 songs had never been seen in print outside Vaughan Williams' notebooks.

Meanwhile the East Anglian Traditional Music Trust was working on its own project to spotlight traditional singing in the North End of Lynn, culminating in 2007 in its publication *North End Voices*[5] and a link-up with BBC Radio Norfolk's own *Celebrate North End* oral history and community project. Important features of these events were workshops for adults and schools to get people actually singing the songs themselves. The associated exhibition and one of the performances arising from these projects took place in St Nicholas' Chapel, thus curiously re-establishing, a century on, an old link with the Revd Alfred Huddle, and his friends James ('Duggie') Carter and Joseph ('Joe') Anderson.

Equally important is the vital role in the research played by the True's Yard Fisherfolk Museum. Its establishment in 1991 followed the discovery of a pair of old fishermen's cottages, once part of the former True's Yard off North Street, which had survived the wholesale redevelopment of the heart of the North End. Spearheaded by the determination of the late Patricia Midgley, a campaign led to their preservation and re-furnishing and the establishment in associated buildings of the museum, with its archive centre and facilities for research. Without True's Yard there would be no permanent visual reminder of the old North End lifestyle and no research base and repository dedicated solely to its recording; Mrs Midgley was deservedly awarded the MBE in recognition of her work. Much more than a museum, True's Yard has become the focus for many people who grew up in the old North End to come in and to talk about their lives there and to help with the day to day running of the operation, which relies heavily on voluntary help.

The family files archived at True's Yard Fisherfolk Museum and the genealogical information now available via the internet have given us facilities not available to Mike Herring and Edgar Samuels. With these to hand, along with the parish registers of St Nicholas' Chapel and of the parish church itself, it has been possible to compile extensive

Lottie Westfield and Lizzie Tilson (née Carter) pictured in 1976 with Elizabeth James. Lottie is on the extreme right. The photograph was taken by their niece Florrie Reid on the afternoon they recorded their reminiscences on tape.
Elizabeth James.

Mrs Pat Midgley, rescuer of True's Yard and founder of the Museum: holding her MBE.
True's Yard.

family trees for most of the names. While recognising that these may yet be incomplete, it has been possible to establish for most of the singers the most likely "candidate" and, in the event of there being more than one, which by reason of age is the most likely choice.

The research into the songs has been greatly assisted by the Full English, the project by the English Folk Dance and Song Society to put the Victorian and Edwardian collectors' material and notebooks online. It has opened up the riches of Vaughan Williams' collection, as well as those of Cecil Sharp, Frank Kidson, George Butterworth, Percy Grainger and others. The Bodleian Library's online collection of broadside ballads has also been a key resource in tracking down the words of songs which were fragmentary or missing. We are also indebted to the EFDSS and the staff of the Vaughan Williams Memorial Library at Cecil Sharp House for their help.

The other notable researcher was the late Roy Palmer, whose books and scholarly research have revealed the cream of Vaughan Williams' years of collecting in several counties and the stories behind the songs he found.

Finally, we have had the benefit of the extensive research and knowledge of Vaughan Williams and Lucy Broadwood themselves and their contemporaries as they first brought these songs to public attention in the journals of the Folk Song Society.

Notes

1 Copy of tape in Lynn Museum collections, accession number KLLM 1968.11. Transcribed by the author in 1976. Mike Herring's original tapes are due shortly to be presented to the archives of True's Yard Fisherfolk Museum, courtesy of their originator, Mike Herring.

2 Copies of Edgar Samuels' unpublished thesis at Lynn Museum, True's Yard Fisherfolk Museum and in the Vaughan Williams Memorial Library at Cecil Sharp House. Samuels also contributed an article to the Vaughan Williams Centenary issue of *English Dance and Song* in 1972 (Vol 34 No 3 (Autumn 1972) pp.92-93 and 96).

3 Samuels recorded some doubt expressed over his identification by persons who believed the picture showed other fishermen, although none of their suggestions coincided with names recorded by Vaughan Williams.

4 The programme was put together and performed by the authors with Alan Helsdon, David Jackson and Robin Tims, with historian Dr Paul Richards talking about the life of the North End in 1905. In the version for Trafalgar Day, we were joined by Martin Greaves of the King's Morris, who danced the jig *Princess Royal* from the Longborough tradition to the tune of *Bold Nelson's Praise*.

5 *North End Voices: The history of folk singing in the fishing community of King's Lynn* (East Anglian Traditional Music Trust 2007).

Appendix 2: Selected Bibliography

Aldritt, K. (2017) *Vaughan Williams, Composer, Radical,* Patriot—*a biography.* Robert Hale Ltd.

Anckorn, G. (1981) *A West Norfolk Camera.* Sevenoaks: Ashgrove Press Ltd.

Bacharach, A.L. (1935) *The Musical Companion.* Victor Gollanz Ltd.

Baily, L. *(1966) Leslie Baily's BBC Scrapbooks Vol 1.* London: George Allan and Unwin Ltd.

Broadwood, L.E. and Fuller Maitland, J.H. (1893) *English County Songs.* London: J.B.Cramer and Co Ltd.

Brooks, P. Childs, A. Felmingham, M. and Groves, T. (1996) *Sheringham and District.* Stroud: Sutton Publishing.

Cannock, S. (2012) *programme notes for The Pilgrim's Progress.* London: ENO.

Cobbe, H. (2002 reprinted 2010) *Letters of Ralph Vaughan Williams.* Oxford: OUP.

Cox, J.C. (1903) *Surrey. London:* Methuen.

Day, J. (1998) *Vaughan Williams.* Oxford: OUP.

De Sola Pinto, V. and Rodway, A.E. (1957) *The Common Muse.* London: Chatto and Windus.

De Val, D. (2011) *In Search of Song: the Life and Times of Lucy Broadwood.* Farnham: Ashgate Publishing Ltd.

Elphick, P. *(1988) Out of Norfolk.* Briston: Orlando Publishing.

Foss, H. *(1950) Ralph Vaughan Williams.* London: Harrap.

Frogley, A and Thomson, A. *(2013) The Cambridge Companion to Vaughan Williams.* Cambridge: Cambridge University Press.

Gregory E.D. (2010) *The Late Victorian Folksong Revival—The Persistence of English Melody 1878-1903.* Lanham, Maryland, USA: The Scarecrow Press Inc.

Grout, D.J. *A History of Western Music.* New York: W.W. Norton and Co. Inc.

Holmes, P. *(1997) Vaughan* Williams, *His Life and Times.* London: Omnibus Press.

Hugill, S. (1961) Shanties of the *Seven Seas.* London: Routledge and Keegan Paul Ltd.

Huntington, G. (2005 edition) *Songs the Whalemen Sang.* Mystic Ct, USA: Mystic Seaport.

Huntington, G. (2014) *The Gam: More Songs the Whalemen Sang.* Essex, Ct, USA: Loomis House Press.

Karpeles, M. (1973) *An Introduction to English Song.* London: OUP.

Kennedy, M. (1964) *The Works of Ralph Vaughan Williams*. London: OUP.

Kennedy, P. (1975) *Folksongs of Britain and Ireland*. London: Oak Publications.

Kidson, F. (1891) *Traditional Tunes—a Collection of Ballad Airs*. Wakefield: S.R. Publishers.

Lloyd, A.L. (1967) *Folk Song in England*. New York: International Publishers.

Lown, J. (2003) *Memories of Old Sheringham*. Sheringham: Lowenbrau Publishing.

Midgley, P. W. (1987) The Northenders—a Disappeared Community. King's Lynn: P.W. Midgley.

Northrop Moore, J. (1987) *Edward Elgar*. London: OUP.

Palmer, R. (1983) *Folksongs Collected by Ralph Vaughan Williams*. London: J.M.Dent and Sons.

Palmer R. (1979) *Everyman's Book of English Country Songs*, London: J.M.Dent and Sons.

Raynor, H. (1980) *Music in England*. London: Robert Hale.

Reeves, J. (1960) *The Everlasting Circle*. London, USA.: Heinemann.

Richards, P. (1990) *King's Lynn*. Chichester: Phillimore and Co..

Sharp, C.J. and Vaughan Williams, R. (1907 reprinted 1965) *English Folk Song: Some Conclusions*. Wakefield: E.P. Publishing.

Shepard, L. (1962) *The Broadside Ballad*. London: Herbert Jenkins.

Shepard L. (1962) *The History of Street Literature*. Newton Abbot: David and Charles.

Vaughan Williams, R. (1934 reprinted 1963) *National Music*. London: OUP.

Vaughan Williams, U. (1964) *R.V.W. A Biography of Ralph Vaughan Williams*. Oxford: Clarendon Press.

Vaughan Williams R. and Lloyd A.L. (1959) *The Penguin Book of English Folksongs*. Harmondsworth: Penguin Books Ltd.

Walker, E. (1907 reprinted 1951) *A History of Music in England*. London: OUP.

Wedgwood, B.and H. (1980) *The Wedgwood Circle*. Westfield, New Jersey, USA: Eastview Editions.

Whall, Capt.W.B. (1910) *Ships, Sea Songs and Shanties*. Glasgow, James Brown and Son.

Kelly's Directories.

Online Resources.

The Full English, EFDSS.

The Bodleian Library collection of Broadside Ballads.

The Vaughan Williams Society.

Newspapers.

The *Lynn News and the Lynn Advertiser* archive in King's Lynn Library.

The *Eastern Daily Press* archive in King's Lynn Library and the Norwich Millennium Library.

Index